RETHINKING THE MEDIEVAL LEGACY

FOR CONTEMPORARY THEOLOGY

This conference was supported by the Margaret Jagels Fund for Catholic Studies at Claremont Graduate University.

Rethinking the
MEDIEVAL LEGACY
FOR CONTEMPORARY
THEOLOGY

Edited by
ANSELM K. MIN

University of Notre Dame Press
Notre Dame, Indiana

University of Notre Dame Press
Notre Dame, Indiana 46556
undpress.nd.edu
All Rights Reserved

Published in the United States of America

Library of Congress Cataloging-in-Publication Data

Rethinking the medieval legacy for contemporary theology /
edited by Anselm K. Min.
pages   cm
Includes bibliographical references and index.
ISBN 978-0-268-03534-1 (pbk. : alk. paper)
ISBN 0-268-03534-2 (pbk. : alk. paper)
ISBN 978-0-268-08698-5 (web pdf)
1. Theology, Doctrinal—History.   I. Min, Anselm Kyongsuk, 1940– editor.
BT21.3.R48   2014
230.09—dc23
2014032977

∞ *The paper in this book meets the guidelines for permanence and durability*
of the Committee on Production Guidelines for Book Longevity of the
Council on Library Resources.

CONTENTS

INTRODUCTION
Rethinking the Medieval Legacy for Contemporary Theology

ANSELM K. MIN

There is no lack of problems, both theoretical and practical, facing contemporary Christian theology. Of all the sciences or disciplines theology is perhaps the most vulnerable to the challenges brought about by social and historical changes because it has to speak about all things according to the logic of God or, as Aquinas put it, *sub ratione Dei*. Any significant changes in any significant area of human life are *eo ipso* challenges to theology because they pose questions about the ultimate significance of human dignity, human solidarity, and human destiny. There are no significant human questions that are theologically indifferent and neutral.

In responding to these questions, however, Christian theology has the cumulative wisdom of the millennia and centuries of experience in Christian communities to draw on. Theology is not left to the individual resources of the isolated theologian, no matter how great these might be, or to his or her individual roles, no matter how important these often are. To a degree far surpassing all other disciplines theology is an endeavor of a believing community with its supra-individual norms and funds of teaching, reflection, and insight. The role of a living tradition in a broad sense is absolutely decisive even if

1

its authoritative definition will always remain controversial. The historical community as a community of shared tradition provides the context for the origination, testing, and reception of all theological developments.

The contemporary world has been raising many issues and challenges to which no serious theologian can remain indifferent, from evolution to ecology to social justice to interreligious understanding to the problem of "horrendous" suffering to the possibility of authentic existence and the possibility of knowing God at all. We also know how theologians have been responding to these challenges over the past century. Most often theological responses have been based on accepting new insights from current philosophies and the social and natural sciences and applying a systematic suspicion to the entire tradition of the believing communities. Tradition as such is often regarded as the chief source of oppression and violence. No one today would defend the tradition in its entirety against the legitimate criticisms and demands of contemporary humanity. It is no wonder that much contemporary theology seeks to be new as distinct from the traditional and to be liberating as distinct from the oppressive.

Given the long-standing self-understanding of Christianity as a living community of tradition, this trend in much contemporary theology is worrisome at least for two reasons, lack of self-criticism and loss of Christian identity. First, it is uncritical mindlessness to ignore the fact that contemporary discoveries and insights also come loaded with peculiarly contemporary prejudices containing their own ideological sources of oppression and violence. We are compelled to critically reflect on the sheer provincialism and shortsightedness of many contemporary intellectual fashions and trends before we theologians rush to "deconstruct" the Christian tradition in light of them. An intellectual movement comes on the horizon with claims to novelty, totality, and radicality and fades into the dustbin of history after a thorough deconstruction by another new movement about thirty years later. It is time that we should all be more sensitive to the historicity of our ideas and the inevitable ideological temptations they conceal.

Second, the first requirement of Christian theology as Christian is not novelty or originality; the originality of a theology may testify to the creativity of the theologian but not necessarily to its Christian identity. A theology may be quite original, but it may also cease to be Christian at all. The Christian identity of a theology lies in its fidelity—which must be creative, if you will—to the enduring tradition of the Christian community, whose founding insights and commitments have developed and enriched themselves through the centuries. Some theologies are found more enduring in their Christian insights and appeal than others, and ideas with a certain universality of such insights and appeal are called "classics" (Tracy). Which of the competing contemporary theologies will prove classical and join the living tradition of the community is precisely for history to tell. For Christian theology the age of the Fathers is one such "classical" period insofar as it is through them that most of the Christian doctrines, still accepted by mainstream Christianity, took their definitive shape, from the Trinitarian to the Christological to the doctrine of sin and grace.

I have been wrestling with the concrete problems of praxis, liberation, and globalization as posed by contemporary social changes while also sensitizing my theological eyes through social and political theories that have exposed these problems. I have discovered the ideological character and shortsightedness of much modern thought while also rediscovering the wisdom of the classical tradition, from the Cappadocians and Augustine to Thomas Aquinas and Nicholas of Cusa. Returning to the insights of the classical tradition did not mean shedding all the valuable insights I have learned from modernity or abandoning the theological sense of problems facing the contemporary world. Modern criticism has made it impossible to accept any tradition including the classical without some dose of suspicion. The classical tradition has made it impossible to accept modernity with its anthropocentric arrogance. It was quite natural, therefore, to pose the question, What are some of the insights of the classical tradition that will help us to cope with our very contemporary problems, fully knowing that those insights have to be discerned and developed in order to prove their relevance to the very concrete problems of our time?

Limiting myself to the Middle Ages, I thought to myself, what if I organized a conference on the theme "Rethinking the Medieval Legacy for Contemporary Theology" for the purpose of retrieving and developing some of the medieval theological and spiritual resources as aids for coping with the challenges facing contemporary theology. What can we learn from medieval theology, spirituality, and culture for theological work today? I sent out a call for papers on this rather general topic to some of the most respected theologians writing today. I left each free to choose any contemporary issue he or she finds compelling as well as any medieval insight that is fruitful in dealing with that issue. The only condition was that participants produce a genuine encounter between an important medieval insight and a compelling contemporary issue. Six distinguished theologians accepted my invitation, with whom I matched six outstanding graduate students from the Department of Religion of Claremont Graduate University as respondents. The result was the exciting conference held at Claremont Graduate University on April 16–17, 2010.

Readers will readily agree, I think, that the problems chosen for discussion are among the compelling ones of our time. How should we conceive of the relation between the recipient of an organ and its donor? Will the medieval theology of perichoresis and communion of saints provide a clue? How should we deal with so many of the horrendous evils that exist today? Will the medieval theology of divine friendship help? What do we do with the historical-critical method of biblical interpretation, with its often scandalous tendencies to debunk all traditional theological interpretation? Will medieval exegesis, with its four senses of scripture and its practice of reading scripture with the tradition, provide a way out? Are the possibilities of authentic human existence limited by radical facticity, individuality, and finitude, as Heidegger claims, or are they radically open as all finitude is subject to the possibilities of creation out of nothing? Will the rediscovery of a theology of creation in Aquinas help us overcome the crisis of Heideggerian authenticity of existence? Nothing seems more urgent for peace today than the mutual theological understanding of Christianity and Islam, yet a genuine theological encounter—not just political or cultural—seems rare. Will the theological struggles of

Aquinas and Cusanus shed some light on our theological understanding of Islam today? Out of the desire to have a God both intelligible and loving on human terms, many theologians speak of him in
univocal terms and continue to commit ontotheological simplicities.
Will a renewed appreciation of Aquinas's analogical approach to
divine names provide the virtuous middle of hope without falling
into the extremes of presumption and despair in the human claim to
know God?

To be more specific, let me turn to the issue of organ transplants.
Is the human person identical with the brain so that other organs like
the heart are merely dispensable parts that may be replaced without
further ado? Is the boundary between one person and another the
same as the boundary between their material bodies? Is it imaginable
to think of one person as dwelling in another person, suffering for the
sake of another, and sharing a communion with another even when
dead? Can organ transplants be understood as something more than
the replacing of an old material part with a new one, as something em-
bodying a communion of the donor and recipient in which one lives
in the other and suffers for the other?

In the first essay, titled "Exchanging Hearts: A Medievalist Looks
at Transplant Surgery," Barbara Newman responds with insights
drawn from the traditional Catholic doctrine of perichoresis, mutual
indwelling or coinherence, first applied to the Trinity and later trans-
ferred to the mystical body of Christ and the communion of saints,
thereby shedding new light on the moral and ontological relationship
between donor and recipient in organ transplants, especially heart
transplants.

Against the prevailing contemporary assumption that the person
is identical with the individual, Newman proposes a perichoretic anthropology based on the theology of the Trinity in which the three
divine persons share one divine nature and dwell in one another. The
divine person is supremely permeable in that each person is indwelt
by the other two: to be a divine person is to be within one another.
The Father is in the Son and the Son is in the Father. This indwelling
extends to the mystical body: Christ dwells in the members of his
body, and they dwell in Christ. As created in the image of the Trinity,

the human person is likewise porous, permeable, and dwells in other persons. To be personal is to be interpersonal; one becomes a person only in, with, and through other persons. Unlike the self-sufficient atomistic individual of the Enlightenment, the Christian views human persons as being one body in Christ and individually as members of one another (Paul).

Newman suggests that organ transplants can be better appreciated on the model of Christ giving himself for the life of the world physically on the cross and sacramentally in the Eucharist, in which the communicant enters into a profound union with the self-giving Christ. It is a mode of profound coinherence of two persons through the sacrifice of one for the life of the other. The medieval practice of praying and suffering for the sinners in purgatory is another example of the intimate communion between the living and the dead in which pains and guilts can also be shared among the members of the mystical body. Many people feel guilty receiving an organ from another person who often has to die in order that that organ can be given. Those who consent to donation of organs do so in the hope of bringing life out of death and honoring the spirit of the deceased donor—profoundly religious motives. Newman argues that these feelings and hopes can be sublimated into profound religious experiences when interpreted in light of the theology of coinherence and communion that governs the mystical body of Christ.

In her essay, "Friendliness, Divine and Human," Marilyn McCord Adams begins with a survey of the significance of friendship as a social institution in the ancient world and its philosophical development through Cicero and details its theological application as a model for thinking about the Trinity in Richard of St. Victor, about Christ's relationship to the church in Aelred of Rivaulx, and about God's astonishing unilateral love of unworthy sinners in Julian of Norwich. The high point of Adams's essay is her application of the model of friendship to her own foremost concern of recent years, the problem of God and "horrendous evil." How is it possible to claim divine friendliness and goodness to those suffering horrendous evils? What theological sense can we make of such evils in the world?

According to Cicero's classical account friendship requires willing and not willing the same things (*idem velle, idem nolle*), which in turn requires knowing the same things. Regarding God's project in this world, this would require the same knowledge of good and evil. However, we cannot expect to achieve God's knowledge of good and evil because we are incapable of seeing God face-to-face or the divine goodness while alive in this world and capable of appreciating the true nature of evil, horrendous evils, only gradually in a pedagogy of growing experience and maturity from the lessons of the paradise lost through Abraham's experience of faith in an incomprehensible God to Job's encounters with evil to Jesus's training of the disciples in maturity through the scandal of the cross and resurrection.

Horrors, for Adams, are beyond both human recognition and control because they are the systematic by-products of the material world. Millions of people suffer horrendous calamities all their lives, which makes it impossible for many to believe in God and leads many to even hate God. In response Adams takes two suggestions from Julian of Norwich. First, just as Julian believed that sin is necessary in this world, yet that God loves us despite our sin and will make everything all right in the *eschaton,* Adams analogously suggests that horrors are necessary by-products of the material world, yet that participants in great horrors are not beyond God's love, God's will and power to help and transform them into worthwhile lives fit for heaven. Second, God would impute his friendliness to his Son Christ to all his creatures, especially participants in great horrors, and see him in every human being. Just as Christ's divine and human knowledge of divine goodness enabled him to deal with the evil of his passion and death, many saints were sustained in their suffering because of their knowledge of divine goodness. Adams suggests that the radical experience of the great virulence of evil by horror participants more closely approaches God's knowledge of evil than does our ordinary experience of evil and shares in God's knowledge of evil. God imputes friendliness to these as well in the full knowledge that such horrendous suffering was a necessary part of God's project in this material world. Like Julian, Adams thinks that God will make it up to all of us for all that we have suffered and thank us, like a grateful friend, for participating in his project in the world. Divine love will award greater honors to those who paid higher prices for that project. This would require for horror participants many stages of therapeutic transformation and purification before they can be fit for the realm of God.

Adams ends with the daring thought that in the *eschaton* all will be glad to have lived their lives on earth in light of God's perpetual friendly love that compensates everyone for their suffering, not glad for the harms we have done, but for what God has made of them and for our role in the divine project, offering all that we have been in a friendly gesture to the divine Friend.

Christian theology has been challenged not only by new advances in medical technology and increasing sensitivity to colossal evils but also from within by the claims of the historical-critical method. By its dismissal of all interpretation of scripture going beyond the intention of the author in his or her historical context and by an exclusive appeal to purely naturalistic assumptions, this method has been playing havoc with all the traditional interpretations based on faith and revelation, threatening the very survival of such foundational Christian beliefs like Christology and the doctrine of the Trinity. It is to these problems that Kevin Madigan responds in his essay, "Can Precritical Biblical Interpretation Cure the Ills of the Critical?," by gleaning lessons from the medieval exegetical experience. He first analyzes the self-understanding of the historical critics and the many serious objections that have been raised to their practice and presuppositions, then goes on to retrieve some of the insights of the premodern, precritical medieval approaches to the Bible and its many different senses, and concludes by arguing that the precritical medieval approaches can cure some of the ills of the historical-critical method, at least in some of its extreme claims.

For Madigan, the distinctive contribution of medieval exegesis lies in two things, the recognition of a plurality of meanings in a biblical text and the exegetical practice of reading the Bible with the tradition. John Cassian was most influential in highlighting the four senses of scripture, literal, allegorical, moral, and anagogical, for medieval hermeneutics. The first deals with the history of God's redemptive activity, the second with the articles of belief, the third with ethical behavior, and the fourth with one's eternal destiny. Jerusalem, for example, can refer to the earthly city in its literal sense, to the church in its allegorical sense, to the soul in its moral sense, and to the heavenly city in its anagogical sense. This method, of course, was applied in a flexible, not a mechanical, way. What is important here is that no medieval interpreter ever thought that the meaning of a biblical text was limited to the intention of the author or the reception by the original audience in its original historical context. This pluralistic approach to exegesis was a way of retrieving the inexhaustible meaning of scripture and making it relevant to different historical situations, especially in preaching, where the allegorical or moral meaning may be more significant than the original literal or historical meaning. This does not mean that a text could be interpreted in any arbitrary way. In some way the multiple senses of scripture had to be grounded in the literal. Still, biblical texts do have multiple meanings as intended by God and human beings. Furthermore, medieval exegetes read the Bible "with the dead," that is, in conversation with previous interpreters and commentators on scripture, drawing on them freely, often verbatim. They took the tradition of biblical interpretation as an authoritative guide, as more than a mere collection of individual opinions.

Can this sort of "precritical" hermeneutics cure the ills of the "critical"? Limiting himself only to those historical critics who claim the historical sense as the only imaginable or true sense of the text, Madigan argues that precritical medieval hermeneutics can cure the ills of the historical-critical method at least in two regards. First, against the critical method, we can say that religious communities do have the right to insist that the biblical text has an excess or surplus of meaning and multiple senses, as the Jewish and Christian tradition of hermeneutics has always recognized. Second, against the critical method, reading the biblical text with the dead—in light of the tradition of interpretations and commentaries of the past, not in the sense of slavishly accepting their conclusions, but in the sense of taking them seriously as sources of potential meanings and relevant questions—can save us from many of the unnecessary restrictions and sterilities of the historical-critical method. Madigan does not mean to say, however, that we have to reject it altogether. Properly criticized and limited, it can be used as a control to keep our religious exegetical imagination honest and limited within certain boundaries.

Another contemporary challenge to Christian theology has come from Heidegger, who held that possibility is higher than actuality but who radically limited Dasein's possibility of being to the contingent facticities into which it is already thrown, to which it is already attuned, and within which it projects its own possibilities, and ultimately to death, the radical possibility of its own impossibility. Restricted to the temporal and worldly limits of one's own existential situation, Dasein's possibilities are totally temporal, contingent, individual, and finite and do not allow for anything radically new, a new way of existing in a different world altogether, not merely living differently in its world, a nonworldly, eschatological way of being. This radical challenge to the possibility of Christian faith is here met by the essay, "*Possibile Absolutum*: The Theological Discovery of the Ontological Priority of the Possible," in which Ingolf U. Dalferth traces the history of the meaning and significance of the modality of possibility from Aristotle to Heidegger and criticizes Heidegger in light of the "revolutionary" significance of the changes in the meaning of possibility brought about by the medieval theology of creation, especially that of St. Thomas.

Since Aristotle, what is possible is based on the actual and ultimately on the actuality of the world taken as given. The medieval theology of creation and divine omnipotence put this priority of the actual radically in question. As a creature of divine omnipotence the world loses its ontological necessity and becomes the realm of the possible rooted in the creative power and will of God. What is at stake in the doctrine of creation is not what is conditionally possible, that is, given the existence of this or that reality in the world, but what is absolutely possible, in the absence of the world itself. The theology of creation provides a radically new paradigm of possibility, the absolutely possible, *possibile absolutum,* locating that possibility in the only actuality relative to absolute possibility, that is, God, since it is still true that possibility must be founded in an actuality. What is possible is everything made possible by God, the impossible everything made impossible by God. The distinction between what is actual and what is possible no longer depends on the given structure of the existing world but only on God's will, which makes some things possible and other things impossible in the world as his creation.

What is possible and what is not depends on the power at issue. What is possible and impossible for human power is different from what is possible and impossible (e.g., change, sin) for divine power. What, then, is possible for God? What is meant by divine omnipotence, by the thesis that God can do "all" things? For St. Thomas, God can do all things that are logically possible, that is, all things that do not involve the contradiction of subject and predicate (e.g., "a man is a donkey"), which defines what is absolutely possible because it is not relative to or conditioned by the actual possibilities of the created world. Not everything that is logically possible, however, is *factibile* or makeable. It must also be something that reflects the nature of the divine agent and something, therefore, that God can will without contradicting his own nature. God can do or make all things that do not involve a logical contradiction, are contingent, and can be willed without contradicting the divine nature. What is possible or makeable is no longer relative to the possibilities of the existing world but only to divine omnipotence who can do or make all things that are not contradictory to the intrinsic nature of the subject and predicate involved or to the nature of the divine agent. This is the theological discovery of the absolutely possible and the ontological priority of the possible over the actual as far as this world is concerned. For Dalferth, "this is nothing short of an ontological revolution, and it opens up a new and deeper understanding of God."

This also means that there is no need to absolutize Dasein's possibilities of being in the radically finite and contingent structure Heidegger attributes to it. Such a structure is not self-explanatory or self-grounding; it is itself contingent on conditions outside its control, possibilities put in its way from outside, conditions prior to itself, both its own thrownness and its projective understanding, conditions that has made Dasein what it is and to which it only responds. It is not its own creation in any absolute sense. If the possible need not be limited to Aristotle's actual world, neither need it be limited to Heidegger's factical possibilities of a Dasein thrown and projecting into a contingent world.

One of the signs of the times is the imperative for mutual understanding and dialogue between different religions, in particular, between Christianity and Islam. The medieval world is a far cry from this globalized one, and it would be anachronistic to expect direct, positive lessons of interreligious hermeneutic from the Middle Ages that will speak to the interreligious problems of our time. Given the history of conquests and crusades since the seventh century, one can easily imagine the degree of hostility, prejudice, and ignorance still existing between the two religions in the high and late Middle Ages. Still, in a conference dedicated to the theme of the medieval legacy to the twenty-first century, the question remains inevitable: Do the medievals have anything positive to teach us in the matter of interreligious understanding?

In his essay, "Can We Talk Theologically? Thomas Aquinas and Nicholas of Cusa on the Possibility of a Theological Understanding of Islam," Pim Valkenberg responds precisely to that question. In a comprehensive textual study he attempts to decipher at least some "faint prefiguration" of something like a genuine theological encounter with Islam. Valkenberg begins by recognizing that Aquinas does not engage Islam at the theological level because he does not see a theological common ground between Christianity and a false prophet. Still, Aquinas does engage Islam on grounds of natural reason by defending the Christian faith in the Trinity, the Sonship of Christ, and Christ's continuing presence in the Eucharist against prevailing Muslim objections and arguing that Christian faith is not irrational. His primary interest was apologetic, not a positive understanding of the other, for which we turn to Nicholas of Cusa.

Nicholas of Cusa's approach to Islam is found in two works, *De pace fidei* and the *Cribratio Alkorani*. In *De pace fidei*, written in the immediate aftermath of the fall of Constantinople in 1453, he pleaded for unity and peace among religions. Cusanus argues, in a way reminiscent of many pluralists today, that no human being can comprehend the infinity of God and that human beings seek God in different rites and call him by different names. Behind differences among religions there is only one faith, *una religio in rituum varietate*. This realization should lead us to peace and harmony among religions on the basis of what unites us.

In his later work, the *Cribratio Alkorani*, written in 1461, Cusanus does not abandon the old polemical tradition seen in Aquinas but also provides a much more positive approach to Islam, employing a *pia interpretatio,* or "faithful" interpretation, that puts the best possible theological construction on the more scandalous passages in the Qur'ān as forcing Christians to have a better understanding of their own faith, especially the incomprehensibility of God. Valkenberg highlights two hermeneutic principles in *Cribratio Alkorani*: "Interpret the Qur'an as intending to give glory to God without detracting from Christ," and "whenever possible, work with the interpretations that the wise among the Muslims assign to the Qur'an." The first rule opens up the possibility of a Christian interpretation of the Qur'ān that does justice to the monotheism common to both religions without jeopardizing the constitutive role of Christ for Christians. The second rule contains the beginning of the awareness that the Qur'ān might be the revealing Word of God for Muslims and that we cannot do justice to the religious function of the Qur'ān without taking seriously the history of Muslim interpretations. These two, for Valkenberg, constitute the basic principles of a Christian theological reading of the Qur'ān and the most important lesson we should learn from the medieval theologians for a genuine theological encounter with Islam today.

In the final essay in this volume, "The Humanity of Theology: Aquinian Reflections on the Presumption and Despair in the Human Claim to Know God," Anselm K. Min assesses contemporary philosophical theologies according to the virtue of hope, finding some guilty of despair because they fail to hope for what they *can* know about God, others guilty of presumption because they claim to know *more* than they can really know about God. Virtue lies in the middle, and we can fail to attain virtue either by deficiency or by excess. We can claim to know too little about God or too much about God. In this sense atheism, agnosticism, and fideism are despairing theologies claiming to know less than human beings can know about God, and rationalism in all its varieties is a presumptuous theology claiming to know more than human beings can ever know about God.

By what standard do we distinguish between too little and too much, between despair and presumption in the matter of knowing God? What constitutes the virtuous middle in our knowledge of God? Drawing on the theology of St. Thomas, Min presents the metaphysics of human knowledge as a hylomorphic being, indicating the nature and limits of human knowledge, followed by a discussion of how such limits apply to the human knowledge of God and how all human predication of divine names has to be analogical, not univocal. He closes with the illustration of five ways in which contemporary philosophical theologies deviate from the norm of human knowledge either by deficiency or by excess, either by despairing to attain even the knowledge that is possible within the limits of human knowledge or by presuming to know God beyond such limits.

It is not easy to observe the nature and limits of human knowledge with respect to God by observing the moments of analogical predication, with all the tensions inherent in them. Min locates the greatness of St. Thomas in his systematic sensibility and his fidelity to this humanity of theology against all the temptations to despair through agnosticism and fideism and to presumption through rationalism and intuitionism.

Thus far I have given a brief, preliminary anticipation of what this book is about. I am more than impressed by the insightful explorations of the medieval legacy as resources still so fruitful and even essential to the many theological problems we face today. Each essay, I am sure, also raises further issues for continuing dialogue.

As should be clear by now, this is not a book on medieval theology as such, its exegesis and commentary in its own historical context. There are many books of this kind we can turn to. Nor is this a book on contemporary theology as such, its constructive task and its many challenges. We also have many books of this kind with which we can engage in dialogue. This is rather a book that seeks to bridge the two worlds by rethinking medieval theology for the surplus of meaning it may yet contain that is relevant to contemporary issues, retrieving its as yet unexplored possibilities as resources for the contemporary theological task. To be sure, the work of retrieval presupposes sound exegesis or proper interpretation of the medieval resources we are trying to mine. I believe the contributors of this volume provide a sound, at least plausible, interpretation of the texts they are exploring, but the point of this volume is to go beyond such exegesis to explore and develop the medieval resources for the task of contemporary theology. Does the result shed light on the contemporary issues to which the volume seeks to respond? Does it also challenge some of our contemporary assumptions? Whether this volume succeeds in this task is for the readers to judge.

AS THE CONFERENCE organizer it is now my delightful duty to thank all the participants for making the conference so worthwhile and productive. In addition to the contributors who gladly accepted my invitation to present, I owe a very special debt of gratitude to the respondents, the six graduate students of Claremont Graduate University, Marlene Block, Duncan Gale, Nathan Greeley, Fabrizio D'Ambrosio, Bruce Paolozzi, and Brad Rubin, whose discerning responses contributed much to the intellectual excitement of the conference. I also thank my colleagues for chairing the sessions: Esther Chung-Kim (Claremont McKenna College), Stephen Davis (Claremont McKenna College), Joseph Prabhu (California State University, Los Angeles), Karen Torjesen (Claremont Graduate University), and Nancy van Deusen (Claremont Graduate University). Bruce Paolozzi, my research assistant, deserves special thanks for doing the preliminary editorial work, as does Shane Ackerman, my new research assistant, for help with the index.

Chapter One

EXCHANGING HEARTS
A Medievalist Looks at Transplant Surgery

BARBARA NEWMAN

*A new heart I will give you, and a new spirit I will put within you;
and I will take out of your flesh the heart of stone and give you a
heart of flesh.*

—Ezekiel 36:26

We are members one of another.

—Ephesians 4:25

The exchange of hearts, a familiar motif in hagiography and romance,
may seem one of the stranger marks of medieval alterity. Lyric poets
routinely send their hearts questing after resistant ladies, who take the
organ hostage with a kiss. When forced to separate, couples pledge
their loyalty by exchanging hearts, which may come back to them
with alarming literalism. Mystics—always female—offer their hearts
to Jesus and receive his in return, sometimes entering his body
through the bloody wound in his side. Jealous husbands kill and ex-
coriate their wives' paramours, feeding their hearts to the ladies in a

secret cannibal feast. On autopsy, a lover's heart reveals the name or image of the beloved or, mutatis mutandis, the tokens of Christ's Passion.

Lovers no longer use these metaphors, nor do the devout. Yet, from one perspective, such narratives should be more intelligible today than ever before. Imagine what a medieval reader would have made of the following tale. In 2004 a man named Sonny Graham, sixty-five, of Hilton Head, South Carolina, married Cheryl Cottle, a widow thirty years his junior. Such unions, though rare, seldom make national headlines. This one did because in 1995 Sonny Graham had received the transplanted heart of Cheryl's late husband, Terry Cottle. After four years of wedded bliss, Graham shot himself in the head and died—just as Terry Cottle had done thirteen years before.[1]

In the three decades since modern transplants literalized the poetic metaphor of exchanging hearts, more and more such tales have emerged, to the consternation of surgeons. A 1999 study by Paul Pearsall and colleagues, published in the journal *Integrative Medicine*, describes ten cases of remarkable personality change among heart transplant recipients, as ascertained from interviews with patients, their families and friends, and donors' families.[2] A middle-aged white factory worker, described by his wife as an Archie Bunker type, makes friends with his black colleagues and develops a passion for classical music. His donor, it turns out, was a young black man killed in a drive-by shooting en route to a violin lesson. A five-year-old boy, given a new heart in infancy, picks out his donor's father in a crowd and runs up to him, calling, "Daddy!" Another young boy with the heart of a drowned girl develops a sudden fear of water, which he always used to enjoy. A man with a woman's heart becomes a better lover and experiences a newfound joy in shopping, while another develops a taste for perfumes and the color pink. A lesbian activist becomes heterosexual and gives up her favorite restaurant, McDonald's, because the smell of meat now disgusts her. Her donor, a vegetarian and heterosexual, had run a health food restaurant. One of the case studies might have come straight from a medieval romance. An eighteen-year-old girl receives the heart of a boy her own age, a songwriter, killed in an auto accident. More than a year later, the boy's parents discover that he had predicted his own death in a song titled "Danny, My Heart Is Yours." When the girl sees the boy's picture, she recognizes in him the longtime lover who died to save her life: "I know he is in me and he is in love with me. He was always my lover, maybe in another time somewhere. How could he know years before he died that he would die and give his heart to me? How would he know my name is Danielle?"[3]

Scientific responses to such anecdotes differ, to say the least. In the study just cited, the authors remark that all seventy-four patients in their sample "showed various degrees of changes that paralleled the personalities of their donors," though not always as dramatically as those described. They posit a theory of cellular memory to explain how "information and energy are transmitted electromagnetically between the brain and heart, [so] that through electromagnetic resonance, the brain may process information derived from the donor's heart."[4] Other studies cite organ recipients who claim to have internalized such donor traits as generosity, artistic talent, piety, aggression, and even the ability to speak a foreign language.[5] Claire Sylvia's 1997 memoir, *A Change of Heart*, narrates her own developing relationship with her donor and presents a range of theories, both scientific and metaphysical, that purport to explain such phenomena.[6] Meanwhile, popular culture has begun to embrace the idea of heart transplants as not only saving but also transforming lives. In the early 1990s, a segment of the *Phil Donahue Show* featured a group of New York–area heart transplant patients who claimed not only to have taken on characteristics of their donors, but to know intimate details of their lives without being told.[7] The 2000 romantic film *Return to Me*, directed by Bonnie Hunt, anticipates the real-life story of Sonny Graham and Cheryl Cottle.[8] In his short story "Whither Thou Goest," Richard Selzer imagines a distraught widow who finds comfort only when she tracks down her husband's heart and listens to it beating in the breast of its new owner.[9]

But such tales also elicit widespread skepticism. A 2004 Israeli study finds that of thirty-five male heart transplant patients, only a third thought they might have experienced personality change caused by their donors' hearts. The researchers ascribe these patients' "fantasies" and "magical thinking" to the physical and emotional stress of surgery.[10] In a study by F. M. Mai, eighteen of twenty transplant patients engaged in denial: seven claimed to have no special thoughts about their new hearts; five said they never wondered about their donors; and six showed denial on both fronts.[11] In an Austrian study of forty-seven patients, 79 percent categorically denied any personality change. As if to prove that Freud's Vienna has not changed very much, the authors of this study see the patients as presenting "massive defense and denial reactions."[12] Even in this group, however, three patients reported personality change in conformity with their donors. The philosopher Jean-Luc Nancy, who received a heart transplant around 1990, described his experience in a trenchant essay titled "The Intruder" (L'Intrus).[13] Though known for his philosophy of "being-with" (*Mitsein*), Nancy expresses surprisingly little interest in his donor, remarking that "the whole dubious symbolism of the gift . . . wears out very quickly."[14] Instead, the "intruder" of his title "is nothing but myself and man himself."[15] His graft, which extended his life without restoring his health, inspires a meditation on the fragmented identity, the long process of self-alienation, induced by the medically altered body.

Whether dramatic or subtle, common or rare, the experiences of those who have undergone a literal change of heart suggest that, even in medical terms, the organ is far more than a muscle that pumps the blood. Understood in cultures around the world as the seat of life, soul, personality, and emotion, the heart remains the most frequent and symbolically charged metonymy for the whole person. The ancient idea of giving one's heart to another takes on new potency now that it has become physically possible. In this essay, I mean to explore the ethics of transplants—in particular, the relationships they establish between the living and the dead—from my perspective as a historical theologian.[16] Seeing through the lens of such Catholic doctrines as the coinherence of the Trinity, the mystical body of Christ, and the communion of saints, I pay special attention to medieval practices based on those doctrines. With Wendy Doniger I believe that "though it has become physically possible to do such operations only in recent decades, people have imagined, for a very long time indeed, the sorts of problems that might arise if one could do such things."[17] This kind of imagining shapes medieval legends about lovers exchanging hearts, as well as the practice of saints offering their own pain to relieve that of others, living and dead. For Christians wrestling with the ethical problems posed by this life-saving, yet disquieting surgery, such legends and practices, in dialogue with contemporary studies, can help us gain a fresh moral and ontological purchase on the problematics of transplants.

Let me return to Pearsall's case histories. What makes his work so important is that for the first time he established an experimental protocol to test claims that had been surfacing within the transplant community for years. In each case, the recipients of new hearts, with their families and friends, were first interviewed about personality changes observed since their transplants. Only later were potential links between these traits and the donors confirmed by interviews with people who had known those donors well. The recipients themselves had no prior contact with their donors' families or friends, nor had they received any information about the donors beyond age and gender.[18] In these patients, therefore, unexpected changes bearing a demonstrable relationship to the donors' qualities could not be dismissed as mere "incorporation fantasies." That is actually one of the kinder terms that physicians have used for such patient reports, when they have deigned to notice them at all. Although patients often express such beliefs, their statements are typically characterized as "animistic," "regressive," and "magic-infused thinking."[19] One physician's assistant defended the hospital's policy of keeping donors anonymous with the remark, "When you give somebody a gift, you don't ask them, 'How's my chess set that I gave you? How's the basketball I gave you?' The same is true with organs. We don't want people saying, 'How's Johnny's heart? Are you taking good care of it?' Some people feel that just because you have their brother's heart in you, they have some influence over your life. And we don't like to foster that feeling at all."[20] Accordingly, many surgeons, lawyers, and economists, and even some bioethicists, have adopted what Renée

Fox and Judith Swazey call a "spare parts" approach, wishing to distance themselves as far as possible from the "superstitious" idea that the dead person lives on in donated organs.

As Don Keyes has noted, the prevailing method of defining death in the transplant community implies a brain-body dualism, with the brain uneasily taking the place of the soul: "There seems to be an implicit assumption that as long as the brain is intact, the self remains intact. Other body parts are interchangeable and transplantable."[21] I argue that this model is seriously flawed. Not only does it fly in the face of our everyday assumptions about psychosomatic wholeness, which are supported as much by biblical theology as by nearly unlimited evidence for the unity of body and mind in the living person. In a more disconcerting way, this primitive dualistic model is undercut by Pearsall's study and a great deal of related evidence, which suggests that some elements of what we call "soul" or "personality" cling to transplanted body parts—especially the heart—even after the death of their owner. Medical research now confirms an insight memorably expressed by the critic Dennis Slattery in *The Wounded Body*: "Perhaps something of our own souls is permanently in our body, in each of its parts. To lose something of ourselves is to lose something of psyche, even of a memory that is embedded deep in every organ."[22] After transplant surgery, patients of all ages and both sexes, most with no history of psychological illness, have unexpectedly found themselves in a personal relationship with their donors, living or dead. Instead of pathologizing their experiences or dismissing them as "fantasies," we might have the courage to admit that a new medical procedure has given us new evidence about our humanity, challenging the limitations of brain-body dualism and, more broadly, of scientific materialism. How might we think more creatively if we acknowledged that patients, as well as surgeons, are now pushing the frontiers of discovery?

Traditional funeral customs have always assumed a continuing link between the body and the personal presence of the deceased. Why else do we go to mourn our loved ones at their graves if any other site might serve as well? Remarkably, the Catholic cult of relics assumes that even saints in heaven work most powerfully through their remains on earth, often centuries after their deaths. The experience of Pearsall's patients suggests that such traditional beliefs should not be taken lightly. If organ transplants can lead, as one psychiatrist puts it, to a "fusion of the ego boundaries of donor and recipient,"[23] this may suggest not that the patient is psychotic but that the boundaries of the ego are not easily separable from those of the body, which the surgery itself has breached. I do not, however, wish to argue on the grounds of this psychosomatic unity that transplants should not occur. Rather, I suggest that prospective donors, families, recipients, and—if it is not too much to ask—medical teams should acknowledge this jarring evidence and make a psychological and spiritual effort to come to terms with it.[24] As a first step, we might reconsider the way we conceptualize personhood.

Nowadays we assume, without much reflection, that a "person" is roughly the same as an "individual." As a theologian, however, I would propose a different starting point: the doctrine of the Trinity, which asserts both the inseparable oneness and the eternal distinction of the three persons. In patristic theology, the Latin *persona,* or mask, was used to translate the Greek *hypostasis,* a subsistent being. A "person" thus came to denote a center of consciousness, or what we might call a "self," over against a "nature," an abstract set of properties characterizing a particular type of being. Theologians formulated the central paradoxes of Christian doctrine through the interplay of these terms, defining the Trinity as three persons sharing one nature and Christ as one person possessing two natures, divine and human. Once these dogmas were in place, both could be extended to define human selfhood. Christian anthropology is founded on the idea of *imago Dei,* the human person created in the image of God. Yet the divine Self is conceived as supremely permeable, for the three persons of the Trinity not only share the same nature. They are also said to "indwell" one another reciprocally—a doctrine known as coinherence, or being-within-one-another.[25] As Jesus in the Gospel of John declares, "I am in the Father and the Father in me" (John 14:11). This divine coinherence extends to the redeemed: "You will know that I am in my Father, and you in me, and I in you" (John 14:20). As a theory of selfhood, coinherence asserts the porousness of human persons on the model of the divine. "The glory which you have given me I have given to them," Christ tells the Father, "that they may be one even as we are one, I in them and you in me" (John 17:22–23). On this model, the essence of personhood is the capacity to be permeated by other selves, other persons, without being fractured by them. A "person" in this sense has little to do with either the self-sufficient Enlightenment self or the decentered, fragmented postmodern self. Rather, the personal is, by definition, the interpersonal. One cannot be a person by oneself but only with, through, and in other persons.[26] Or in St. Paul's words, "We, though many, are one body in Christ, and individually members one of another" (Rom. 12:5).

The great twentieth-century Anglican writer Charles Williams— poet, novelist, and theologian—explored the profound implications of coinherence as a spiritual practice, even founding a lay religious order called the Companions of the Co-inherence.[27] In his view, this overarching reality involves bodies no less than souls. Hence he ends his book *The Descent of the Dove*, subtitled *A Short History of the Holy Spirit in the Church*, with an observation about pregnancy— a subject on which church historians usually have little to say. "At the beginning of life in the natural order," Williams wrote, "is an act of substitution and co-inherence. . . . The child for nine months literally co-inheres in its mother; there is no human creature that has not sprung from such a period of such an interior growth. . . . It has been the habit of the Church to baptize it, as soon as it has emerged, by the formula of the Trinity-in-Unity. As it passes from the most material co-inherence it is received into the supernatural."[28] Pregnancy is the only circumstance in which one human being actually dwells in the body of another—or at least it was until the advent of transplant surgery. Today, therefore, coinherence may provide the most ontologically useful way to understand the new relationship between persons that is established through transplants. I would propose that the gift offered by an organ donor is far more than a functional "spare part" to replace a broken one, like a new hard drive in an old computer. Rather, it is a gift of self in a much deeper sense, a literal enactment of the dictum that "we are members one of another" (Eph. 4:25). Like a child in its mother's womb, the transplanted heart represents the sojourn of one person within another. But, while the first instance of coinherence ends with a birth, the other begins with a death.

For medieval writers, the exchange of hearts likewise originates as a corporeal metaphor of love. More specifically, it denotes the lover's mysterious and transforming presence within the beloved. At first the motif is used playfully by troubadours and romance poets. Over the course of time, however, it reveals a surprising pull toward literalizing the gift. From the twelfth century on, poets imagine the heart under amorous provocation taking leave of the lover's body. Ablaze with delicious pain or bitter joy, it goes to dwell with the lady, who takes it captive with a kiss. Forced to part at dawn, illicit lovers pledge fidelity by exchanging hearts along with their rings. In Chrétien de Troyes's *Yvain*, a newlywed knight departs on a quest but leaves his heart behind with his wife. As Chrétien says comically:

> We know the body can't survive
> without a heart, yet he's alive!
> His body has no heart inside!
> So it can never be denied
> that such a wonder came about,
> because he's still alive without
> his heart, which, though enclosed before,
> will not go with him any more.[29]

In Chaucer's *Troilus and Criseyde*, as the heroine debates whether to take Troilus as her lover, she falls asleep and dreams that an eagle, "feathered white as bone," sets his claws beneath her breast, extracts her heart, and replaces it with his own, amazingly causing no fear or pain—"and forth he flew, with heart there left for heart."[30] The dream foreshadows and facilitates their actual affair. Another exchange of hearts occurs in the thirteenth-century romance, *Flamenca*. Meeting again after a separation, the hero, Guillem, asks his beloved, "How is my heart doing?," and she replies:

"This is a strange new thing indeed
and comes of love and subtlety—
I keep your heart in place of mine
and you keep mine, in such a way
that I suffer mine to live in you,
and in the same way you suffer yours
to live in me through pure desire."[31]

The exchange of hearts does not only symbolize mutual love but can also convey darker meanings of pain, betrayal, and sacrifice. Abelard tells Heloise that she is "immortally entombed" in his heart, from which she will never emerge while he lives.[32] When a lover is faithless—as Criseyde is to Troilus—the survivor can only perish miserably, having lost not one heart but two. In a gruesome cluster of romances, the so-called eaten heart tales, a poetic exchange of hearts ends with a material gift.[33] The dying lover in Jakemes's *Romance of the Castellan of Couci and the Lady of Fayel* asks his valet to remove his heart, embalm it, and send it to his beloved in a silver casket. But the gift is intercepted by her jealous husband, with fateful consequences. He secretly gives the heart to his chef, who prepares an exquisite dish for his wife to eat. On learning what she has just devoured, the lady resolves to turn her unwitting cannibal act into a Last Supper by starving herself to death:

"Alas! What a sorrowful gift
is his heart, which he has sent me!
He showed me truly it was mine,
so mine should just as well be his!
So it is! I will prove it well,
for I will die for love of him."[34]

It is no coincidence that in tales like this one, what begins as a metaphysical gift of love ends in a physical act of cannibalism. Stuart Youngner has proposed that "in an entirely concrete sense, organ transplantation *is* a form of nonoral cannibalism, that is, the taking of the flesh and blood from one person into another."[35] Living persons can make a symbolic gift of the heart, but (unlike a kidney) the actual gift requires a sacrificial death—which in the Christian tradition has always been the supreme proof of love. In 1972, when members of the Uruguayan rugby team found themselves stranded in the Andes after a plane crash, the survivors justified their practice of cannibalism by linking it to the Eucharist. "It's like Holy Communion," one explained. "When Christ died he gave his body to us so that we could have spiritual life. My friend has given us his body so that we can have physical life."[36] Disturbing as the analogy might be, the Eucharist is indeed a rite of symbolic cannibalism; without sacrifice there could be no communion. Transplant patients—"survivors" of another fearsome but life-giving rite—might suffer less guilt if they could acknowledge their donors as honestly as this Catholic athlete acknowledged his dead teammate. But, whatever the context, the choice to benefit knowingly from another's death should not be an easy one. For this reason medieval saints often became hyperscrupulous about receiving communion. In response, churchmen defended both partaking with gratitude and abstaining from a sense of unworthiness.[37] Much like communicants in the Middle Ages, transplant patients today sometimes feel guilt and gratitude so intense they can be paralyzing.[38] Such feelings are not "morbid," though they are often presented as such in the literature. On the contrary, they demonstrate spiritual maturity and moral sensitivity. Yet Christians, at least in principle, have already accepted the knowledge that "another died so that I might live." Honoring that context, with the principle of coinherence and exchange that governs the mystical body, could make it easier for patients to manage such troubling emotions.

Medieval tradition followed the exchange of hearts into a similar realm, linking it with both the Eucharist and personal sacrifice. From the mid-thirteenth century, hagiographers began to imitate secular poets, noting that holy women exchanged hearts with Jesus just as romance heroines did with their lovers. This grace is first reported of Lutgard of Aywières, a Cistercian nun who died in 1246.[39] Whether her life established a model or simply marked a trend, the exchange of hearts soon became a regular feature of women's vitae. More than thirty saints were ultimately said to have received this grace, among them, Gertrude of Helfta, Catherine of Siena, Dorothy of Montau, Teresa of Avila, and Margaret Mary Alacoque.[40] An exchange of hearts served to confirm the coinherence of a saint with Christ. Often the exchange would occur as the mystic received communion. In one miracle story, when St. Juliana Falconieri lay dying in 1341 she was too ill to swallow the host, so she asked the priest to place it on a corporal above her heart. No sooner had he done so than it vanished— and at the same instant the saint died, smiling, in the kiss of her Beloved.[41] Such a death can be viewed as a variant on the exchange of hearts: the saint receives the eucharistic Christ into her heart even as, dying, she enters his.

The most famous and complex of these tales concerns St. Catherine of Siena (d. 1380). Ten years before she died, as her biographer Raymond of Capua reports, Catherine was praying the words of Psalm 50—"Create in me a clean heart, O God"—when Christ appeared to her, opened her side, and extracted her heart. This was no mere vision, Raymond insists, but an experience so physically compelling that when she next went to confession Catherine said "she no longer had a heart within her breast." Her confessor laughed, but she persisted: "It is a fact, Father. As far as I can judge from what I feel in my body, I seem no longer to have any heart in it."[42] For the next few days she repeated this claim—until Christ returned with his own heart, "ruby in colour and ablaze with light," and placed it within her breast. For Raymond, the material reality of this miracle was all-important. Hence he notes that Catherine's "companions informed myself and many others that they had often seen the scar" from her incision,[43] while she herself claimed that she could no longer commend her heart to Christ because he already possessed it.

For Catherine, this divine transplant was the first stage of a life-long process. After an active ministry caring for the poor and sick, making peace between feuding city-states, and trying to persuade the pope to return from Avignon to Rome, Catherine was heartbroken when Gregory XI did return in 1377 only to die soon afterward, provoking the election of two rival popes and inaugurating a schism that would last for forty years. When all else she could do had failed, Catherine finally gave her heart, pulsing with Christ's blood, as a remedy to heal his ailing bride. In a farewell letter written with her own hand, she tells Raymond how, at God's urging, she had offered her life for the church. "Oh eternal God," she prayed, "accept the sacrifice of my life within this mystic body, holy Church! I have nothing to give except what you have given me. Take my heart and squeeze it out over the face of this bride!" In response, "God eternal, turning the eye of his mercy [on me], tore my heart out by the roots and squeezed it out over holy Church. He had drawn it to himself with such force that if he hadn't encircled the vessel of my body with his strength (not wanting it to be broken), the life would have gone out of it."[44] As she prayed thus, Catherine suffered what seems to have been an actual heart attack. She describes feeling "as if my memory and understanding and will had nothing to do with my body" while simultaneously enduring demonic attacks and perceiving divine mysteries. In a second and final letter, composed later the same day, she adds that at the time "the pain in my heart was such that my tunic was torn apart wherever I could get hold of it, while I reeled about the chapel as if I were in convulsions. . . . The terror and physical pain were such that I wanted to run. . . . But all of a sudden I was thrown down, and, once down, it seemed to me as if my soul had left my body. . . . I remained that way for such a very long time that the family was mourning me as dead."[45] The end was in fact very near. A few days later Catherine suffered a second attack, after which she lay paralyzed until her death.

There need be no contradiction in seeing this near-death experience as a mystical sacrifice *and* a massive heart attack, though interpreters have been reluctant to offer such interpretations.[46] Nor does one need to be privileged as the cause of the other. Catherine's asceticism, especially her prolonged failure to eat, undoubtedly weakened her heart, and the pain she suffered gave her the opportunities for sacrifice that her ardent soul craved.[47] What seems strangest about her account is not just its quintessentially late medieval fusion of extreme pain with ecstatic prayer, but the idea that she could heal a desperately sick woman (albeit an allegorical one) by squeezing her heart's blood into her face. Catherine's thought seems akin to the folk belief that leprosy could be cured by the blood of an innocent virgin or a child.[48] The idea of transferring such a remedy to the church could have occurred only to someone who was steeped in blood piety, inclined to both physical and metaphysical realism, and utterly devoted to the cause of reform. Having already exchanged hearts with Christ, Catherine offered her new heart for the good of his mystical body, in a willed and ultimately fatal sacrifice. For this act she might today be exalted as the patron saint of donors.

Surgeons, of course, do not extract hearts from the living—or at least that is not their intent, despite lingering controversy over the criterion of "brain death."[49] Nevertheless, the decision to donate organs is often fraught, whether it is made by a living donor or, more painfully, by relatives after the sudden death of a young person. About 70 percent of all families approached for organs consent,[50] usually in the hope of bringing life out of death and honoring the spirit of the deceased. These are deeply religious motives, whether or not the families profess any faith. In Denys Arcand's 1989 film, *Jesus of Montreal*, organ donation is used as an explicit analogue for the resurrection. When the actor performing Christ in a passion play is killed in a production accident, his heart resurrects a dying man, his corneas give sight to the blind, and so forth. Even so, removal of organs from the newly dead (or, some would say, the nearly dead) violates ancient and profound taboos. Almost every culture has strictures against mutilating corpses, and the shocked and grieving survivors may be unable to anticipate how they will feel about their decision after the fact. Their trauma can be heightened if multiple organs are taken, as is often the case.

In Richard Selzer's story, cited earlier, the young widow expresses anger and horror when she hears a radio preacher holding forth on the resurrection of the flesh. "Tell me this," she asks. "What about Samuel Owen on your resurrection day? Here he is scattered all over Texas, breathing in Forth Worth, urinating in Dallas *and* Galveston, digesting or whatever it is the liver does in Abilene. They going to put him back together again when the day comes, or is it to the recipients belong the spoils? Tell me that."[51] As Selzer doubtless knew, this was the same objection that pagans raised against the early Christian belief in bodily resurrection: how could the flesh be restored to its pristine

wholeness after it had been devoured by wild beasts or eaten by can-
nibals?[52] Transplant surgery raises the specter of a new kind of dismemberment, appalling even to some who believe intellectually that
the procedure is benign. In an essay titled "Why Organ Transplant
Programs Do Not Succeed," Leslie Fiedler points out that the
Frankenstein monster, that irrepressible myth of our popular culture,
is a patchwork of what would now be called "cadaveric organs."[53]

In view of such fears, I want to consider an alternative way of
viewing the link between one person's harm and the health of others.
The medieval doctrine of purgatory is best known today as a system
of otherworldly bribes that justly earned Luther's wrath. But, long
before it evolved into a cash nexus, purgatory provided some comfort
for survivors by giving them concrete actions they could take to help
their beloved dead. The "Poor Souls" languishing there were thought
to be among the saved but not yet sufficiently purified to stand in the
presence of God. They needed first to be cleansed by a time of
suffering—which could be considerably shortened if the living were
kind enough to share their burden. Hence priests sang extra masses
for them; survivors made gifts of prayers, alms, and fasting; and saints
took it on themselves to suffer not only for their departed friends and
kin, but for poor sinners at large.[54] Pain came to be seen as a currency
that could be used to buy relief for the pain of others, whether they
were afflicted by physical illness, mental anguish, or purgatorial torments. In effect, the practice of suffrages for souls is a gift exchange
that, like St. Catherine's gift of her heart, literalizes the metaphor of
the church as Christ's body. The fact of coinherence is presupposed:
since "we are members, one of another," pain as well as guilt could
be displaced from one limb of the mystical body onto another. But
the practice also promised benefits for the living. In a world where
medical care was neither highly effective nor widely available, the gift
of suffering as suffrage could be a strategy for the endurance of
chronic disease and disability. It was a way of turning extreme helplessness into help for others, need into gift, abjection into power—
thus introducing an altruistic dimension into what might otherwise
seem an unavoidably slow and horrible loss of self.

Alice of Schaerbeek, a Cistercian nun of Ter Cameren, died in 1250. Her biographer, perhaps Abbot Arnold II of Villers, wrote her vita about twenty years later, relying on her sister and her maid as sources.[55] What intrigued him about Alice was that she spent the last years of her life, perhaps as much as a decade, in a leper's hut. There, within earshot of the monastery bells, she offered the ravages of her illness for the living and the dead until it finally carried her off. Alice's heavenly bridegroom, the author writes, wished to have her all to himself, so he sequestered her "as a sign of perfect love" by smiting her with leprosy. Rhetoric of this kind should arouse suspicion, for nothing is easier than to glamorize someone else's suffering. Nevertheless, in between evocations of horror and rhapsodic consolations we can discern the pragmatic use that Alice found for her pain. The author prefaces the onset of leprosy, the first major turning point in Alice's vita, with a dream in which she sees a golden cross descending from heaven. At the second turning point, before her last and most agonizing year, he hails the "violence of charity" with which she begs God to "relieve the purgatorial pain of all the dead, and likewise purge the living of all sins," on condition that she alone might bear "the vengeance of all for the sake of each."[56] *Poena* and *vindicta* are judicial terms; as Alice explains to her sister, she endures these punishments for the sins of others, not her own. At precisely the point when she can no longer leave her hut to walk to church, her disintegrating body becomes a microcosm of the church, as she makes a transition from contemplative martyrdom to vicarious penance. When she loses her right eye to leprosy, she offers it as a suffrage for the newly elected king, asking God to enlighten the eye of his understanding—literally giving an eye for an eye.[57] Soon afterward she gives her left eye as a "fruit of penance" for the success of Louis IX's crusade.[58] Though Alice had no control over the loss of her sight, the belief that she could trade her blindness for another's enlightenment goes a step beyond resigned or even joyful acceptance. It transforms an appalling biological process into a gift.

Other saints behaved in comparable ways, transforming both self-inflicted pain and the torments of illness into suffrages. Arnulf of Villers, a lay brother, flogged himself bloody for his friends. As he rhythmically scourged himself he would chant a ditty: "'Got to be braver, got to be manly; . . . friends need it badly; this stroke for this one; that stroke for that one; take *that* in the name of God.' As the flogging went on and on, he kept remembering and naming now this particular brother, now those various friends, and now these devout women, . . . [f]logging hard and begging hard that the Lord transmit to each a gracious forgiving of some sin of theirs, or a lightening of some trouble."[59] Around the same time, Margaret the Lame, a recluse of Magdeburg, made a gift of the depression she endured on account of her disability and social ostracism.[60] Lidwina of Schiedam (1380–1433), a Dutch saint born in the year Catherine of Siena died, was afflicted with horrible complications from a skating accident. An invalid from fifteen until her death at fifty-three, she was said not only to release souls from purgatory, but even to heal the sickness of others with effluvia from her putrefying body.[61] Such practices may now seem grotesque and repulsive—witnesses at best to the medieval tendency Esther Cohen calls "philopassianism," the love of pain as a moral good.[62] Even if literal rather than symbolic organ transplants had been possible in the thirteenth century, a leper like Alice would have been an unlikely donor. Yet her tale is not merely tragic or bizarre, for the principle she practiced can reach beyond the conditions of her life. Today's "purgatories" may be the dialysis wards and intensive care units where desperately ill patients languish, waiting for usable organs that may or may not come in time to save them.

Intriguingly, Catholic bioethicists opposed transplants in their early, experimental years. The effective principle was that a body could be surgically "mutilated" only for the good of the whole. For instance, a cancerous organ might be removed, but a healthy kidney could not be taken for transplant. In 1944, however, Bert Cunningham turned the tables with his controversial thesis, *The Morality of Organic Transplantation*, which argued that the "whole body" whose welfare must be considered is not the individual but the mystical body of Christ—another version of coinherence. Hence "a person may licitly mutilate him- or herself for the good of the neighbor."[63] For example, Cunningham argued, a mother might give up a cornea to help her blind child, though the result would be a significant loss of vision. Even a one-eyed donor might sacrifice the cornea from his good eye and, in consequence, plunge into total blindness.[64] If Cunningham had known about Alice the Leper, he would surely have approved. Neither the medical profession nor the church ever adopted so extreme a view, but after prolonged debate Cunningham's underlying position was accepted by most ethicists.

Today the most obvious debating ground is the gift of kidneys from live donors, especially volunteers who are and remain strangers to their recipients. Anyone can understand such a gift to save a relative, spouse, or dear friend. But gifts from strangers are unnerving because they test the viability of coinherence, or the common good, rather than personal love as the motive for so intimate a sacrifice. In a 2009 *New Yorker* essay, "The Kindest Cut," Larissa MacFarquhar profiles a group of volunteer donors and explores the powerful clash of feelings elicited by their gifts. While most people admire this form of altruism, others find it freakishly masochistic. "Cold-blooded altruism," MacFarquhar muses, "seems nearly as sinister as cold-blooded malevolence."[65] It is a bit too close, perhaps, to the practice of medieval saints. When the philosopher Hans Jonas characterized organ donation as a "supererogatory" gift, one that goes "beyond duty and claim,"[66] he used a term the church has traditionally applied to the saints' "treasury of merits." Being more than sufficient for their own salvation, these can be applied at will to the account of souls in purgatory. In this connection the last of MacFarquhar's profiles is telling. Kimberly Brown-Whale, who called her local transplant center after hearing on television that someone needed a kidney, is a Methodist pastor who works with the poor and owns practically nothing. Having adopted two children from foster care, she suffered hair-raising hardships with her family in the African mission field. On the morning of her surgery, she left home alone, deciding not to wake her husband because he had had a long drive the day before. As for the man who received her kidney, he never called, and she knew nothing about him. After the operation, Brown-Whale refused all pain medicine and was back at work in a week. Rather than agree with most volunteer donors, who warn that "it's not for everyone," she asked MacFarquhar, "Well, why not? . . . Give it a try. We can do more than we think we can. If you're sitting around with a good kidney you're not using, why can't someone else have it? . . . Gosh, I've had flus that made me feel worse."[67] Though organ donors come in all varieties, the reporter chose to highlight one who would meet nearly anyone's criteria for sainthood.

I have tried in this chapter to present what might be called the imaginary of organ transplants—the myths, images, fears, and values that surround not just the surgery itself, which is fairly new, but the ancient pattern in which it partakes. That pattern is one of sacrifice and communion, coinherence and gift exchange. Unless it is acknowledged and honored, the promise of "medical miracles" could end up dehumanizing donors and patients alike. Transplants save lives, yes— but only at the cost of risk and discomfort to the living, mutilation and dismemberment of the dying, and potentially heightened anguish for the survivors. Even as this surgery becomes more common, it continues to challenge our sense of personhood by blurring the most fundamental boundaries we know—between self and other, between living and dead.[68] Both of these boundaries are more porous in traditional cultures than they have seemed to the post-Enlightenment West, which is one reason a backward glance at medieval beliefs and practices can paradoxically show us a way forward.[69] The alternative, as the sociologist Renée Fox wrote in her eloquent farewell to the field, is a utilitarian "spare parts" approach that massively cheapens the gift of life, turning it into a commodity and diminishing the sense of awe that hovered around transplants in the pioneer days. Where they are commercialized and routinized, they are also profaned—a word Fox does not hesitate to use.[70] Although transplant surgery is a moral good, it is what Charles Williams called a "terrible good"[71]— like the Eucharist and the cross, like the heartrending gift of St. Catherine and the generosity of Alice the Leper. No matter how many transplants are performed, each remains a sacred act both for those who give life and for those who receive it—with all the ambiguity of the Latin *sacer*, "marked for sacrifice." For a body wounded by the surgeon's knife is indeed a sacred body, one in which "the wound may be the violent presence of the numinous, or the sacred that enters us through the actions of others."[72] Remembering this context may help us hold off the coming of a new marketplace in human flesh.

NOTES

This chapter was first published in *Spiritus* 12 (2012): 1–20. I thank the editor, Douglas Christie, and the Johns Hopkins University Press for permission to reprint it in slightly altered form.

1. "Man with Suicide Victim's Heart Takes Own Life," Associated Press, April 6, 2008, www.msnbc.msn.com/id/23984857/ (accessed April 12, 2010).

2. Paul Pearsall, Gary E. R. Schwartz, and Linda G. S. Russek, "Changes in Heart Transplant Recipients That Parallel the Personalities of Their Donors," *Integrative Medicine* 2 (1999): 65–72.

3. Ibid., 66.

4. Ibid., 72. Of the 74 transplant patients, only 23—including all 10 of those profiled in the article—received heart transplants. Changes in the recipients of other organs were less durable and profound.

5. Pietro Castelnuovo-Tedesco, "Transplantation: Psychological Implications of Changes in Body Image," in *Psychonephrology 1: Psychological Factors in Hemodialysis and Transplantation*, ed. Norman B. Levy (New York: Plenum, 1981), 219–25 (222), with references to earlier literature.

6. Claire Sylvia with William Novak, *A Change of Heart: A Memoir* (Boston: Little, Brown, 1997), 219–35.

7. Stuart J. Youngner, "Some Must Die," in *Organ Transplantation: Meanings and Realities*, ed. Stuart J. Youngner, Renée C. Fox, and Laurence J. O'Connell (Madison: University of Wisconsin Press, 1996), 32–55 (51–52).

8. See also Nancy Weber's romance novel, *Brokenhearted* (New York: Dutton, 1989).

9. Richard Selzer, "Whither Thou Goest," in *Imagine a Woman and Other Tales* (New York: Random House, 1990), 3–28.

10. Y. Inspector, I. Kutz, and D. David, "Another Person's Heart: Magical and Rational Thinking in the Psychological Adaptation to Heart Transplantation," *Israel Journal of Psychiatry and Related Sciences* 41, no. 3 (2004): 161–73.

11. François M. Mai, "Graft and Donor Denial in Heart Transplant Recipients," *American Journal of Psychiatry* 143 (1986): 1159–61.

12. B. Bunzel, B. Schmidl-Mohl, A. Grundböck, and G. Wollenek, "Does Changing the Heart Mean Changing Personality? A Retrospective Inquiry on 47 Heart Transplant Patients," *Quality of Life Research* 1 (1992): 251–56.

13. Jean-Luc Nancy, *L'Intrus* (Paris: Galilée, 2000); English ed.: "The Intruder," trans. Richard A. Rand, in Jean-Luc Nancy, *Corpus* (New York: Fordham University Press, 2008), 161–70.

14. Nancy, "Intruder," 166. On "being-with," see Jean-Luc Nancy, *Être singulier pluriel* (Paris: Galilée, 1996); English ed.: *Being Singular Plural*, trans. Robert D. Richardson and Anne E. O'Byrne (Stanford: Stanford University Press, 2000).

15. Nancy, "Intruder," 170.

16. For a similar exercise, see Caroline Walker Bynum, "Material Continuity, Personal Survival and the Resurrection of the Body: A Scholastic Discussion in Its Medieval and Modern Contexts," in *Fragmentation and Redemption: Essays on Gender and the Human Body in Medieval Religion* (New York: Zone, 1991), 239–97.

17. Wendy Doniger, "Transplanting Myths of Organ Transplants," in Youngner, Fox, and O'Connell, *Organ Transplantation*, 194–220 (195).

18. Pearsall, Schwartz, and Russek, "Changes," 71.

19. Castelnuovo-Tedesco, "Transplantation," 223; C. Don Keyes, "Body and Self-Identity," in *New Harvest: Transplanting Body Parts and Reaping the Benefits*, ed. C. Don Keyes and Walter E. Wiest (Clifton, NJ: Humana Press, 1991), 161–77 (170, 172); Renée C. Fox and Judith P. Swazey, *Spare Parts: Organ Replacement in American Society* (New York: Oxford University Press, 1992), 43.

20. Ina Yalof, *Life and Death: The Story of a Hospital* (New York: Random House, 1988), 48.

21. Keyes, "Body and Self-Identity," 171.

22. Dennis Patrick Slattery, *The Wounded Body: Remembering the Markings of Flesh* (Albany: State University of New York Press, 2000), 4–5.

23. Castelnuovo-Tedesco, "Transplantation," 223.

24. Nurses and anesthesiologists have been considerably more willing than surgeons to do so, using such nonclinical terms as *soul* and *spirit*. See, e.g., Youngner, "Some Must Die," 46–47.

25. I use this term synonymously with the Greek *perichoresis*, "dancing around (one another)," and Latin *circuminsessio*, "sitting within (one another)." Both terms are comparatively rare. The theology of Trinitarian *perichoresis* was developed especially by Gregory of Nyssa in the fourth century and John of Damascus in the eighth. For a good recent discussion, see Catherine Mowry LaCugna, *God for Us: The Trinity and Christian Life* (New York: HarperCollins, 1991), 270–78.

26. The anthropologist McKim Marriott uses the interesting term *dividuals,* in lieu of *individuals,* to describe the same fluidity of personal boundaries in Indian thought. "Hindu Transactions: Diversity without Dualism," in *Transaction and Meaning: Directions in the Anthropology of Exchange and Symbolic Behavior,* ed. Bruce Kapferer (Philadelphia: Institute for the Study of Human Issues, 1976), 109–42 (111).

27. Barbara Newman, "Charles Williams and the Companions of the Co-Inherence," *Spiritus* 9 (2009): 1–26.

28. Charles Williams, *The Descent of the Dove: A Short History of the Holy Spirit in the Church* (1939; repr. Grand Rapids, MI: Eerdmans, 1974), 234.

29. Chrétien de Troyes, *Yvain, or The Knight with the Lion,* trans. Ruth Harwood Cline (Athens: University of Georgia Press, 1975), lines 2475–82, p. 74.

30. Geoffrey Chaucer, *Troilus and Criseyde,* II.925–31, in *The Riverside Chaucer,* ed. Larry Benson (Boston: Houghton Mifflin, 1987), 502 (modernized).

31. *The Romance of "Flamenca,"* ed. and trans. E. D. Blodgett (New York: Garland, 1995), lines 7393–99, pp. 380–83 (my translation).

32. Constant J. Mews, *The Lost Love Letters of Heloise and Abelard: Perceptions of Dialogue in Twelfth-Century France* (New York: St. Martin's, 1999), Letter 22, p. 204.

33. Jean-Jacques Vincensini, "Figure de l'imaginaire et figure du discours: Le motif du 'Coeur Mangé' dans la narration médiévale," in *Le "cuer" au Moyen Âge (réalité et sénéfiance)* (Aix-en-Provence: Centre Universitaire d'Études et de Recherches Médiévales d'Aix, 1991), 439–59; Milad Doueihi, *A Perverse History of the Human Heart* (Cambridge, MA: Harvard University Press, 1997).

34. Jakemes, *Le Roman du Castelain de Couci et de la Dame de Fayel,* ed. Maurice Delbouille (Paris: Société des anciens textes français, 1936), lines 8143–48; my translation.

35. Youngner, "Some Must Die," 49. Original emphasis.

36. Piers Paul Read, *Alive: The Story of the Andes Survivors* (Philadelphia: Lippincott, 1974), 91.

37. Jef Lamberts, "Liturgie et spiritualité de l'Eucharistie au XIIIe siècle," in *Fête-Dieu (1246–1996): Actes du colloque de Liège, 12–14 septembre 1996,* ed. André Haquin (Louvain-la-Neuve: Université Catholique de Louvain, 1999), 81–95.

38. This is what Fox and Swazey call "the tyranny of the gift": *Spare Parts,* 35, 39–42.

39. Thomas of Cantimpré, *Life of Lutgard of Aywières* I.12, trans. Margot H. King and Barbara Newman, in *Thomas of Cantimpré: The Collected Saints' Lives*, ed. Barbara Newman (Turnhout: Brepols, 2008), 227.

40. André Cabassut, "Coeurs, changement des," in *Dictionnaire de spiritualité ascétique et mystique, doctrine et histoire*, 17 vols. (Paris: Beauchesne, 1932–95): II.2, cols. 1046–51.

41. "De B. Juliana Falconeria," cap. 17, *Acta Sanctorum*, 19 June, IV, 770; Peter Browe, *Die eucharistischen Wunder des Mittelalters* (Breslau: Müller & Seiffert, 1938), 30.

42. Raymond of Capua, *Die Legenda Maior (Vita Catharinae Senensis) des Raimund von Capua*, II.6.179, ed. Jörg Jungmayr, 2 vols. (Berlin: Weidler, 2004), 1:258; Raymond of Capua, *The Life of Catherine of Siena*, trans. Conleth Kearns (Wilmington, DE: Michael Glazier, 1980), 174.

43. *Legenda Maior* II.6.180, ed. Jungmayr, 1:258; *Life of Catherine*, trans. Kearns, 175.

44. Catherine of Siena, *The Letters of Catherine of Siena*, Letter T371, trans. Suzanne Noffke, 4 vols., Medieval and Renaissance Texts and Studies (Tempe: Arizona Center for Medieval and Renaissance Studies, 2000–2008), 4:362.

45. Letter T373, *The Letters of Catherine of Siena*, trans. Noffke, 4:365–66.

46. The same might be said of the stroke cum epiphany experienced by Thomas Aquinas shortly before his death; after that event he could no longer write because all he had said of God seemed to him "like straw." Neither a secular interpreter nor an incarnational theologian should be shocked by the coincidence of such revelations with catastrophic physical events. See, e.g., Carol Zaleski, *Otherworld Journeys: Accounts of Near-Death Experience in Medieval and Modern Times* (New York: Oxford University Press, 1987).

47. For radically differing interpretations of Catherine's inedia, see Rudolph M. Bell, *Holy Anorexia* (Chicago: University of Chicago Press, 1985), 22–53; and Caroline Walker Bynum, *Holy Feast and Holy Fast: The Religious Significance of Food to Medieval Women* (Berkeley: University of California Press, 1987), 194–207.

48. This motif occurs in several romances, including *Der arme Heinrich* by Hartmann von Aue, *La Queste del saint Graal*, and the Middle English *Amis and Amiloun*.

49. Stuart J. Youngner et al., "Psychosocial and Ethical Implications of Organ Retrieval," *New England Journal of Medicine* 313 (August 1, 1985): 321–24; Keyes, "Body and Self-Identity," 172–77; Fox and Swazey, *Spare Parts*, 59–63.

50. Ruth Richardson, "Fearful Symmetry: Corpses for Anatomy, Organs for Transplantation?," in Youngner, Fox, and O'Connell, *Organ Transplantation*, 66–100 (91).

51. Selzer, "Whither Thou Goest," 8–9. Original emphasis.

52. Caroline Walker Bynum, *The Resurrection of the Body in Western Christianity, 200–1336* (New York: Columbia University Press, 1995), esp. 94–114.

53. Leslie A. Fiedler, "Why Organ Transplant Programs Do Not Succeed," in Youngner, Fox, and O'Connell, *Organ Transplantation*, 56–65 (62).

54. Jacques Le Goff, *The Birth of Purgatory*, trans. Arthur Goldhammer (Chicago: University of Chicago Press, 1984); Brian Patrick McGuire, "Purgatory, the Communion of Saints, and Medieval Change," *Viator* 20 (1989): 61–84.

55. Arnold II of Villers (?), *Alice the Leper: Life of St Alice of Schaerbeek*, trans. Martinus Cawley, OCSO (Lafayette, OR: Guadalupe Translations, 2000), v–xxii.

56. Ibid., chap. 21, pp. 19–20 (translation modified).

57. Ibid., chap. 23, pp. 21–22.

58. Ibid., chap. 27, p. 24.

59. Goswin of Bossut, *Life of Arnulf, Lay Brother of Villers*, I.11, in *Send Me God: The Lives of Ida the Compassionate of Nivelles, Nun of La Ramée, Arnulf, Lay Brother of Villers, and Abundus, Monk of Villers*, trans. Martinus Cawley, OCSO (Turnhout: Brepols, 2003), 147–48.

60. Johannes O.P. of Magdeburg, *The Life of Margaret the Lame*, trans. Gertrud Jaron Lewis and Tilman Lewis, in *Living Saints of the Thirteenth Century*, ed. Anneke B. Mulder-Bakker (Turnhout: Brepols, 2011), 313–96; Anneke B. Mulder-Bakker, *Lives of the Anchoresses: The Rise of the Urban Recluse in Medieval Europe*, trans. Myra Heerspink Scholz (Philadelphia: University of Pennsylvania Press, 2005), 148–73.

61. Bynum, *Holy Feast and Holy Fast*, 124–27.

62. Esther Cohen, "Towards a History of European Physical Sensibility: Pain in the Later Middle Ages," *Science in Context* 8 (1995): 47–74.

63. David Kelly and Walter E. Wiest, "Christian Perspectives," in Keyes and Wiest, *New Harvest*, 199–221 (200), summarizing Bert Joseph Cunningham, *The Morality of Organic Transplantation* (Washington, DC: Catholic University of America Press, 1944).

64. Cunningham, *Morality*, 105–6.

65. Larissa MacFarquhar, "The Kindest Cut," *New Yorker* (July 27, 2009): 38–51 (40).

66. Hans Jonas, "Philosophical Reflections on Experimenting with Human Subjects," in *Experimentation with Human Subjects*, ed. Paul A. Freund (New York: George Braziller, 1970), 1–31 (16).

67. McFarquhar, "Kindest Cut," 51.

68. Doniger, "Transplanting Myths," 210; Renée C. Fox, "Afterthoughts: Continuing Reflections on Organ Transplantation," in Youngner, Fox, and O'Connell, *Organ Transplantation*, 254–57.

69. Cf. Heather Webb: "The medieval heart, in its radical openness to the world, in its generous capacity to overreach the limits of its containing body and to enter into communion with the external world, represents perhaps a less accurate model in its details, but a truer model in terms of where it sets [its] parameters: not within the body but at the margins of our social networks and the borders of our beliefs, no matter where they may lie." *The Medieval Heart* (New Haven, CT: Yale University Press, 2010), 185.

70. Fox, "Afterthoughts," 262; see also Fox and Swazey, *Spare Parts*, 206–9.

71. Charles Williams, *Descent into Hell* (1937; repr. Grand Rapids, MI: Eerdmans, 1980), 16.

72. Slattery, *Wounded Body*, 7.

Chapter Two

FRIENDLINESS, DIVINE AND HUMAN

M A R I L Y N   M C C O R D   A D A M S

IDEALS OF FRIENDSHIP

Christian religion focuses on persons in relationship: divine persons—Father, Son, and Holy Spirit; Jesus, the God-man; and merely human beings. In seeking to characterize and/or norm personal interactions, the Bible reaches for multiple social models: God is patron king, while humans are fellow servants and subjects; God is father/mother, while humans are adopted children, one another's siblings; God or God-man is husband, the people of God his chosen bride. Among others, medieval theology finds friendship, personal friendliness, particularly salient for explaining how divine personal relationships *are*, and for showing what divine-human and human-to-human relationships are *meant* to be.

Classic Varieties

Medieval thinkers did not, of course, invent the social category of friendship. The Hebrew Bible identifies Abraham (Gen. 18:16–33) and Moses as friends of God (Exod. 33:11; Deut. 34:10), and John's Jesus calls his disciples "friends" (John 15–17, esp. 15:13–15). Homer

43

memorializes the famous friendship of Achilles and Patroclus and bears witness to a variety of "friendly" social practices.[1]

In the ancient world, friendship broadly conceived was *an institution (or family of institutions) for exchanging benefits* (originally, *charis,* something that prompts joy and delight).[2] Life is too uncertain to proceed on a strict "fee for services" basis. Any hope of survival and flourishing requires us to enter into alliances with others on whose general benevolence we can presume, as they can on ours, for material assistance, for advice and support, for the general promotion of our aims.[3] *Reciprocity* is obligatory. Even if ties of friendship are forged out of need and as a result of means-end calculations, they are also underwritten by natural tendencies. Friendship's goals are best served when friends take each other's interests to heart as if they were their own.[4] *Trustworthiness* is key if friends are to count on one another to protect and promote each other's interests in foul weather (when the climate is competitive or hostile) as in fair or to help when misfortune places demands on the friend's resources without any immediate prospect of return. Trustworthiness is also needed to inspire confidence or at least dispose one to give the other the benefit of the doubt in the face of accusations and real or apparent offenses.[5] For friendship to increase security, there must be *a presumption of stability:* even in the face of offense, the burden of proof rests on the partner who would dissolve the relationship.[6] Likewise, in ancient societies friendship is *transitive:* if you are my friend, your friends are my friends, your enemies my enemies, so that each partner brings a network of obligations of varying degrees.[7] Friendship's responsibilities are many and great. To the extent that friendship is voluntary, prudence advises caution. One should not make friends too quickly without testing candidates for character and resourcefulness.[8]

Ancient societies recognized and enforced friendship institutions at several levels. If self-interest—more generally, a bias toward "me and mine"—is natural,[9] (i) *family members* assert the strongest entitlements to friendship, bound as they are presumed to be by blood ties and common interests. Natural instinct was supposed to generate friendship of parents toward offspring to whom they give both life and nurture. Children are obliged to support aging parents by way of reciprocal exchange.[10] This kind of friendship comes in degrees and extends to all blood relatives in proportion to kinship affinities. (ii) *Civic friendship* widens the circle. When political organization shifted from clan to city-state (or *polis*), the new unit was likened to a family, whose citizens are kin, the fatherland a parent who must be repaid for birth and nurture, whose interests could be pressed at the expense of smaller family units.[11] (iii) *Marriage* was another distinctive kind of friendship based on exchange of favors, first between the couple's families[12] but subsequently between husband and wife, who offer one another—among other things—the *charis* of sexual gratification.[13] Because friendship is transitive, marriage makes families friends and presumptive kin—a semifiction given substance by the indirect blood ties established in the couple's children.[14] (iv) *Personal friendships* may overlap with family and city but may also be established with foreigners. They are initiated from one side by spontaneous favor and maintained by exchange over a lifetime of varying circumstances.[15] (v) Finally, there is *friendship with the gods,* at one level commercially conceived of as a *do-ut-des* swapping of sacrifices for supernatural favors.[16]

Literature, legend, and history illustrate that friendship is rife with opportunities for conflicting loyalties. Not only do the claims of family and marriage, personal friends and state check the pursuit of *self*-interest. They compete with one another. What if being true to the one means betrayal of another? Or, equally disastrous, what if one's friends are vicious and demand partnership in crime?

Idealizing Model

Such institutions were alive and well in medieval society, and theological estimates were doubtless shaped by actual social practice. Just as influential, however, were the idealized pictures of friendship forwarded by philosophers. Prominent among these was Cicero's treatise *On Friendship*, which dismisses commercial and need-based notions and declares that true friendships are characteristically initiated between equals who are self-sufficient, independently well endowed.[17] True friendships are possible only among the good, who—if not yet perfect—already possess such virtues as wisdom, loyalty, integrity, equity, and liberality in a high degree.[18] What sparks such relationships is neither desperation for the necessities of life nor prospects of upward mobility but nature. Humans share a universal natural tendency toward connection with others of the same kind. Humans are naturally endowed with inclinations to love, to benevolence with charity.[19] Actual familiarity evokes and reinforces such dispositions.[20] Solitude is contrary to nature.[21] Humans join the beasts in preferring blood relatives to strangers and fellow citizens to foreigners.[22] But good men find nothing so attractive as virtue in others.[23] The mutual appreciation of one another's character, the sharing of such excellent life stirs the embers of benevolence and charity, warms friends to an enjoyment without which life would not be worthwhile.[24] Virtue and friendship are mutually reinforcing: virtue begets and sustains friendship,[25] which is in turn a context in which good character thrives and grows.[26] Moreover, such interchange and affection fosters generosity that will go to any lengths for the other,[27] that draws each not only to love and to cherish but also to revere the other.[28] True friendship drives toward equivalence of agency—such perfect harmony of opinions and will[29] that one could say there is "one soul in two bodies."[30] If benevolence reaches out to all and sundry, Cicero estimates, such intensity of affection and harmony can be sustained only between two or at most among a few.[31] This type of friendship, Cicero declares, is an end in itself. Many advantages flow from it, but they are not the goal toward which friendship is the means.[32]

True friendship never asks or consents to anything dishonorable.[33] True friendship is utterly candid, devoid of flattery or hypocrisy.[34] True friendship gives the friend the benefit of the doubt, so, far from lodging accusations, it refuses to believe others' charges and suspicions unless and until the evidence becomes incontrovertible.[35] True friendship is relaxing, less restrained, more genial.[36]

True friendship, Cicero insists, goes beyond the Golden Rule. It does not "adopt the same feelings towards friend and self" because it is much more extravagant in promoting the friend's cause than one's own.[37] Much less is it governed by "do as you're done by," weighing and balancing off benevolences expended and received. Such petty cost accounting would be incompatible with its spirit of abundance and generosity.[38] So, far from "valuing the friend as he values himself," true friendship subjects self-estimates to correction, cheering the depressed or underconfident, challenging when the reckoning goes wrong.[39]

Nevertheless, true friendship is regulated by wisdom, which proportions benevolence to give the friend as much as it can commensurate with his ability to receive.[40] Paradigm friendship is based on equality that puts partners on a level plane. Where there are de facto inequalities, the dignity of the higher now elevates the lower, now condescends to the latter's station by turns.[41]

True friendship ought to be permanent. Yet, Cicero finds, nothing is more difficult than for friendship to continue to the very end of life.[42] Friendships based on advantage are broken up by changing tastes and emerging conflicts of interest.[43] Political arguments disrupt consensus; hard times alter dispositions; attention narrows under the burdens of old age.[44] Morally the most serious cause of dissolution is one partner's turning away from virtue.[45] Yet, if treason or outrageous scandal call for an immediate withdrawal of affection,[46] Cicero would rather see bonds of friendship "sundered by a gradual relaxation," "unravelled rather than broken,"[47] "burned out rather than stamped out."[48] Likewise, one should try to avoid the appearance of friends becoming enemies.[49] The best way to steer clear of such difficulties is to be careful about making commitments in the first place[50] by testing potential comrades for relevant virtues,[51] by allowing wisdom to check the headlong rush of benevolence,[52] and by delaying alliances with persons until a relatively stable character has been formed.[53]

Theological Applications

Medieval imagination found the friendship model extremely versatile.[54] In the twelfth century, Richard of St. Victor uses friendship love in the Godhead as a premise from which to demonstrate the Trinity, while Aelred of Rivaulx points to friendship between Christ and the church and among those who help one another seek to follow him. In the fourteenth century, Julian of Norwich ponders the astonishing

friendliness between Godhead and fallen human beings. My concluding section takes its cue from Julian and explores how friendliness
might be a way to conceive of divine goodness to persons whose lives
have been shattered or twisted by participation in horrendous evils.

TRINITARIAN FRIENDSHIP

Writing in 1148, Richard of St. Victor proposed in his book *On the
Trinity* to *demonstrate* the triunity of God with bold and concise
arguments. Everyone agreed: God is all-powerful, of immeasurable
wisdom, and goodness. Richard's distinctive move was to reason
from considerations of divine friendliness. His "Ciceronian" contention was that if perfect wisdom and power could exist in solitude,[55]
divine goodness could not! Richard identifies the heart of goodness,
not with justice or mercy, but with *charity* (*caritas*) and *benevolence*,
happiness (*felicitas*) and *joy*. Charity is always other-directed, indeed
involves the will to love another[56] and the will that the other be loved
as oneself.[57] Likewise, benevolence acts to share benefits;[58] perfect
benevolence reveals itself in largeness of spirit, such freedom from
greed as wishes to hold nothing back.[59] Because omnipotence is able
to confer infinite abundance,[60] it would be shameful for God to keep
immeasurable goodness all to himself.[61] On the contrary, it would be
God's greatest glory to share it.[62] Likewise, the highest happiness necessarily requires outward-bound charity. The highest joy essentially
involves the mutuality of love shared.[63] Nevertheless, "in the Highest,
the flame of love burns no hotter than highest wisdom dictates."[64]
Because neither divine charity nor divine benevolence can help being
governed by divine wisdom, God would not give the full measure of
divine riches to anyone unworthy of them. Charity ought not take
unlimited delight in what isn't perfectly delightful.[65] Likewise, perfect
benevolence would not release any *inordinate* flow of gifts, overspill-
ing the receiver's capacity.[66] Richard draws the obvious conclusion:
the only apt receiver of such divine largesse would be another divine
person.[67] The divine lover and beloved are thus distinct but equally
worthy divine persons[68]—equally powerful, wise, good, and blessed.[69]

Because there cannot be more than one divine essence, their *"equality"* is paradigmatic, consisting in the identity of their substance nature.[70] Because the divine lover seeks a worthy consort eternally by the necessity of the divine nature, the couple are equally incorruptible, immutable, and uncircumscribable.[71] Their relationship thus enjoys the paradigmatic *permanence* of eternity.

Divine goodness "twins"[72] itself to share its greatness (*magnitudo*) and to create a "communion of majesty."[73] Charity finds a worthy object of its delight, the two bestow on one another an affection of highest desire,[74] and "solitary majesty" gives way to the sweetness of mutual love and appreciation.[75] Yet divine goodness does not consummate charity unless the two produce a third, a common love object, so that they can share in loving the very same thing.[76] Without a common love object, happiness would lack some sweetness because sharing would be restrained.[77] Glory would be shamed by withholding possible benefit.[78] Moreover, charity and benevolence require this third to share with the first two in that paradigmatic equality which owns one and the same divine essence,[79] so that—as Christians confess—there are three coequal persons, one God.

FRIENDSHIP BETWEEN CHRIST AND THE CHURCH

Quite possibly the same year that Richard of St. Victor produced *On the Trinity*, Aelred of Rievaulx wrote a highly complementary treatise *Spiritual Friendship*, whose announced purpose was to "baptize" Cicero, the better to lay out a Christian theology of friendship, pouring down from God through Christ and raising us up to fellowship with God.

Utopic Beginnings

For Aelred, the starting point is divine self-sufficiency: God is supremely powerful, divine goodness itself enough for God's joy, happiness, and glory. God has no need of creatures to secure divine being or well-being.[80] It is not by natural necessity that creatures come forth from Godhead. Rather what makes the divine decision to create un-surprising is the fact that wealth spawns liberality. God is the self-sufficient source of everything else: God is the cause of all being, the life of all sensation, and the wisdom of all intelligence.[81] Aelred traces the alleged natural tendency toward connection among all crea-tures[82]—whether inanimate, nonrational, human, or angelic—to the unity and integrity of God's comprehensive providential plan.[83] An-gels were created for "Ciceronian" friendship—for society among pleasant and harmonious companions, whose wills and desires agree.[84] Humans, also, were made for society among equals. Aelred corrects Greek models when he rejects gender inequalities. On the contrary, God created Eve from Adam's rib to show that they are both of the same substance and so equals as true friendship requires.[85] For hu-mans, an isolated life without the giving and receiving of love in friendship would be bestial[86] and devoid of happiness.[87] Where friends are concerned, Aelred favors plenitude over parsimony: the more, the merrier.[88]

Unity, Perverse and Shattered: The Consequences of Adam's Fall

Cicero has taught us this: nature plants charity, a desire for friend-ship, in the human heart; experience increases it.[89] Christian theology explains how Adam's fall corrupts human social inclinations, cools charity, and stirs concupiscence, self-centeredness, and a decided preference for private advantage over the common good.[90] Such psycho-spiritual disorganization explains why we constantly find ourselves in situations with conflicting loyalties. This also accounts for the predominance of false kinds of friendship.[91] No wonder that the better part of practical wisdom is to adopt a divided policy of charity towards all but friendship only for the tried and true.

Among the false, Aelred numbers "carnal" friendships which spring from mutual harmony in the vice of inordinate attachment to sensory beauty and pleasure. While they last, the law of *idem velle, idem nolle* drives them to reinforce each other's passions, each urging the other on.[92] Aelred denounces such friendships as "puerile," because their affection is ungoverned by reason. In consequence, he finds them unstable, dying down as quickly as they flared up.[93]

Likewise false is the traditional "worldly" friendship "born of a desire for temporal advantage or possessions."[94] Prudence *seems* to commend these, because of their practical ante mortem advantages (see the opening discussion).[95] Often, the duty of reciprocal exchange engenders special affection,[96] and sometimes relationships begun this way can evolve into something better.[97] Nevertheless, Aelred could not be more opposed to economic conceptions of friendship as a "trade" "bought with money."[98] Both their currency and their emphasis are wrong. That is why "worldly" friendships easily degenerate into deceit and intrigue or vanish in the winds of changing fortune.[99]

Spiritual Harmony

By contrast, Aelred declares, true friendship is spiritual friendship, which is principally to be desired for its own sake, its completion or perfection its own reward.[100] Its media of exchange are not silver and gold, power or position, but psycho-spiritual benefits such as counsel in perplexity, consolation in adversity,[101] prayer without ceasing,[102] and empathetic identification in grief and shame as much as in honor and joy.[103] Spiritual friendship is a virtue, bought with love and won by competition in generosity.[104]

For Aelred, Christ is the ground—the source, the middle, and the end—of true friendship. Christ is its beginning, who inspires friends' love for each other.[105] Christ is friendship's paradigm, in that he laid down his life for his friends.[106] True friendship ascends by degrees to Christ, who gives himself as our Friend to love and who endlessly showers us with his charm, sweetness, and affection.[107] True friendship is perfected in Christ, so that friend clinging to friend in the Spirit of Christ is made one with Christ in heart and soul.[108] Each wills to will only what Christ wills, and each wills to nil only what Christ nils. Thus suspended in Christ, true friendship can never conflict with legitimate norms.

On the contrary, true friendship is a safe haven in a fallen world, like the monastery, an ark within which the fall is being reversed.

Because it aims at spiritual advance, true friendship begins among the good, progresses among the better, and is consummated among the perfect.[109] The wicked cannot enter upon it but only those who already lead just, sober, and godly lives.[110] Friends covenant to be partners in training the passions to the cardinal virtues (prudence, temperance, justice, fortitude), together "sign on" to submit to the disciplines needed for the cure of the soul.[111] To be fit for such work, friends have to be trustworthy, because candor is required. Friends must have no reluctance to open themselves for the other's correction, no hesitation to confess their failings, no shame in acknowledging progress won.[112] Likewise friends need a safe place to share secrets and evolve plans.[113] The sweetness of shared affection is the best anti-dote to self-centeredness, because it readies them to love the other more than self,[114] indeed—like Christ—to lay down life for friends.[115]

Aelred accords spiritual friendships eschatological significance, because they amount to an "already" amidst the "not yet" in divine restoration of cosmic harmony. Participating in them brings us a double benefit, because it makes us friends of one another and at the same time friends of God.[116] For, on the one hand, friends achieve harmony with one another by helping one another grow toward *idem velle, idem nolle* with Christ. On the other hand, because the love of Christ is both source and medium, ever-present, always mid-wifing our love for one another, spiritual friendship is an ever-deepening participation in the knowledge and love of Christ.[117] In the advanced stages, spiritual friends pass beyond mere virtue to spiritual zeal, from spiritual zeal to a revival of the spiritual senses, and from heightened spiritual sensitivity to intimacy with God.[118] Aelred trans-forms Cicero's idea of permanence into a vision of the communion of the saints, where love is literally stronger than death, and the harmo-nious unity of friends begun on this side of the grave lasts eternally.[119] Moreover, in the world to come, the transitivity of friendship makes friends of Christ all friends with one another, so that God will be all in all.[120]

Aelred's symbol for the unity of friends is a kiss. Just as a bodily kiss involves the impression of the lips in such a way that the breaths are mingled and united, producing a sweetness that binds lovers together,[121] so a spiritual kiss involves contact, not of the mouth, but of the hearts' affections, which so mingle the spirits with one another and with the Spirit of God that there is one spirit in many bodies.[122]

LOPSIDED FRIENDSHIP

For Julian of Norwich, divine-human friendship is definitely friendship among unequals. Where Godhead is concerned, there is the size gap: in comparison with divine being, all that is made is like a hazelnut, so small and flimsy as to be on the verge of disintegration. It exists only because God loves it.[123] Likewise, Julian emphasizes, in relation to Mother Jesus, we never advance beyond infancy or early childhood.[124] She is astonished that Our Lord Jesus, "the most supreme, mighty, noble, and worthy of all, should also be the most lowly, humble, friendly, and considerate."[125]

Godhead expresses friendliness toward Adam's race through many gestures. First, God created us for joyful life together and finds deep satisfaction in making the human soul. The size gap means that Godhead is not simply an alter ego on the outside. Omnipresent Godhead indwells; the Trinity and Christ take up residence and make themselves at home in our souls.[126] Omnipresent Godhead continually enfolds us. Godhead is the ground of our Being. The only way God could abandon us would be by making us cease to be.[127] Second, Godhead befriends Adam's race by joining it. On Julian's conception, Godhead joins our higher spiritual nature to God the Son at creation and our lower corporeal nature to him at incarnation.[128]

Instructed by Holy Church, Julian was convinced that sin, which we struggle against so unsuccessfully, must be a serious threat to divine purposes and to our eternal well-being.[129] In her showings, God gives her to know otherwise. We are sinners, because we lack the power and skill to bring our two natures (both of which are good) into proper alignment. God confirms that she will continue to sin to the day that she dies.[130] But God assures her that sin is necessary, and that at the last day God will do something that will make everything all right.[131]

Meanwhile, it is a further expression of royal friendship that God "holds onto us so tenderly when we are in sin."[132] Sin is the hardest hell, the worst scourge that the soul can suffer.[133] Sin "is the cause of all this pain."[134] Yet sin does not make God angry with us, Julian explains, because anger and friendship are mutually opposed.[135] Anger is incompatible with divine power and divine wisdom and with the integrity of divine love. Where there is no divine wrath, there is no forgiveness either. On the contrary, God never blames us; God excuses us.[136]

Nor does divine extravagance stop there. Julian reports:

> God showed that sin need be no shame to a man but can even be worthwhile. For just as every sin has its corresponding penalty because God is true, so the same soul can know every sin to have its corresponding blessing because God is love. Just as various sins are punished with various penalties according to their seriousness, so may they be rewarded with various joys in heaven if they have brought punishment and sorrow on earth. For the soul that comes to heaven is precious to God, and the place is so holy that the goodness of God will never allow the soul who gets there to have sinned without that sin being compensated. Ever known, it is blessedly made good by God's surpassing worth.[137]

Julian's showings indicated one way that God will accomplish this. She reckons that

> the greatest honor a great king or noble lord can do a poor servant is to treat him like a friend, especially if, in public and private alike, it is seen to be both genuine and spontaneous.[138]

When we get to heaven, God will preempt any apologies or expressions of humility on our part with the greeting, "Thank you for your suffering, the suffering of your youth."[139] Such a public expression of divine gratitude will pay us honor that will cancel the shame of sin and fill us with eternal joy and freshness of pleasure.[140]

Likewise, Jesus Christ is full of friendly gestures, beginning with his eagerness for incarnation, his cheerful desire is to do the hardest thing, the most difficult deed of knightly valor, to suffer if possible times without number to win over and to satisfy the soul.[141] Jesus shows a Lover's friendship when he suffers his passion and begs to have us as his reward.[142] Jesus also bears us a mother's friendship, when he carries us in his womb entered from the wound in his side, when he bears us through his passion (Julian says, we are ever being born from him but never delivered), when he feeds us from his own body, when he lets us learn the hard way to correct our faults and shows us the nanny's tender loving care.[143]

The full friendliness of Godhead toward Adam's race comes out in the Parable of the Lord and the Servant, which is so striking as to be worth quoting in full:

> I saw physically before me two people, a lord and his servant. And God showed me its spiritual meaning. The lord is sitting down quietly, relaxed and peaceful: the servant is standing by his lord, humble and ready to do his bidding. And then I saw the lord look at his servant with rare love and tenderness, and quietly send him to a certain place to fulfill his purpose. Not only does that servant go, but he starts off at once, running with all speed, in his love to do what his master wanted. And without warning, he falls headlong into a deep ditch, and injures himself very badly. And though he groans and moans and cries and struggles he is quite unable to get up or help himself in any way. To crown all, he could get no relief of any sort: he could not even turn his head to look at the lord who loved him and who was so close to him. The sight of him would have been a real comfort, but he was temporarily so weak and bemused that he gave vent to his feelings, as he suffered his pains.[144]

The fall is sin, which is a result not of rebellion but incompetence on the servant's part. Sin befuddles the servant so that he cannot recognize divine presence and good or pleasure.

Julian's rich analysis brings out two points that are important here. First, according to the parable, the Lord's friendliness toward the servant remains constant, even though the servant is neither aware of it nor in any condition to reciprocate. Evidently, friendliness does not everywhere and always have to be a two-way street. Second, according to its God-given interpretation, the servant stands, not merely for our supposed primal ancestor Adam, but for Everyman and for Christ.[145] Julian makes her point more precise when she declares, "Jesus is everyone that will be saved, and everyone that will be saved is Jesus!"[146] And she draws the conclusion that "because of his great and everlasting love for mankind, God makes no distinction in the love he has for the blessed soul of Christ and that which he has for the lowliest to be saved."[147] God counts the agency of any human being to be saved as equivalent to the agency of Christ himself. What we have here is a doctrine of imputed friendliness.

There is imputed friendliness, and there is actual friendliness. It is the human calling—or at least the vocation of those to be saved— more and more to become friendly toward God. Even in youth, Julian was extravagant, when she prayed to understand Christ's passion, to do the friend's part by being present at the foot of the cross, to suffer with him, even to feel his pains in her own body.[148] Julian prayed for the three wounds: contrition, compassion, and a sincere longing for God. And she asked God for a near-fatal illness in youth, the better to go through the spiritual exercises of fighting off the Fiend at the hour of death and emerge able to love God the better.[149] God met one friendly move with another by granting her what she asked. The showings and their interpretation were acts of divine friendship given to reassure, not only Julian, but every "even Christian."[150]

Julian learned that what God would find actually friendly is trusting him to be for us,[151] being patient with our sufferings—even with our sinfulness—because they redound to God's glory and our benefit, and clinging to Jesus when we need help.[152] God also finds it friendly when we work away at our prayer. The reason is that God is the ground of our praying: God moves us to pray for what God wants to give us. Prayer that asks for what God wills us to have is a way of moving toward *idem velle, idem nolle,* a step toward actual equivalence of agency even from a Ciceronian point of view.[153]

HORRIFYING FRIENDSHIP

The above review shows how in medieval theology the friendship model gets applied and reapplied. Richard of St. Victor argues for Trinity within the Godhead as a society of ideal friends. Aelred of Rivaulx and Julian of Norwich apply the notion of friendliness to the human spiritual journey from our fallen natural state in this world toward fit citizenship in heaven. Aelred stresses how human friends help each other grow in the knowledge and love of Christ, while Julian stresses how being friendly enough to trust in divine friendliness is key to spiritual progress.

The Problem of Horrors

I turn now to explore how the notion of friendliness can help with what I have elsewhere styled the problem of horrendous evils.[154] Like Aelred and Julian, I begin with the assumption that in the world as we know it the human condition is nonoptimal and divine-human relations are nonoptimal. My own diagnosis of the root of our nonoptimality problems is that God has made us material persons in a material world of real and apparent scarcity, and that this situation makes us radically vulnerable to horrendous evils. I define *horrendous evils* or *horrors* as "evils the participation in which—whether as a victim or a perpetrator—constitutes prima facie reason for believing that the participant's life cannot—given their inclusion in it—be a great good to him or her on the whole," or "evils that are prima facie life ruining because they seem to take away any possibility of positive meaning in the participants' lives." Paradigmatic horrors include the rape of a woman and axing off of her arms, psycho-physical torture whose ultimate goal is the disintegration of personality, cannibalizing one's own offspring, child abuse of the sort described by Ivan Karamazov, parental incest, participation in the Nazi death camps, the explosion of nuclear bombs over populated areas, schizophrenia, severe and persistent clinical depression, being the accidental and/or unwitting agent in the disfigurement or death of those one loves best.

In the world as we know it, horrors are not rare. Barring miracles, they are inevitable systemic by-products of this material world when it includes material persons in it. Likewise, human societies inevitably spawn horror-producing systemic dysfunctions, so that we are all at least collectively complicit in the perpetration of horrors. Unsurprisingly, human history is strewn with horrors. The pressing question becomes, what could God have meant by creating us in a world like this?

With Julian's friendly prompting, I want to try the following answer on for size: namely, that God means to be friendly by creating us for life together and that God aims for plot resolution in which we all live together harmoniously in friendship with God and one another. To be more specific, I am interested in a version of the "Two Age" theory according to which the divine plan has two stages. First, God makes us for life together in this material world, because God loves this material world and loves it preeminently by loving us, because we are material persons and this is our natural home, and because God wants to live together with us on our home turf. Second, because life together in this material world is so harsh and demanding as prima facie to forfeit the human good and to abort divine aims, God purposes future life together in a modified environment where we will no longer be vulnerable to horrors—in a context in which evident divine presence will so convince us that we are safe and that we are loved, that we will be able to live together in peace and harmony like—because together with—the Trinitarian society of friends.

The Knowledge of Good and Evil

On Cicero's account, ideal friendship involves interchangeable agency. But harmony of wills (*idem velle, idem nolle*) presupposes the knowledge that underwrites it. Where God's projects in this world are concerned, that would require a knowledge of good and evil—not merely knowledge by description, whether of the abstract sort in which philosophy courses trade or of the narrative type treated by literature, but knowledge by acquaintance which tastes and sees how really, really good and how really, really bad things in this world are.[155]

Sharing God's Outlook?
Where divine-human friendship is concerned, actual equivalence of agency is not fully possible. The size gap is one obvious reason. The Bible itself challenges, "who has known the mind of the Lord?," warns that "God's ways are higher than our ways" (Isa. 55:8–9), Divine thoughts more numerous than the sand of the sea, too high for us to attain (Ps. 139:6, 17–18). Medieval school theologians translated this point into philosophy: humans should not aim to will what God wills because our cognitive capacities are too limited to know what God knows; rather humans should will what God wills us to will.

Where relevant knowledge of good and evil are concerned, our problems run deeper. There is the real and present danger that human capacities are not robust enough to experience the best goods or the worst evils without being destroyed in the process. Biblical authors tremble at the prospect of divine goodness: there is not enough to human beings to see God and live (Exod. 33:20; Isa. 6:5). Job anticipates (what in fact happens): that he would come unraveled and be unable to utter a coherent sentence were God to appear to face Job's complaints (Job 9:19–20, 34–35; 42:1–6). Admirably foolhardy desert fathers bent their human natures out of shape in all kinds of ways, counting human flourishing rubbish in comparison with seeing God face-to-face. The school theologian Thomas Aquinas declared that an upgrade of human cognitive capacities—both radical and miraculous—would be required for us to attain to beatific vision, our supranatural end.

So also with the knowledge of evil. It is one thing for a child to learn by the experience of a mildly burned or slightly blistered finger why it is a bad idea to touch hot stoves. But horrors typically wreck and ruin human agency by dazing, deranging, or stalemating our meaning-making capacities. Horrors by definition prima facie rob the participant's life of the possibility of positive meaning. Knowledge of good and evil in a world that is horror-studded yet God-infested is something Godhead is up to but more than humankind can take.

The Pedagogy of Friendship.

Unsurprisingly, the God of Genesis 2–3 knows this and warns Adam and Eve not to eat of the tree of the knowledge of good and evil (Gen. 2:16-17; 3:2-3). It is the serpent's temptation that invites Eve to become like God, knowing good and evil (Gen. 3:4–5). Adam and Eve are still children. Life in Paradise creates the illusion of safety, of everything being laid on and no dangers looming. Protecting children from harsh realities, introducing them to real-world problems gradually as their growing capacities become more able to handle them, is good pedagogy to this day.

Nevertheless, numerous Bible stories suggest that mature friendship with God requires a rite of passage in which God's human partners are forced to get real about what life together with God in this world really means. (i) Adam and Eve fall from naïveté, lose their illusions about what it means to be personal animals, material persons in a world like this.[156] Childbirth is painful. Hard labor is required to earn bread. Nature is inhospitable. So, far from being friendly, relations among humans and God's other creatures are hostile (Gen. 3:14–19). And—contrary to the serpent—personal animals all die.

(ii) Abraham is a friend of God, one with whom God shares plans and from whom God takes council (Gen. 18:17–33). God blesses Abraham with companionship, wealth, and power. But God tests Abraham by delaying fulfillment of the divine promise of offspring numerous as the stars until he is one hundred years old (Gen. 21:5) and then commanding Abraham to sacrifice Isaac on Mount Moriah (Gen. 22:1-14). The reality is that trafficking with God demands not only being willing to leave home (Gen. 12:1), but also to sacrifice the people one loves the most; not only being willing to lose earthly prizes, but—at God's behest—to destroy what looks like the only means of God's fulfilling divine promises.

(iii) Job is introduced—at the beginning of the story—as a paradigm patriarch, a friend of God, full of reverence and gratitude. Job has tasted and seen this world's goods: he is rich and prosperous, the father of ten children, a wise and respected community leader. He has played the patron's part, noblesse oblige, befriending widows and orphans, and so on (Job 1:1–5, 29–31). His happy situation in life gives him knowledge of divine goodness at a remove: from its effects on him and by the hearing of the ear. But he has not seen God (Job 42:5–6). Likewise, Job's knowledge of evil is secondhand. He has not tasted and seen just how bad life in this world can be. Job's crash-course acquaintance with horrors, followed by the theophany in which he sees divine goodness, deepens his knowledge of good and evil and in consequence his friendship with God. Throughout his chapters-long torment, Job retains enough integrity to play the part of the seemingly betrayed friend calling God to account for letting him down. God takes Job's performance for what it is—friendly—and rewards him by catapulting him into the role of priestly intercessor for the friends whose knowledge of good and evil was so superficial that they knew not what they said (Job 42:7–9).

(iv) Likewise, Jesus's earthly career is for the disciples a period of bonding and trust building, filled with signs and wonders, public teachings and private tutorials. But they do not rise to maturity as Jesus's friends (John 15:14–15 has to be proleptic) before they undergo crucifixion-resurrection rites of passage. Triduum events first force them to drain their cup of spiced and foaming wine, rudely awaken them to their own moral flimsiness and failures, to the treachery of their nation's leaders who vow no king but Caesar (John 19:15) and misguide the people into calling down the Messiah's blood on their heads (Matt. 27:25), to the brutality of crucifixion and to the crush of imperial power. Following Jesus leads to much worse than they had asked or imagined. Resurrection is equally disruptive as it explodes their pathetic underestimation of divine resources to make good on the worst things.

Unprepared Acquaintance.

Unfortunately, the material world in which we find ourselves is no respecter of human learning curves or pedagogical order. Horrors are its systemic by-products, and the dynamics that produce them are not within human power reliably to recognize or control. Millions of people have been born into calamity and endured lives of unrelieved misery all the way to the grave. Millions of others have had lives interrupted, their personalities and life projects shattered in ways that prove humanly impossible to put back together again. Millions more respond to life experiences in ways that turn them into moral monsters—into the Hitlers and Stalins and Pol Pots, who herd others forward to perish on the slaughter bench of history. For millions, there is no actual friendship with God, immature or otherwise. Many are religiously ignorant. Traumatized others find belief in God psychologically impossible. Still others believe that God exists but hate God for permitting or causing them and others to experience hell on earth. Wouldn't it be ridiculous to suppose that friendliness plays any role in what is at stake between God and them?

Friendliness, Unrecognized and Imputed.
Here Julian of Norwich offers two friendly suggestions. First, Julian's parable shows the lord remaining friendly toward the servant, even when he has fallen into the pit and is too stunned and dazed to recognize it. Julian reports how God insisted that sin is necessary but showed her how God holds us tenderly in our sins and assured her that at the last day God will make everything all right. Analogously, I suggest, in this world horrors are naturally inevitable systemic byproducts of material persons in this material world, but unrelieved participation in horror puts neither victims nor perpetrators beyond God's will and power to do them good, to give them lives that they will count great goods to them on the whole, and to transform them into persons fit for heaven. Horrors may make ante mortem trust impossible and even twist horror participants into God haters. But horrors do not really mean that God hates us, and they cannot finally separate us from God's love (Rom. 8:31–39).

Second, Julian's parable alerts us to the notion of imputed friendliness: Julian's God counts Adam's agency (and that of every human being to be saved) as equivalent to Christ's, even though it is not actually equivalent. Horrors demand that we foreswear Julian's caution that holds back from explicit universalism and delights in the eternal hellish quarantine of the fiends.[157] If God is going to be good to all horror participants, I suggest, divine love will count the agency of every human being as equivalent to Christ's.

In his Godhead, Christ shares the Trinity's knowledge of good and evil. In his human nature, Christ both tastes and sees divine goodness—according to scholastic Christologies, he has the beatific vision throughout his human career[158]—and participates in passion week horrors. His Godhead and his human tasting and seeing of divine goodness strengthen him to look evil in the face and stare it down, so that Christ's human nature knowledge of good and evil runs deep. Perhaps some saints actually approximate such dialectical knowledge, where their glimpses of divine goodness enable them to confront evils, and, conversely (as in Job's case), their experience of evil catapults them into a resizing of divine goodness, which has to be at least as good as evils here below are bad! For the saints, such knowledge of divine goodness cushions their encounters with evils. They are able more and more to face how bad things can be, because they more and more experience how boundless goodness is there to overcome it.

Horror participation that wrecks and ruins agencies gulps down the poison without any counteracting antidote. It shatters, bends, and twists. I suggest, that—ghastly and distorted as it is—such participation in horrors also shares deeply in God's knowledge of evil. It tells truths that Christ's human career or the Maccabean martyrs (4 Macc. 5–18) or St. Francis of Assisi can't declare. Once again, their knowledge of evil is counterbalanced, and according to the stories they retained enough integrity to remain faithful to God to the end. What wrecked and ruined horror participants are, is in a way, a more radical exposé of the virulence of evil to prima facie destroy the image of God in human beings. In at least this dimension, it approaches more closely to divine knowledge of evil. For God created this world with eyes wide open to its ruinous potential for human beings. My contention is that God imputes friendliness to these wrecked and ruined horror participants also, willy-nilly, whether or not they actually meant it, even if they actually meant the opposite.

Eternal Honors.

According to Julian, God will make it up to us for all that we have suffered—not least, the scourge of being the messed up agents that we have been—by playing the part of a grateful friend. For by being material persons in this material world, we have, willy-nilly, been part of God's project of life together in the material world that is our natural home. Like Julian, I imagine, God will thank us for getting through it. Even among wrecked and ruined agencies, costs may be higher or lower. It is worse to be contorted into a moral monster—to be a Hitler or a Stalin or a Pol Pot—than to be one of their victims shoveled alive into the crematorium. It is worse to be Judas than to be Mary Magdalene at the foot of the cross or even one of the twelve who runs for his life. My suggestion is that divine love will award greater honors to those who paid higher prices for God's project of life together in this world.

Retrospective Friendliness.

Since participation in horrors wrecks and ruins agencies, horror participants will require numerous post mortem therapeutic stages of personality reform and restructuring, perhaps—as Hick suggests—many careers' worth of reeducation by Mother Jesus, before they can be fit citizens of the realm of God. For horror participants (both Hitler and his victims), drastic transformation would have to happen before they could recognize and trust that life together in friendship is and has been God's meaning all along.

My suggestion is that because the life to come *is* a long run, we all will come to recognize divine friendliness. Like Julian (but pace Miroslav Volf),[159] I imagine that God will never cover up our past careers, not because God will be out to blame us or to shame us, but because they constitute a judgment on God's project. Each human life will have told some truth about what life together in this material world was really like, what it would cost human beings. I suggest that God counts our being the media of such verdicts as a friendly gesture. Like Julian, I imagine that God eternally honors us for these truths that we have willy-nilly told.

Some will say that I have already gone way too far. My final and perhaps most daring thought is this: that—convinced of God's perpetual friendliness and seeing enough of how God has made good on everything and how God compensates everyone for horror participation—we will move beyond accepting ourselves and the lives that we lived, and become retrospectively willing, perhaps even retrospectively glad to have lived them. Not glad about the harm to others or glad to have been agents of their prima facie ruin, not glad to have caricatured God's image in ourselves and those around us, but glad for what God has made of it, and glad to have played a part in God's project. Perhaps eventually we will offer all that we are and have been in a restrospectively friendly gesture to God.

NOTES

1. See John T. Fitzgerald, "Friendship in the Greek World Prior to Aristotle," in *Greco-Roman Perspectives on Friendship*, SBL Resources for Biblical Study 34, ed. John T. Fitzgerald (Atlanta, GA: Scholars Press, 1997), 13–34, esp. 19–26.

2. Mary Whitlock Blundell, *Helping Friends and Harming Enemies: A Study in Sophocles and Greek Ethics* (New York: Cambridge University Press, 1989), 31–33.

3. Ibid.

4. Ibid., 35–36.

5. Ibid., 37.

6. Ibid., 37–38. See Fitzgerald, "Friendship in the Greek World Prior to Aristotle," esp. 29–33, for ancient texts that complain of the scarcity of trustworthy befriendable persons.

7. Blundell, *Helping Friends and Harming Enemies*, 48.

8. Ibid., 34.

9. Ibid., 39.

10. Ibid., 43. Friendship between parents and children looms large for Aristotle in his discussions in the *Nicomachean Ethics* VIII.1, 1155a16–18; VIII.7, 1158b13–15; VIII.12, 1161a11–1162a14; VIII.14, 1163b13–27.

11. Blundell, *Helping Friends and Harming Enemies*, 43–44. Compare Aristotle, *Nichomachean Ethics* VIII.1, 1155a19–21; VIII.9, 1159b25–35.

12. Blundell, *Helping Friends and Harming Enemies*, 46.

13. Ibid. Compare Aristotle, *Nicomachean Ethics* VIII.7, 1158b13–29 and VIII.12, 1162a15–28, where he counts marriage as a type of friendship between unequals.

14. Blundell, *Helping Friends and Harming Enemies*, 46–47.

15. Ibid., 45. See Fitzgerald, "Friendship in the Greek World Prior to Aristotle," 20–26, where he expands on the duties of so-called guest-friendships. Similar institutions forged political links in the feudal period in Europe; see Gerd Althoff, "Friendship and the Political Order," in *Friendship in Medieval Europe*, ed. Julian Haseldine (Gloucestershire: Sutton Publishing, 1999), 91–105, esp. 92–95.

16. Blundell, *Helping Friends and Harming Enemies*, 47. Aristotle equivocates about whether and how friendship across such inequalities as obtain between us and the gods; see the *Nicomachean Ethics* VIII.7, 1158b29–1159a13; VIII.12, 1162a4–7.

17. *De amicitia* IX.31, XIV.51. See also Aristotle, *Nicomachean Ethics* VIII.3, 1156a1–1156b20.

18. *De amicitia* V.18–19, VI.21. See also Aristotle, *Nicomachean Ethics* VIII.3, 1156b7–9; VIII.4, 1156b33–1157a19; VIII.4, 1157b1–4.

19. *De amicitia* V.19–20; XXIII.88. See also Aristotle, *Nicomachean Ethics* VIII.1, 1155a16–21.

20. *De amicitia* IX.29, 32.

21. *De amicitia* XXIII.87.

22. *De amicitia* VIII.27, XIV.50, XXI.81.

23. *De amicitia* VIII.28.

24. *De amicitia* VI.22, IX.29, 31–32, XIV.49, XXVII.102. See also Aristotle, *Nicomachean Ethics* VIII.3, 1152b7–23.

25. *De amicitia* V.20.

26. *De amicitia* XXII.83.

27. *De amicitia* XXII.82.

28. *De amicitia* XXII.82.

29. *De amicitia* IV.15, VI.20. See Aristotle, *Nicomachean Ethics* IX.6, 1167a21–1167b8, where agreement among friends is political, about what is to be done!

30. *De amicitia* XVII.61.

31. *De amicitia* V.20. See Aristotle, *Nicomachean Ethics* VIII.6, 1158a10–17; IX.5, 1166b30–1167a20; IX.10, 1170b20–1171a21.

32. *De amicitia* IX.32, XIV.51. See Aristotle, *Nicomachean Ethics* VIII.4, 1156b33–1157a16.

33. *De amicitia* XII.40, XIII.44.

34. *De amicitia* XVIII.65–66, XXV.92.

35. *De amicitia* XVIII.65–66. See Aristotle, *Nicomachean Ethics* VIII.4, 1157a20–24.

36. *De amicitia* XVIII.66.

37. *De amicitia* XVI.56–57.

38. *De amicitia* XVI.56, 58. Aristotle, *Nicomachean Ethics* VIII.13, 1162b6–13.

39. *De amicitia* XVI.56–57, 59. But see Aristotle, *Nicomachean Ethics* IX.8, 1168a28–1169b33, and IX.12.1171b32–37, where he considers whether a person ought not to be his own best friend and love himself the most. Even self-sacrifice and foregone advantages express self-love insofar as they increase the agent's nobility.

40. *De amicitia* XX.73.

41. *De amicitia* XIX.69–70, 71–73. See Aristotle, *Nicomachean Ethics* VIII.6, 1158b1–1159b24, where he belabors the issue of equality vs. inequality between friends.

42. *De amicitia* X.33.

43. *De amicitia* X.33–34, 74.

44. *De amicitia* X.33–34. See also Aristotle, *Nicomachean Ethics* VIII.5, 1157b13–17; VIII.6, 1158a1–9.

45. *De amicitia* X.35; XXI.78–79. Aristotle's position in *Nicomachean Ethics* IX.3, 1165a37–1165b37, is more emphatic: when people cease to be moral peers, they can no longer be friends. This happens both when a friend turns to vice and when one outstrips the other in moral growth and achievement.

46. *De amicitia* XXI.76.

47. *De amicitia* XXI.76.

48. *De amicitia* XXI.78.

49. *De amicitia* XXI.77.

50. *De amicitia* XXI.78–79; XXII.85.

51. *De amicitia* XVIII.65.

52. *De amicitia* XVII.63; XXI.79.

53. *De amicitia* XVIII.74.

54. See James McEvoy, "The Theory of Friendship in the Latin Middle Ages: Hermeneutics, Contextualization, and the Transmission and Reception of Ancient Texts and Ideas, from c. AD 375 to c. 1500," in Haseldine, *Friendship in Medieval Europe*, 3–44.

55. Richard of St. Victor, *De trinitate* III.16.204. References are to Richard of St. Victor, *La Trinité*, trans. S. J. Gaston Salet (Paris: Cerf, 1959).

56. *De trinitate* III.2.168.

57. *De trinitate* III.11.190.

58. *De trinitate* III.4.174.

59. *De trinitate* III.4.176; III.6.178; III.14.198.

60. *De trinitate* III.8.182.

61. *De trinitate* III.4.174.

62. *De trinitate* III.4.176; III.6.178; III.14.198.

63. *De trinitate* III.3.172.
64. *De trinitate* III.8.180.
65. *De trinitate* III.2.168; III.7.180.
66. *De trinitate* III.4.176.
67. *De trinitate* III.8.182.
68. *De trinitate* V.22.346; V.24.362.
69. *De trinitate* III.10.186; cf. III.21.214.
70. *De trinitate* III.8.182, 184; III.9.186, 188; III.23–24.216, 218; VI.9.394.
71. *De trinitate* III.10.186; cf. III.22.216.
72. Richard's own word; see *De trinitate* III.17.206.
73. *De trinitate* VI.6.388.
74. *De trinitate* III.19.208, 210.
75. *De trinitate* III.4.174; III.14.198, 200.
76. *De trinitate* III.11.190, 192; III.14.200; III.18.208; III.19, 208, 210; VI.6.388.
77. *De trinitate* III.12.194; III.17.206.
78. *De trinitate* III.14.198, 200.
79. *De trinitate* III.21–24.212–18.
80. Aelred, *Spiritual Friendship*, trans. Mary Eugenia Laker, Cistercian Fathers Series (Kalamazoo, MI: Cistercian Publications, 1974), I.61.
81. *Spiritual Friendship* I.61.
82. *Spiritual Friendship* I.61–62.
83. *Spiritual Friendship* I.61–63.
84. *Spiritual Friendship* I.63.
85. *Spiritual Friendship* I.63.
86. *Spiritual Friendship* II.71, 82.
87. *Spiritual Friendship* III.110.
88. *Spiritual Friendship* III.111.
89. *Spiritual Friendship* I.61–63.
90. *Spiritual Friendship* I.63.
91. *Spiritual Friendship* I.64.
92. *Spiritual Friendship* I.59.
93. *Spiritual Friendship* II.83. Aristotle counts friendships based on pleasure and friendships based on utility as "incidental" friendships, not friendships in the truest sense. Nevertheless, he does emphasize how pleasure plays a role in true friendships based on the goodness or virtue of the companions. See *Nicomachean Ethics* VIII.3-4, 1156a6–1157a16.
94. *Spiritual Friendship* I.60.
95. *Spiritual Friendship* II.84.
96. *Spiritual Friendship* I.60.
97. *Spiritual Friendship* III.92.
98. *Spiritual Friendship* II.83; III.108.

99. *Spiritual Friendship* I.60.

100. *Spiritual Friendship* I.60; II.84–85.

101. *Spiritual Friendship* II.84.

102. *Spiritual Friendship* III.131.

103. *Spiritual Friendship* III.119.

104. *Spiritual Friendship* III.108. See also Aristotle's comment that friendship either is a virtue or implies virtue (*Nicomachean Ethics* VIII.1, 1155a3–5).

105. *Spiritual Friendship* II.74.

106. *Spiritual Friendship* I.58; II.72.

107. *Spiritual Friendship* II.74–75.

108. *Spiritual Friendship* III.114, 132.

109. *Spiritual Friendship* II.79.

110. *Spiritual Friendship* III.93.

111. *Spiritual Friendship* I.61, 65.

112. *Spiritual Friendship* II.72.; III.111.

113. *Spiritual Friendship* II.72.

114. *Spiritual Friendship* II.72; III.111.

115. *Spiritual Friendship* I.58; II.72.

116. *Spiritual Friendship* II.73.

117. *Spiritual Friendship* II.73.

118. *Spiritual Friendship* III.114; III.131.

119. *Spiritual Friendship* II.70; III.111.

120. *Spiritual Friendship* III.132.

121. *Spiritual Friendship* II.75–76.

122. *Spiritual Friendship* II.76.

123. Julian of Norwich, *Revelations of Divine Love*, trans. Clifton Wolters (Baltimore, MD: Penguin Books, 1966), chap. 5, 68.

124. *Revelations of Divine Love*, chaps. 57–61, 164–73.

125. *Revelations of Divine Love*, chap. 7, 72–73.

126. *Revelations of Divine Love*, chaps. 54–46, 157–61.

127. *Revelations of Divine Love*, chaps. 54–55, 157–60.

128. *Revelations of Divine Love*, chap. 56, 160–61.

129. *Revelations of Divine Love*, chap. 50, 139.

130. *Revelations of Divine Love*, chap. 37, 117–18.

131. *Revelations of Divine Love*, chap. 27, 103–4; chaps. 31–32, 107–10.

132. *Revelations of Divine Love*, chap. 40, 121.

133. *Revelations of Divine Love*, chaps. 39–40, 120–23; chap. 63, 175.

134. *Revelations of Divine Love*, chap. 27, 104.

135. *Revelations of Divine Love*, chap. 27, 104.

136. *Revelations of Divine Love*, chap. 28, 105; chaps. 45–46, 131–33; chap. 49, 137.

137. *Revelations of Divine Love*, chap. 38, 118–19.

138. *Revelations of Divine Love*, chap. 7, 72.

139. *Revelations of Divine Love*, chap. 14, 85.

140. *Revelations of Divine Love*, chap. 14, 85.

141. *Revelations of Divine Love*, chaps. 20–23, 94–99.

142. *Revelations of Divine Love*, chaps. 20–23, 94–99.

143. *Revelations of Divine Love*, chaps. 57–60, 164–71.

144. *Revelations of Divine Love*, chap. 51, 141.

145. *Revelations of Divine Love*, chap. 51, 141.

146. *Revelations of Divine Love*, chap. 51, 149.

147. *Revelations of Divine Love*, chap. 54, 157.

148. *Revelations of Divine Love*, chap. 2, 63; chaps. 17–18, 89–92.

149. *Revelations of Divine Love*, chap. 2, 63–64; chap. 66, 182–83; chap. 69, 185–86.

150. *Revelations of Divine Love*, chap. 68, 184–85.

151. *Revelations of Divine Love*, chaps. 41, 123; chaps. 73–74, 191–95; chaps. 85–86, 210–12.

152. *Revelations of Divine Love*, chaps. 76–77, 197–200.

153. *Revelations of Divine Love*, chaps. 41–43, 123–28.

154. See Marilyn McCord Adams, *Horrendous Evils and the Goodness of God* (Ithaca, NY: Cornell University Press, 1999), and *Christ and Horrors: The Coherence of Christology*, Current Issues in Theology (New York: Cambridge University Press, 2006).

155. No, I have never agreed with those who reply to the "contrast" argument (i.e., to be able to conceive of good we have to be able to conceive of evil) that God could have supplied Adam and Eve with novels that told stories of treacherous people and evil deeds. In my view, experience in paradise would have furnished them with no basis for understanding just how bad such things would be.

156. I take this reading of the Genesis fall story from a conversation with my friend Christopher Rowland, Dean Ireland Professor of New Testament Studies at the Queen's College, Oxford.

157. *Revelations of Divine Love*, chap. 13, 83–84.

158. See Marilyn McCord Adams, *What Sort of Human Nature: Medieval Philosophy and the Systematics of Christology*, Aquinas Lecture 1999 (Milwaukee, WI: Marquette University Press, 1999).

159. Miroslav Volf, *The End of Memory: Remembering Rightly in a Violent World* (Grand Rapids, MI: Eerdmans, 2006), esp. 177–214.

Chapter Three

CAN PRECRITICAL BIBLICAL INTERPRETATION CURE THE ILLS OF THE CRITICAL?

KEVIN MADIGAN

I would like to begin my reflections today by recollecting with you the encounter between the so-called Ethiopian eunuch and the evangelizer Philip as remembered, reconstructed, or imagined in Acts 8:26–39. Philip, under instructions from an angel, happens upon this man, perhaps a God-fearer or a pious Jew, on a desert road. Apparently, he had been to Jerusalem to worship and was now returning home. When Philip finds him, the Ethiopian is reading a text from a scroll of Isaiah. He is in fact reading from that part of Isaiah which we know as chapter 53, which refers to one "led like sheep to a slaughter," deprived unjustly of his life and put to death (Isa. 53:7–8). Philip asks him, "Do you understand what you are reading?" (Acts 8:30), to which the Ethiopian famously replies, "How can I, unless someone explain it to me?" He then tosses Philip a gift question: "Is the prophet talking about himself, or someone else?," and Philip of course is able to run a long way with it, explaining the oracle Christologically as a reference to Jesus and the "good news" associated with his ministry.

As a thought experiment, we might wonder together how a similar exchange might unfold in a college or university classroom today. What would happen if a student were to ask his instructor to

71

explain the meaning of this periciope? It is, I think, virtually certain that the instructor, whatever his religious commitments, if any, would explain this passage in a very different way. For one thing, he would not rely at all, probably appropriately, on the Christological hermeneutic that allowed Philip to make sense of the text. Rather, the student would be told that, in order to appreciate the meaning of the text, he should first place it in its original historical context. Accordingly, the Isaianic text would then be understood as a classic and characteristic expression of Second Temple restoration eschatology. No mention would be made of Jesus of Nazareth, except perhaps to observe that he, too, like Isaiah, was a prophet immersed in the world of, and profoundly shaped by, that same eschatology. Like the author of this part of Isaiah (which the student would, not wrongly, be told is a pastiche composed by at least two and maybe three writers), Jesus hoped for the imminent restoration of Israel, the impending, decisive, and final incursion of God in history, the reconstruction of the Temple and the natural world, the resurrection of the dead, the judgment of the dead and living, and the definitive establishment of the kingdom of God on earth. The instructor might observe that this apocalyptic eschatology, fueled in part by the long experience of foreign domination, was widespread among Jewish communities in Judea. He might add that Jesus of Nazareth was likely one of many prophets or teachers or warriors, some of whose names we know from that very New Testament, as well as secular literature from the first century, who were motivated by deep conviction that all of the events of the end time just described were soon to occur.[1] The instructor likely would not, and in my view probably should not, in today's educational context, especially but not only in secular colleges and universities, attempt to connect the figure prophesied in Isaiah with the historical figure of Jesus, except perhaps to observe that in the long history of the reception and interpretation of the Book of Acts in the history of Christianity such a connection was commonly and indeed usually, and possibly normatively, made in sermons and biblical commentaries alike.

So. One story, two very different readings. These dual readings tell us a lot about the act of interpretation. First, the text is evidently ambiguous, or put differently, capable of multiple meanings and readings. Second, it seems clear that, in order to make any sense of this text at all, one has to put it in *some* interpretive framework. Both the Ethiopian and our hypothetical student seem to lack such an interpretive framework and to be in need of a master interpreter. In this case, each of the two readings is dependent upon distinct modes of approaching the biblical text, one Christological, the other commonly denominated, tautologically, as "historical-critical."

In my view, each of these readings is legitimate or "valid" in its interpretive context, be it a religious community or an educational one. But to admit that is to confess how odd I am, or, to depersonalize my point, how rare is the capacity to tolerate without mental reservation, without cognitive dissonance, two competing, even conflicting and probably incompatible readings of the text. Why this should be the case has everything to do with the claims made by practitioners of the two different approaches to the Bible. More particularly, it originates in the profoundly (just how deeply I will discuss presently) aggrieved perception on the part of many religious readers that the claims made by some if not most practitioners of the historical method, and the materialistic and naturalistic presuppositions that ground and inform it, occlude or even rule out, as violations of the "true meaning" of the text, *any* alternative reading of the text. This would include, in their view, the Christological—or any religious—interpretation of it, or any reading of the text which might function as an entrée to transcendence.

Given this state of affairs in the current interpretation of the Bible, my aim in this chapter is threefold. First, I would like to analyze both the self-understanding of historical critics of the Bible and some of the serious and deeply felt objections made by a great many religious readers to the practice and presuppositions of the historical-critical method. I want to add incidentally here that no one should make the mistake of reading what is emphatically not between the lines: I have no interest in criticizing, much less repudiating or consigning to oblivion, the historical method and all its works; I simply seek to understand it and its critics better. Second, presuming for now the power of the argument that the sometimes totalistic claims of method *can* and sometimes, if not often, *do* impoverish the meaning of the biblical text and occasion existential quandaries for religious readers, many of whom also accept the results and even methods and presuppositions of historical study, I would like to hearken back to premodern or "precritical"[2] interpretive approaches to the Bible and to analyze its very different ways of perceiving the text, approaching it hermeneutically and interpreting it. Third, I would like to address, in a preliminary way, the question, can the precritical or medieval approach to the Bible, or its concrete exegetical products like sermons and commentaries, cure the perceived or real ills of the historical-critical method?

THE HISTORICAL-CRITICAL METHOD AND ITS DISCONTENTS

Contrary to popular perception and to current polemics, most historical critics are aware that they, like their precritical predecessors, have assumptions when they approach the biblical text. Only the philosophically innocent believe they are approaching the text in a purely neutral, absolutely objective, or entirely value-free fashion. No, the real issue is not the naive straw man of those who loathe historical criticism; the issue is how self-aware and explicit the critic is in his assumptions. Most respectable historical critics (and I take it as given that most in the academy are respectable, though some have not been, such as researchers who in the nineteenth century wished to disprove the existence of Jesus of Nazareth, a negative enterprise that some wit dubbed "the lower criticism"). Most will, if pressed, volunteer that, fundamentally, they accept Troeltsch's three renowned axioms for historical study: first, the principle of methodological doubt, which holds, given that any conclusion may be revised, historical study can never achieve complete certainty but instead can give us relative degrees of probability; second, the principle of analogy, which presumes, correctly in my view, that the laws of nature were the same when the writings of the Bible were composed and heard as they are now; and third, the principle of correlation, which holds that, since the events of history depend on one another and are interrelated, no single event can be isolated from the succession of events, or be immune to the historical laws of cause and effect.[3] To these three axioms, some critics, like the Hebrew Bible scholar John Collins, would add the principle of autonomy or independence, which maintains that no religious or secular authority can establish a framework within which the historical scholar must work and which would almost certainly limit or curb the conclusions to which the evidence and data lead, by, for example, insisting that results must conform to predetermined dogmatic formulas.[4] Incidentally, since, regardless of religious commitment, all historical critics accept these assumptions, it is, at least in theory, irrelevant, *for the purposes of historical inquiry,* whether the critic be Jew, Protestant, Catholic, or agnostic or anything else. After all, those purposes demand, if possible, that the inquiry proceed unfettered by any religious commitments or theological assumptions. As a historian, he is as little interested, ideally, in vindicating religious or dogmatic assumptions as he is in destroying them.

Needless to say, these theoretical commitments do not always work out so neatly in practice. Think of the debunking of nineteenth-century romantic notions of the life of Jesus, in which European critics, as if looking in a reflecting pool, saw themselves and their aspirations in the life of this ancient Near Eastern Mediterranean peasant teacher. But lest those suspicious of the historical method feel smug about this, we must hasten to remind ourselves that it was a quintessentially historical critic, Albert Schweitzer, who so perceptively exposed and deconstructed the ideology of these scholars—an example of the Troeltschian self-corrective potential intrinsic to the historical enterprise.[5] Nonetheless, at least in theory, historical critics attempted to approach the text without interest in predetermined conformity to any dogma or to its meaning for religious communities but rather what it meant. To invoke Ranke here, they were and are interested in discovering the data as they actually were (*wie es eigentlich gewesen*).[6]

Finally, most critics would also perceive, with much truth, that these assumptions are rooted, historically and philosophically speaking, in the larger early modern movement we describe by the umbrella term *the Enlightenment* and embrace its confidence, *for the purposes of historical explanation,* in the rules of reason, nature and science— complex terms which, though each would require generous explana- tion in an elaborate treatment of our subject, are clear enough, I believe, for our purposes. Many German scholars would want, in ad- dition, or instead, to trace the origins of historical criticism back to the Reformation. Here the argument is that the Reformers, suspicious of magisterial interpretations of some texts, felt they had the perfect right to ask what the texts meant without accepting what the religious authorities said they meant.

Thus, for example, it could be asked if (referring especially to the first chapter of Philippians) whether the terms *bishop* and *deacon* had the hierarchical meaning the church imposed on them in the sixteenth century or whether they had a very different sense at the time they were written.

What happens once these assumptions are put into practice in actual historical-critical study of the Bible? Of course it depends on who you ask. But it is only fair first to ask the practicing historical critic. Then we will ask the critics' critics.

Most historical critics will tell you that they attempt to encourage an encounter with the Bible that is not in essence different from the way in which they would encourage a student to engage with, say, the writings of Homer or Plato. Each body of literature ought to be understood, they argue, in the context of the time in which it was produced, be it the ancient Near East or classical Athenian culture. In the case of the Bible especially, historical critics understand the sacred text (whether the collection be Jewish, Catholic, or Protestant) as a collection or library of different books—and here the Greek for Bible, *ta biblia* (The Books) is useful, as well as impressively showy, to trot out here. In this sense, it is unlike the classics of other traditions— unlike, say, the Mahabharata or some other religious epic. The Bible we know differs from other classics in that it was written in various different languages, which, importantly, make the Bible more alien than it seems in translations into English and European vernaculars. It contains many different viewpoints, sometimes on identical reli- gious matters, as well as prescribed practices and narratives which contradict one another. In fact, the Bible as a whole has no single meaning; only its individual books do, and even the meaning of these is extremely difficult, sometimes impossible, to recover. In the early modern period, it became fashionable among the Reformers and their followers to say that the Bible's meaning is plain and clear. But with hindsight, that seems naive, as it relies upon an extremely selective and partial canon-within-the-canon, which violates the complexity and the foreignness, not to mention the integrity, of the canon. Nor is the meaning of this collection given by its mysterious assembly into a single collection, beginning, but certainly not ending, in the second through fifth centuries—that is, its assemblage into a canon, which took a long time for the orthodox to fix, and on which Jews, Catholics, and Protestants still disagree. Beyond this the Bible is, or can be, extremely unreliable on its face historically, cosmologically, and in all senses scientific.

Quite evidently, historical criticism is preoccupied, some (though not I) would say unhealthily obsessed, with the question of origins. In this sense, historical critics are usually said to be interested in "genetic" questions: When was a book written? By whom? What was its readership or audience like? How and by what historical processes, or stages, did a particular book or collection of books come into being?

In attempting to ascertain the "original intention" of an author or text, historical-critical interpretation has distinguished between the final written form of the text and pretextual, often oral, sources. As historical critics would themselves admit, they are often more interested in underlying, or precanonical, sources than the final canonical form of a book. Thus to take the two most familiar examples, no historical critic any longer regards the Pentateuch as written by a single author, such as Moses.[7] Rather, it was composed of at least four sources, designated by letters (in this case J, P, E, and D, the "deuteronomistic" source which is sometimes distinguished into two or even three strands) that indicate their emphasis: P, for example, is particularly interested in priestly qualifications, prerogatives, practices, and functions. This, of course, is the famous "documentary hypothesis," usually if not entirely correctly associated with Julius

Wellhausen, who was actually not the first to perceive distinct religious and theological strands that were woven together by editors at a time much later than their original, probably oral composition.[8]

Similarly, scholars of Matthew and Luke now realize that, contrary to eighteen centuries of opinion, Mark is not an epitome of Matthew but rather one of its sources, as it is of Luke. In addition, an anonymous sayings source, called Q (from the German *Quelle*, for "source"), fed into its composition, as well as material special to each of the two evangelists. These sources, Mark, Q, and the material unique to the writers of the second and third gospels (whose names are unknown, having been associated with Matthew and Luke early in the second century), were then assembled, edited, and reworked into their final form, according to their understanding of the messiahship of Jesus of Nazareth and the needs of the communities for which they had composed their good news—their gospels.[9]

In short, historical criticism has emphatically not been primarily interested in what a biblical text means, or could mean, to modern readers or religious communities. Instead, it is interested in an original meaning of the text and what it might have meant to its original hearers or readers.

Perhaps most disturbingly to some, historical-critical study regards its object as produced by humans—fallible humans (to use another tautology). It ignores, brackets, or in more radical forms denies, irresponsibly in my view as this question goes outside the historian's purview, that the text was in any way inspired, authorized, or dictated by supernatural forces—by God, that is. In short, the text, in the hands of the historical critic, qua historian, ceases to be a divine oracle and becomes, not unlike the *Posterior Analytics* of Aristotle, say, or Vergil's *Aeneid*, a human and only a human artifact.

Incidentally, and again contrary to common opinion, the historical enterprise was launched by Jews and Catholics, as well as Protestants, who might be said to have perfected it. One need only mention the name of Spinoza, or the French Catholic Oratorian Richard Simon, to make the point. Lest we believe that suspicion of historical critics is a unique feature of our own day, it is worth reminding ourselves that both men would pay a heavy price by the

believing communities of which they were also a part for their historical brilliance. Analogously, both Julius Wellhausen and others
would pay the price in lost academic chairs in the communities where
their historical magnificence would cause them to pay so dearly.

Let me attempt to drive home explicitly some of the problematic
or disturbing implications of this wholly inadequate historical summary. Before the advent of historical criticism, the Bible was understood as a repository of *all* knowledge, not just religious and historical, but scientific. Thus Luther famously dismissed Copernicus's
heliocentric view of the solar system because, as was plain for those
with eyes to see, the sun rose and set. The Bible told him so. But historical criticism of the Bible, once absorbed and if accepted, profoundly corroded faith in its reliability as either a historical or scientific document. Even the religious knowledge it putatively taught
stood on sand, as critics ruthlessly detected incompatible strands of
tradition, irreconcilable propositions, and, beginning with the first
two chapters of Genesis, two cosmogonies which in no way could be
reconciled. In short, cognitive propositions and truth claims swiftly
lost their authority when the historian wielded his critical scalpel. The
notion of historical or scientific accuracy came to be seen, correctly
I believe, as an assumption imposed on scripture by tradition. Second,
no critic felt he had to invoke the supernatural when a historical
explanation, relying on the principle of cause-and-effect seemed to
offer a more natural or plain and fully sufficient explication—and
thus demanded no recourse to a supranatural cause.

With this, the doctrine of inspiration, which has slender justification, at best, in the Bible itself, came to be profoundly challenged,
as did the more modest but still immensely problematic category of
revelation. Third, historical criticism demolished the notion, held in
Christian history at least since Origen (185–253), that the collection
of books in the scripture was a unity and testified to a single truth.
I conclude this section by observing that, had Philip somehow magi-
cally been endowed with this knowledge, he would have been wholly
unable to respond to the Ethiopian eunuch. Today the Christological
hermeneutic he employed as a key to understanding Isaiah would be
rudely ruled out of court by his historical critics as a later, Christian

imposition upon the Jewish text which does unacceptable violence to its original meaning.

THE "ILLS" OF THE HISTORICAL-CRITICAL METHOD

Let me begin my second question by asking how critics of the historical method respond to the question, What happens once Troelschian assumptions are put into practice by the critics of the historical study of the Bible? Here I knew I would get a different response; what surprised me, as I did my research, was the depth of rejection of, almost the revulsion with, the assumptions and results of such study. A quick inspection of my bibliography is sufficient to speak to the profundity of the repudiation. Some critics gently suggest "concrete alternatives" or a "postcritical" paradigm to the challenges posed by the historical method. Others have wondered if their denominational leaders may even resort to the method as a means of interpretation. Still others, more alarmed, suggest that biblical criticism finds itself in a desperate "plight," brought to the edge of a "pagan precipice"; still others, even more horrified, suggest there is a "crisis" in the field, while one critic has composed the "obituary notice"[10] for the method in the title of his book, *The End of the Historical-Critical Method.* Others have implied that it is less a methodology than an ideology.[11] What is it about historical criticism that makes it so profoundly objectionable in the eyes of these authors?

As John Barton has observed, "Perhaps the central accusation against the historical critical method that one hears nowadays concerns its Enlightenment origins."[12] Indeed, it is true that many see in the rise of the historical-critical method a major battle in the war of modernity and Christianity. Here we must begin by observing the anomaly that traditional ecclesiastical interpreters have joined hands with poststructural analysts in their critique of the historical method. As Barton explains, both poststructuralist and religious critics argue that the claims of disinterested or objective historical inquiry have been shown to be unfounded because, so it is alleged, no one is, or could be, wholly disinterested. All, so it is said, have "an axe to grind," and therefore the "pretense of academic neutrality" ought to be jettisoned. At least those with explicit commitments are honest about them; historical critics, who pretend to be neutral, actually smuggle their convictions and commitments, sometimes destructive ones, under the cover of distinterested neutrality. Barton goes on to observe that if these critics are correct, the exclusive preoccupation for original meanings would then lose its justification. The original meaning of the text would lose its special status, for this is no reason to privilege it above other meanings the text has acquired throughout history. Even to assume that historical facts can be recovered is, for some, delusional and self-deceptive.[13] In short, historical critics have come together with postmodernists in "banish[ing] the expression 'really means' to the outer darkness."[14]

Implied in the rejection of the expression "really means" is that the biblical text has an excess of meaning or a fuller sense, a *sensus plenior* (which I use in its nontechnical sense here), that is hardly captured or exhausted by historical-critical investigation. Scripture has a fuller meaning that can be found than that which depends wholly upon inquiry into the circumstances that produced it. In this sense, it corresponds to rabbinic understandings of *remez, drash,* or *sod,* where some fuller, and potentially deeper, meaning than the historical is perceived in and drawn from the text. The community of historical critics is just one interpretive community. Other communities, particularly religious communities reflecting upon the primary language of the Bible, have their own, and in their view, equally valid history of interpretation that in no way is obligated to capitulate to the positivistic results and Enlightenment assumptions of historicism. By insisting that the historical sense is the only true and valid one, historical critics are, in effect (as one critic has observed), asserting "a secular analogy to a religious revelation: they are claiming to have a definitive insight into the meaning of things, even things that they have never directly experienced and that are interpreted very differently by those who have."[15] Historical critics thus shift "the locus of truth from the practicing community to the nonpracticing and unaffiliated individual." Only the observer peering in from the outside has access to the true meaning of the text. In this sense, it is a "secular

equivalent of fundamentalism." The historical critic would be well
advised, if this is true, to make room for other senses of the text,
which are developed by communities and traditions different from
and proceeding on different (but no less valid) assumptions from his.
It is simply hubristic to pronounce noncritical interpretations in error
because they don't harmonize perfectly with the community that
originally produced them—*a* community that did not have a Bible
and may not even have had the written text on which the historical
critic parasitically thrives. The critical community must realize it is
just that—a community, "dependent upon other communities of interpretation for the very object of its inquiry and historically for its
motivation as well."[16]

Ideally, it must also be aware that the text it studies has a history,
something of which its critics believe it is either blithely unaware or
ignorant; again ideally, it should acquaint himself with and respect it.
The history of interpretation cannot be dismissed, in oracular fashion,
as the history of misinterpretation, or precritical and thus wholly
irrelevant to his mature task, the history of reception being a mere
relic from the infancy of the study of the Bible. The history of the
interpretation itself is testament to the fundamental fact that, as Erich
Auerbach observed, the text stands desperately in need of interpretation,[17] and thus the history of that enterprise cannot be dismissed
arrogantly as a history of the violation of the book. Because, as even
the historical critic will acknowledge, the text is ambiguous and
opaque and because readers' and communities' circumstances change
over time, interpretations necessarily must change and yield a multiplicity of possibilities for meaning and understanding.

Many religious readers, and practically all evangelical and funda-
mentalist ones, are, as I have already intimated, profoundly alarmed
that the historical critic excludes, arbitrarily in their view, the principle or possibility of supernatural incursion and causation in history,
the possibility or reality of divine revelation, the unity of scriptural
affirmation and the rejection of cognitive religious truth. Making
points that many historical critics agree with, evangelical writers observe that historical critics are not, and cannot be, philosophically
neutral, cannot deal with issues concerning the supernatural or mi-

raculous, cannot disprove the factuality of a biblical historical event, and cannot entertain the possibility that the scriptures are divinely inspired and thus a source of supernatural revelation or a record of miraculous redemptive history.[18] They understand the history *internal to* the Bible but are profoundly ignorant *of* the history of the Bible as assembled, standardized, and commented upon. Historical critics need to recognize that their work is itself historically particular, is itself a tradition, and must therefore refrain from insisting that all other traditions, and all other senses of the text, surrender to its. They, after all, constitute a community of interpretation, and it is not self-evident that their totalistic claims to the truth must be accepted by other communities simply because they take and apply texts without dogmatic reference to their original historical context. Historians must learn to interact more fruitfully with other communities of interpreters who do not share their assumptions or accept, and sometimes repudiate, their exegetical results—and certainly their monopolistic claims and practices.

While interested in the history of biblical interpretation before there was a Bible, or, more precisely, early Jewish or Christian history, they show no interest in the history of scriptural interpretation. But, of course, in concentrating on original context, critics ignore that texts, including biblical texts, are constantly recontextualized; they survive the conditions that originally produced them and are, all along then, in need of new reading and new application to current circumstances and community problems. Concentrating on the period of the composition of the texts, critical scholars, unlike, say, practitioners of the canonical method, overlook the meaning of the assembled or canonical Bible and are innocent of its immense significance in the history of religion and culture.

Evidently, its irreverence and subversiveness is a source of intense irritation. Historical critics, by insisting that it is only through their lens that the Bible can be understood, lapse into grave and innocent error. They claim a monopoly on the interpretive process that is in no way warranted by the history of its primary use over twenty centuries as a source of revelation, models of sanctity, and guide to normative behavior and is in fact at odds with, if not subversive of, those modes of reading the text. "They assume," one commentator has concluded, that "the observer's observation is truer than the practitioner's practice." The effect in academic practice, this commentator continues, is to set up a new hierarchy, "a 'new clerisy' . . . of academic theorists who, unlike the people they study, know what they are doing." Only insofar as he separates himself from ritual and believing communities, so the historical critic assumes, can we come to understand the truth of things. The site of truth shifts, then, from the practicing community to the "nonpracticing and unaffiliated individual."[19]

Left unsettled, or even unaddressed, in these potent critiques is how the pluralism of senses can avoid "degenerating uncontrollably into relativism,"[20] allegorical alchemy, or fractionation. Nor is it usually recognized that historical critics have put the brakes on both postmodernistic impulses to an infinity of meanings and the abuse of the text, by means of allegorical alchemy, of religious readers. But that is hardly to begin to deny the power or deeply felt character of the religiously motivated criticism of the historical method. The question I would like now to pose, as I move to the next section, is whether and in what ways medieval hermeneutics might cure the ills of the modern.

READING THE BIBLE WITH THE DEAD: MEDIEVAL HERMENEUTICS AND PRECRITICAL COMMENTARIES AND SERMONS

Browsing around one's library these days, it is quite apparent that many people think medieval hermeneutics may hold a cure. Whole new series have been launched of ancient and medieval interpretations of scripture in English translation, born out of frustration with the perceived sterility of the historical method. But before we can endorse this as an antidote to the putative ills of that method, we must remind ourselves, all too briefly, of the character of precritical hermeneutics and exegetical practice.

Precritical hermeneutics are complex. It would be absurd to attempt a comprehensive treatment here. What I would like to do is to analyze the theory most commonly associated with the Middle Ages, the so-called fourfold or four-sense theory.

The question of how many senses of scripture there were, and what each meant, achieved authoritative definition at the end of the ancient period in Christianity in the writings of the monk John Cassian (360–435). Most ancient commentators worked with the practical distinction between literal and spiritual senses. Origen had theoretically designated three senses: literal, moral, and spiritual (*On First Principles* 4.2.4), though scrutiny of his surviving commentaries indicates he did not follow this principle slavishly. In his *Conferences*, Cassian became the first to argue that, theoretically, scripture contained or expressed four senses: literal, allegorical, moral or tropological, and anagogical or eschatological. Eventually, this understanding was versified as follows:

> Littera gesta docet, quid credas allegoria,
> Moralia quid agas, quo tendas anagogia.

This little couplet basically meant that the literal sense has to do with the history of God's redemptive activity, the allegorical level with articles of belief, the moral with ethical behavior, and the anagogical with one's eternal destiny. Thus, for example, when Jerusalem is mentioned in the Bible, it would refer literally to the earthly city, allegorically to the church, morally to the soul, and anagogically to the heavenly city. Cassian's *Conferences* was one of the few texts recommended in the *Rule of Benedict*. As a consequence, his theory was absorbed in Benedictine cloisters in the early Middle Ages and passed on to interpreters for a millennium. Again, few interpreters applied this principle mechanically; many were content to distinguish in their commentaries between two or sometimes three senses. Actually, it was rather rare, in practice, for a medieval commentator to interpret a particular verse in all four senses. Nonetheless, that is not crucial. What is important, for our purposes, is simply to observe that no medieval interpreter imagined that the meaning of any scriptural book, chapter, or verse was ever limited to what its human author intended or its original audience received as its meaning in their original cultural and historical context. The allegorical method, which the church did not invent, had been appropriated and baptized by it. All Christian interpreters recognized that allegory (or, with the Antiochenes, *theoria*) gave the church access to a meaning that was not frozen in time or fixed. With the allegorical method, the church had inherited, and had brilliantly exploited, a way of making the scriptures inexhaustible. To it the ancients had bequeathed a means by which, until the modern era, it could make the scriptures perennially relevant, above all, perhaps, in preaching. Indeed, other, allegorical or moral meanings might be far more significant than the original literal or historical meaning.

This is emphatically not to suggest that medieval interpreters thought or believed that the text could mean absolutely anything, or open up an infinite field of potential interpretations. As Beryl Smalley has proven, the literal sense gained a sort of ascendancy as the Middle Ages progressed.[21] Though all agreed that scripture had multiple senses or layers, interpreters became increasingly determined to ground the three spiritual senses ever more securely in the literal sense. Thomas Aquinas's famous definition and discussion of the literal sense in the opening sections of his *Summa* is merely the most well known instance of this. Despite this emphasis, premodern interpreters, as Henri de Lubac, in response to Smalley, pointed out, continued to regard the scriptural text as having multiple meanings intended by their author, in this case, God, as well as a human being.[22]

It is also crucial for our purposes to remind ourselves that medieval exegetes typically wrote their commentaries or homilies surrounded by a cloud of scriptural witnesses. Or to put it another way, borrowing from the title of a recent book, they read the Bible with the dead[23]—that is, with previous interpreters of scripture—and this is the case with both Jewish and Christian commentators. Medieval exegetes typically had the writings of ancient commentators on scripture open before them and felt free to draw on them, sometimes verbatim, as they wrote their own commentaries. That is, they read the *tradition* of scriptural interpretation, and used it as an authoritative guide, as they wrote their own commentaries and homilies.

From this all too brief glimpse at medieval hermeneutical method and exegetical practice, we can finally address ourselves to the question that this chapter began by posing. Can precritical hermeneutics cure the ills of the critical? Needless to say, I can only gesture at a response here, but I will not use that as a justification to avoid the question, only to indicate the sort of response of which I am capable in this context.

First of all, my title presumes there *are* ills. This seems to me true only if a historical critic claims the meaning he uncovers is the only imaginable or true sense of the text. Yet some do, and it seems to me obvious that religious communities of readers are right to insist that the biblical text actually has "an excess of meaning" and multiple senses that a severe historical critic illicitly attempts to limit.

In this sense, I think contemporary religious readers can rightly point out that Jewish and ecclesiastical readers have *always* held that the meaning of the text has given rise to multiple readings and has been believed, hermeneutically, to have multiple senses. Thus, in that sense, I do think that recovery of the medieval legacy of multiple senses can begin to cure the ills of the most ideologically egregious and practically nonsensical forms of historical criticism.

I also think that it is important to follow the example of the medieval tradition and to read the biblical text with the dead, with the tradition of exegesis. I do not think that we need to accept their conclusions or the results of their practical criticism. But I think it is useful to read them as illustrative of various potential meanings and as a springboard for asking questions about the text—as conversation partners, if you like. In this connection, I would like to see Christian exegesis become more like rabbinic interpretation, which depended on presentation of a host of authorities, often in disagreement, but which did not rush to harmonize them and felt free to leave questions of interpretation open.

In this sense, too, I think the famous Tridentine decree on scripture and tradition, interpreted liberally, can be usefully applied to present-day readings of scripture. Both scripture and its readers through history ought to be received with reverence, *pari affectu,* in conversation with one another, and with the contemporary reader.

Reading the Bible with the dead can liberate us from the shackles and sterility of the historical-critical method. At the same time, the historical-critical method can be used as a control, to keep religious readers honest and to establish some broad field within which the game of exegesis can be played. Thus, in the end, I think religious readers dismiss the historical-critical method and its results at their peril. At the same time, I conclude by responding to the question with which I began with a qualified yes: precritical exegesis can cure the ills of the historical-critical method, at least in its most ideologically and practically extreme forms.

NOTES

1. E. P. Sanders, *Jesus and Judaism* (Philadelphia: Fortress Press, 1985).

2. For all the implications of "precritical," as applied to exegesis, see the provocative essay by David Steinmetz, "The Superiority of Pre-Critical Exegesis," *Theology Today* 37, no. 1 (April 1980): 27–38.

3. Ernst Troeltsch, "Historical and Dogmatic Method in Theology," in *Religion in History,* ed. James Luther Adams and Walter F. Bense (Minneapolis: Fortress Press, 1991), 11–32.

4. Jon D. Levenson, "The Bible: Unexamined Commitments of Criticism," *First Things* 30 (February 1993): 24–33 (30).

5. Albert Schweitzer, *The Quest of the Historical Jesus: A Critical Study of Its Progress from Reimarus to Wrede,* trans. W. Montgomery (New York: Macmillan, 1959).

6. Leopold Ranke, "Preface: Histories of the Latin and Germanic Nations from 1494–1514," in *The Varieties of History: From Voltaire to the Present,* ed. Fritz Richard Stern (Cleveland: Meridian Books, 1956), 57.

7. See chapter 12 of R. N. Whybray, *The Making of the Pentateuch: A Methodological Study* (Sheffield: JSOT, 1987).

8. Ernest W. Nicholson, *The Pentateuch in the Twentieth Century: The Legacy of Julius Wellhausen* (Oxford: Clarendon Press, 1998).

9. See the classic textbook, Burnett Hillman Streeter, *The Four Gospels: A Study of Origins, Treating of the Manuscript Tradition, Sources, Authorship, and Dates,* 4th ed. (London: Macmillan, 1930); and the annotated bibliography by Thomas R. W. Longstaff and Page A. Thomas, *The Synoptic Problem: A Bibliography, 1716–1988* (Macon, GA: Mercer University Press, 1988).

10. The term is not mine. See Alan F. Johnston, "The Historical-Critical Method: Egyptian Gold or Pagan Precipice?," *Journal of the Evangelical Theological Society* 26, no. 1 (March 1983): 3–15 (8).

11. Johnston, "The Historical-Critical Method," 3–5; Mark G. Brett, *Biblical Criticism in Crisis? The Impact of the Canonical Approach on Old Testament Studies* (New York: Cambridge University Press, 1991); Henry Joel Cadbury, "The Peril of Archaizing Ourselves," *Interpretation* 3, no. 3 (July 1949), 331–37; O. C. Edwards, "Historical-Critical Method's Failure of Nerve and a Prescription for a Tonic: A Review of Some Recent Literature," *Anglican Theological Review* 59, no. 2 (April 1977): 115–34; Stephen Garfinkel, "Applied Peshat: Historical-Critical Method and Religious Meaning," *Journal of the Ancient Near Eastern Society* 22 (1993): 19–28; Eta Linnemann, *Historical Criticism of the Bible: Methodology or Ideology?*, trans. Robert W. Yarbrough (Grand Rapids, MI: Baker, 1990); Gerhard Maier, *The End of the Historical-Critical Method*, trans. Edwin W. Levernz and Rudolf F. Norden (St. Louis: Concordia, 1977); Gerhard Maier, "Concrete Alternatives to the Historical-Critical Method," *Evangelical Review of Theology* 6, no. 1 (April 1982): 23–36; James P. Martin, "Toward a Post-Critical Paradigm," *New Testament Studies* 33, no. 3 (July 1987): 370–85; Chester C. McCown, "The Current Plight of Biblical Scholarship," *Journal of Biblical Literature* 75, no. 1 (March 1956): 12–18; Richard John Neuhaus, ed., *Biblical Interpretation in Crisis: The Ratzinger Conference on Bible and Church* (Grand Rapids, MI: Eerdmans, 1989); Robert D. Preus, "May the Lutheran Church Legitimately Use the Historical-Critical Method?," *Affirm* (Spring 1973): 31–35; Joachim Rohde, *Rediscovering the Teaching of the Evangelists*, trans. Dorothea M. Barton, new ed. (London: SCM Press, 1968); Georg Schelbert, "Defaming the Historical-Critical Method," trans. Linda Maloney, in *Church in Anguish*, ed. Hans Küng and Leonard Swidler (San Francisco: Harper & Row, 1987), 106–24; E. F. Scott, "The Limitations of the Historical Method," in *Studies in Early Christianity*, ed. Shirley Jackson Case (New York: Century Co., 1928), 3–18; Willard M. Swartley, "Beyond the Historical-Critical Method," in *Essays on Biblical Interpretation: Anabaptist-Mennonite Perspectives* (Elkhart, IN: Institute of Mennonite Studies, 1984), 237–64.

12. John Barton, "Historical-Critical Approaches," in *The Cambridge Companion to Biblical Interpretation*, ed. John Barton (Cambridge: Cambridge University Press, 1998), 9–20. See esp. 12–13.

13. Ibid., 12–17.

14. Ibid., 17.

15. Levenson, "Unexamined Commitments of Criticism," 33.

16. For these observations, see Levenson, "Unexamined Commitments of Criticism," 29–33.

17. Erich Auerbach, *Mimesis: The Representation of Reality in Western Literature*, trans. Willard R. Trask (Princeton, NJ: Princeton University Press, [1953] 2003).

18. See esp. Johnston, "The Historical-Critical Method," 12–13.

19. Levenson, "Unexamined Commitments of Criticism," 29.

20. Ibid., 33.

21. This is essentially the thesis of her groundbreaking book: Beryl Smalley, *The Study of the Bible in the Middle Ages* (Oxford: Clarendon Press, 1941). See the Ancient Christian Commentary on Scripture series (IVP); or *The Church's Bible* (Eerdman's).

22. Henri de Lubac, *Medieval Exegesis: The Four Senses of Scripture*, trans. Mark Sebanc (Grand Rapids, MI: Eerdmans; Edinburgh: T & T Clark, 1998–), 3 vols. to date.

23. John Lee Thompson, *Reading the Bible with the Dead: What You Can Learn from the History of Exegesis That You Can't Learn from Exegesis Alone* (Grand Rapids, MI: Eerdmans, 2007).

Chapter Four

POSSIBILE ABSOLUTUM
The Theological Discovery of the
Ontological Priority of the Possible

INGOLF U. DALFERTH

FROM THE SCIENCE OF BEING TO THE
SCIENCE OF THE POSSIBLE

"There is a science," says Aristotle in *Metaphysics* IV 1003 a, 21, "which investigates being as being" (τό ὄν ᾗ ὄν). In contrast to special sciences such as physics or mathematics, which investigate the attributes of a part of being, first philosophy or metaphysics, as it came to be called in the Aristotelian tradition, is the science that studies *what is insofar as it is* (περὶ τοῦ ὄντος ᾗ ὄν).[1]

Some two thousand years later and in sharp contrast to Aristotle, Christian Wolff defines philosophy in his *Discursus praeliminaris de philosophia in genere* (1731) as the science of the possible *insofar as it can be:* "Philosophia est scientia possibilium, quatenus esse possunt."[2]

And in the twentieth century we hear from philosophers like Heidegger that "higher than actuality stands *possibility*,"[3] and theologians like Jüngel propose an ontological "priority of possibility over actuality"[4] because "God is to be conceived as the one who makes the possible to be possible and the impossible to be impossible. As the one who does this . . . God distinguishes himself from the world. And in that he distinguishes himself from the world, God lets the world be actual."[5]

This change from the priority of the actual over the possible to the priority of the possible over the actual is significant. It is one thing to investigate *what is insofar as it is,* quite another to study *what is possible insofar as it is possible.* What is the significance of this change, and how did it come about? My answer is that it manifests an onto-logical revolution that took place between the twelfth and the four-teenth century and whose impact on our thinking and doing to this very day cannot be overestimated, and that this revolution would have been unthinkable without theology.[6]

POSSIBILITY IN ARISTOTLE

Since the time of Aristotle it has been clear that one cannot study being without reference to modality. Nothing is what it is without being it in a certain mode. This is true of beings (metaphysical and physical modalities) as much as it is of propositions (alethic modali-ties). But which modes of being have to be taken into account in the study of being as being? Merely possibility and necessity and their contraries and contradictories (impossibility, non-necessity, contin-gency), or also actuality (reality), truth and falsity (*vera/falsa*), *bona/mala, scita/ignota, concepta, credita, opinata, dubitata,* as William of Ockham proposed in the spirit of Aristotelianism in the fourteenth century?[7] And even if we confine ourselves to the alethic modalities *necessary, contingent, impossible, possible,* how are they to be under-stood? Modal terms notoriously have many senses (*pollachos lego-mena*). Aristotle's various and inconsistent attempts to systematize the (metaphysical or alethic) modalities have opened up different ave-nues of reflection.

In the *Analytica priora* I.2, 25a1, he distinguishes three modal terms which can be predicated of being: *necessary, possible* (= that which is not impossible), and *actual* or *contingent* (= that which is not necessary and not impossible); and this threefold division can still be found in Kant's theory of modality which distinguishes between *possibility, existence,* and *necessity* as the three basic ways of a subject's relation to the content of a judgment.

In *De interpretatione* 12, 21b26 ff., on the other hand, Aristotle accepts only *necessity* and *possibility* as modes, whereas *actuality* is that which is modified by the modal terms; and in this he is followed by most contemporary modal theories, which accept only two modalities, *necessity* and *possibility,* even though there is no difference in grammatical structure between "p is real" ("It is the case that p") and "p is necessary" ("It is necessarily the case that p"). But the difference shows in negation. Whereas "It is not the case that p" is equivalent to "It is the case that not p," "It is not necessary that p" is not equivalent to "It is necessary that not p."

In *De interpretatione* 12–13 and the *Analytica priora* (I.3, 13) Aristotle distinguishes between *necessity* and *possibility* but defines possibility as *contingency* (in the broad sense), that is, as *that which is not necessary and not impossible.* But he also uses a more general notion of *possibility* defined as *that which is not impossible.* The latter notion merely excludes impossibility but includes necessity, that is, *that which is impossible not to be.* The former notion (contingency), on the other hand, does not include everything that is not impossible but excludes the necessary. Thus the first notion of possibility includes necessity whereas the second doesn't.

However, the notion of possibility is even more ambiguous than Aristotle's account as represented so far suggests. Subsequent discussions through the centuries up to Leibniz have brought out that there are at least two further notions of possibility besides the two outlined:

1. The *possibile* in the broadest sense (Mp), which is the contradictory of the *impossibile* (–Mp)
2. The *possibile* in the sense of Aristotle's *endechomenon* (–Np & –(–Mp)), which is *neither necessary nor impossible*

3. The *possibile* in the sense of the *contingens* (p & M–p) in Leibniz's sense, which is neither necessary nor impossible *but exists even though it could not have existed*
4. The *possibile* in the sense of the *mere possibile* (–p & Mp) or *esse in potentia*, which is neither necessary nor impossible *and does not exist*

The last two versions of possibility can only be distinguished by recourse to the difference between *being* (*esse*) and *nonbeing* (*non-esse*), and this is why *actual* or *actuality* is sometimes counted as a third modality of being. Aristotle's account in *De interpretatione* 12 and *Analytica priora* I.2, 25A 1–3, gave rise to couching this difference in terms of *modi recti et obliqui*, that is, *absolute* and *relational modalities*. Relational modalities such as *possible, necessary, impossible, non-necessary* always qualify a being or becoming, that is, an *einai (esse)* or a *gignesthai (fieri);* they cannot stand on their own but are relative to the absolute modalities (*esse, fieri, non-esse;* or: p, –p) which they modify. However, strictly speaking, absolute modalities are no modalities at all but that which is modified by modal terms. Modal terms are modifiers and cannot be used meaningfully in an absolute way. Modes are always modes *of something:* Only *what is actual* can be possible, and only *what is* can be necessary. Without actuality there is no possibility or necessity.

This is also true of the *mere possibile* which understands possibility (*possibilitas*) as a potency (*potentia*);[8] for every potency is the potency *of something or someone*. Nothing can be *mere possibile* unless it is related to an actual reality. But then what is possible differs from what is actual only by being not yet or no more actual: Possibility is *possible actuality,* actuality takes place in time, and hence all possibility is the possibility of something past, present, or future. Thus no genuine possibility can remain forever unrealized, as the so-called Principle of Plenitude holds.[9] Aristotelian possibility in all its various senses does not involve reference to simultaneous alternatives but is understood in a statistical or temporal frequency way: Whatever is possible, was, is, or will be actual.[10]

A DIALECTICIS LIBERA NOS, DOMINE

It is not surprising that this account of modality was hard to accept for Christian thinkers. Al-Farabi (872–951) reports that Christian bishops allowed the study of Aristotle's *Organon* only to the end of the theory of categorical syllogism; the theory of modal syllogism was not permitted because this was considered to be detrimental to and dangerous for the Christian faith. This critical stance toward Aristotle's theory of modality continued well into the eleventh century.[11] His view that actuality has priority over possibility was taken to be incompatible with divine omnipotence and to create aporias in the understanding of divine providence, foreknowledge, and freedom. In his *De divina omnipotentia,* Peter Damian (1007–72) narrates that he discussed with young monks in Montecassino the *quaestio frivola:* "Numquid potest Deus hoc agere ut, postquam semel aliquid factum est, factum non fuerit?"[12] The monks cited Hieronymus who had warned a young woman, "Audenter loquor, cum omnia possit Deus: suscitare virginem non potest post ruinam."[13] For if one follows Aristotle that "quidquid nunc est, quamdiu est, procul dubio esse necesse est,"[14] then what is now the case is necessary and hence cannot be changed, not even by God.

However, the argument confuses the *necessitas consequentiae* (N(p–>p)) with the *necessitas consequentis* (p=>Np). The inference p=>Np is a modal shift fallacy and to be rejected for logical reasons. But such arguments are also unacceptable for theological reasons, as Peter points out, because they unduly constrain God's omnipotence and, as he puts it, "eum penitus impotentem reddant."[15] If modal arguments interfere with divine omnipotence, so much the worse for them.

DEO NIHIL EST IMPOSSIBILE

Here is the linchpin of the entire debate. Since the days of Homer it was accepted that θεοί δέ τε πάντα δύνανται (*Odyssey* X, 306). "Nihil est," as Cicero puts it, "quod deus efficere non posit."[16] Jesus was taken to say the same when he replied to the Pharisees that what is impossible with men is possible with God (Luke 18:27). But if everything is possible for God, what exactly is the reference range or distribution of this "everything": Does it mean all that is impossible with men? Or all that is possible? Or all that is either possible or impossible? Tertullian saw the problem and stated more precisely: "Deo nihil est impossibile, nisi quod non vult."[17] It is God's will that determines what for God is possible or impossible, and God's will is absolutely free and not constrained by any necessity or impossibility. Anselm put it as usual in a precise way in *Cur Deus homo?* II,17: "Omnis quippe necessitas et impossibilitas ejus subjacet voluntati: illius autem voluntas nulli subditur necessitati aut impossibilitati."

However, this still leaves open the question whether what is possible is so because God wills it or whether God wills it because it is possible? Thomas Aquinas answered, "Deus dicitur omnipotens, quia potest omnia possibilia absolute, quod est alter modus dicendi possible" (*ST* I, q. 25, a. 3 resp.).

POSSIBILITAS AND POTENTIA

This argument deserves to be examined in more detail. It belongs in the context of the debate about the creation of the world that led to a new theological interest in the modalities in the twelfth century. Contrary to the antidialectical attitude of the eleventh century (*A dialecticis libera nos, Domine*), John of Salisbury (1120–80) points out in his *Metalogicon* (IV.4) that the *ratio modorum* (knowledge of the modalities) is of great importance (*pernecessarium*) for the study of Holy Scripture. And a similar interest can be seen in Abelard, who introduced the distinction between *de re* and *de dicto* in the logic of modalities.

However, Aristotle's *Metaphysics* and *Physics* became available in the West only in the thirteenth century, and hence also his metaphysical theory of modality outlined in *Metaphysics* IX (theta) that distinguishes between *energeia* (*actualitas*) and *dynamei on* (*poten-*

tia).[18] Possibility is the *potentia* to be actual or to do something actually. Thus every change in the actual involves a change from the possible to the actual, and what cannot become actual, cannot be possible. Already Avicenna (980–1037) distinguished between *possibilitas* and *potentia,* between the *possibility* of something or someone ("It is possible to φ") and the *potency* or competence of something or someone to be or to do something ("It is possible for a to φ"). In either case the possibility or potency was understood to be *relative to some actuality:* Possibility is always the possibility of something actual, and the same is true of potency.

POSSIBILE ABSOLUTUM

In *Metaphysics* IX (theta) Aristotle had introduced these modal distinctions in order to be able to describe and analyze the manifold changes in the *kosmos.* This helped Christian thinkers to understand *becoming in the world,* but it was of no help in understanding the *becoming of the world,* that is, the *creatio ex nihilo.* In Aristotelian terms this required postulating an actual potency that actualizes the possibility of the world. But this *possibility of the world* could no longer be understood as the *possibility of the actual world* but had to be presupposed *as possibility:* It was no longer a relative possibility but an absolute possibility, a *possibile absolutum.*

This led to a completely new paradigm of modal thinking. The possible was no longer defined by reference to the actual, the impossible no longer in terms of its incompatibility with the actual world (physical impossibility) or the actuality of the world (metaphysical impossibility). On the other hand, there was still the principle that there is no possibility, necessity, or impossibility as such. But since it could no longer be the possibility or necessity of the actual world, it had to become the possibility or necessity of the divine creator of the world: Absolute possibilities came to be seen as the eternal ideas in the divine mind. The possibility of the world is understood not relative to the actual world but to the divine mind of the creator; similarly impossibility is understood independently of any reference to the actual world merely by reference to the creative mind of God: Possible is now everything that is *possible for God,* that is, *made possible by God;* and similarly impossible is everything that is *impossible for God,* that is, *made impossible by God.*

By combining the distinction between creator and creation with the modal distinctions in this way, a new scheme or pattern of modality became established. For what is possible for God (e.g., human goodness and justice) may be either a possibility or an impossibility for us; and what is impossible for God (sin) may be an impossibility or (in a perverted way) a possibility for us. Thus one can no longer say in an unqualified way that what is impossible for us is possible for God: it may also be an impossibility for God if it is made impossible by God. Similarly what is possible for us may be a possibility or an impossibility for God, even though in the latter case it should correctly be called an *impossible possibility* for us. The decisive point is that the distinction between the possible and the impossible is no longer dependent on any reference to the created world but solely to God. God is creator as the poet of the possible who distinguishes between the possible and the impossible by making that unique possibility actual from all the simultaneous alternatives before him which best corresponds to God's will for his creation. Those alternative possibilities are not there already for God merely to choose from them, but neither are they tethered to the actual world created by God. Rather, they result from God's creative act of distinguishing between the possible and the impossible and, at the same time, between one possibility and other possibilities in the very act of making that possibility actual that corresponds best to God's will for his creation.

This is the revolution I have mentioned. Possibilities are now tied to God's very act of creating from which they result, that is, to the creative act of distinguishing in a threefold way between the possible and the impossible, one possibility and other possibilities, and the possible and the actual. They are no longer seen as possibilities of the created world or, in a later Scotist sense, as an independent world of possibilities from which God only can choose thus making his choosing dependent on the prior actuality of the possible. Possibilities are essentially possibilities produced by God in the very act of creating everything that is different from God—the possible (by distinguishing between the possible and the impossible), a plurality of possibilities (by distinguishing among the possibilities between those God actualizes and those he doesn't), and the actual (by distinguishing between the possible and the actual). It follows that to speak of the possible is to speak of God, and to speak of the impossible and the actual also.

UTRUM DEUS SIT OMNIPOTENS

How this change comes about can clearly be seen in Aquinas. In quaestio 25a 3 of the *Summa theologiae* Thomas asks *utrum deus sit omnipotens* (whether God is omnipotent). The objection lists various arguments (God cannot move, we can; God cannot sin, we can), but the most interesting one is objection 4:

> Further, upon the text, "God hath made foolish the wisdom of this world" (1 Corinthians 1:20), a gloss says: "God hath made the wisdom of this world foolish [Vulgate: "Hath not God," etc.] by showing those things to be possible which it judges to be impossible." Whence it would seem that nothing is to be judged possible or impossible in reference to inferior causes, as the wisdom of this world judges them; but in reference to the divine power. If God, then, were omnipotent, all things would be possible; nothing, therefore impossible. But if we take away the impossible, then we destroy also the necessary; for what necessarily exists is impossible not to exist. Therefore there would be nothing at all that is necessary in things if God were omnipotent. But this is an impossibility. Therefore God is not omnipotent.[19]

If the possible or impossible must be judged not in reference to the natural causes, that is, as relative possibilities, but in reference to divine power, that is, as absolute possibilities, and if God is *omnipotens,* then *omnia erunt possibilia,* hence nothing is impossible and nothing is necessary but everything merely contingent. This is the opposite view of the Stoics, who held everything possible to be necessary, and it virtually coincides with the Epicurean view that nothing is necessary but everything contingent.

Thomas solves the problem in the following way.

> I answer that, All confess that God is omnipotent; but it seems difficult to explain in what His omnipotence precisely consists: for there may be doubt as to the precise meaning of the word *all* when we say that God can do all things (*omnia posse Deum*). If, however, we consider the matter aright, since power is said in reference to possible things, this phrase, "God can do all things," is rightly understood to mean that God can do all things that are possible (*omnia possibilia*); and for this reason He is said to be omnipotent.[20]

However, to say "Deus possit omnia possibilia, et ab hoc omnipotens dicatur" looks like a circular argument that explains nothing. Thomas therefore offers a defense in terms of the two different senses of *possibile* in Aristotle's *Metaphysics* V.12 (1019b34).

In the first sense, *possibile* means "*possibile secundum potentiam,*" that is, possible relative to a competence or potency. For example, "Peter can swim" states that Peter has the ability, competence, or potency to swim. Whatever is possible for human beings in this sense is said to be a *possibile homini*. In this sense, *omnia posse Deum* would mean that whatever is possible for a *natura creata* is also possible for God. But this is false, because it says both too much and too little. Not everything that is possible for us is also possible for God (sin); and God would not be God if God's power would not extend farther than the sum of the powers (potencies) of the creatures.

In the second sense to be found in Aristotle, the *possibile* means *possibile absolute:* "Deus dicatur omnipotens quia potest omnia possibilia absolute." Now "a thing is said to be possible or impossible absolutely, according to the relation in which the very terms stand to one another, possible if the predicate is not incompatible with the subject, as that Socrates sits; and absolutely impossible when the predicate is altogether incompatible with the subject, as, for instance,

that a man is a donkey." Thus the absolute possible is the noncontradictory, the absolute impossible everything where the predicate contradicts the subject: "man is a donkey." If impossible is what Aristotle
defines, that is, that whose contradiction is necessarily true, then the
possibile absolutum is not a possible in the sense of *potentia* but *possibilitas,* that is, a logical possibility.[21]

With this in mind Thomas can now state his answer in two steps:
First, God is called omnipotent *quia potest omnia possibilia absolute.*
God can create everything that is free from contradiction, everything
that is *logically possible.* His power is not restricted to the possibilities
of the actual world. On the contrary, God is completely independent
of the actual world.

Second, however, not everything that is a *noncontradictory possibility* is a *possibility that can be created.* Rather, "since every agent
produces an effect like itself, to each active power there corresponds
a thing possible as its proper object according to the nature of that act
on which its active power is founded." Thus only this can be created
by God that can be a *simile* of the divine being.

> The divine existence, however, upon which the nature of power in
> God is founded, is infinite, and is not limited to any genus of being;
> but possesses within itself the perfection of all being. Whence,
> whatsoever has or can have the nature of being, is numbered among
> the absolutely possible things, in respect of which God is called
> omnipotent. Now nothing is opposed to the idea of being except
> non-being. Therefore, that which implies being and non-being at
> the same time is repugnant to the idea of an absolutely possible
> thing, within the scope of the divine omnipotence. For such cannot
> come under the divine omnipotence, not because of any defect in
> the power of God, but because it has not the nature of a feasible or
> possible thing. Therefore, everything that does not imply a contra-
> diction in terms, is numbered amongst those possible things, in re-
> spect of which God is called omnipotent: whereas whatever implies
> contradiction does not come within the scope of divine omnipo-
> tence, because it cannot have the aspect of possibility. Hence it is

better to say that such things cannot be done, than that God cannot do them.[22]

Thus Thomas argues that God can create everything that is an *ens absolute possibile,* that is, a *factibile.* This *factibile* has three basic properties: It is *possible:* its description does not involve a contradiction; it is *contingent:* it cannot be actual without being created (i.e., it is in need of a *causa essendi*); it is a *simile* of the divine nature: it is something which God can will to be without contradicting his own nature.

In short, not everything that is noncontradictory is a *factibile* for God but only those *possibilia* whose existence God can will without self-contradiction. God not only defines the *possibilia* but also which of the *possibilia* are *factibilia;* and all of this without any reference to created actuality but before anything is created. This is nothing short of an ontological revolution, and it opens up a new and deeper understanding of God.

THE PRIORITY OF THE POSSIBLE OVER THE ACTUAL

First, the *possibile absolutum* is the *ens absolute possibile* that is both logically possible and a *Deo factibile.* Therefore, the contingently actual world is not merely a *possible world* but the possible world *that is willed by God to be actual.*

On the one hand, possibility is defined in purely formal or logical terms without reference to the actual world and hence no longer understandable in terms of the temporal frequency interpretation of modality. That is to say, the modalities can now be defined in a purely formal way:

possibility (Mp):	what is true in at least one possible world
impossibility (–Mp):	what is false (not true) in all possible worlds
necessity (–M–p):	what is true in all possible worlds
contingency (M–p & Mp):	what is true in at least one possible world and false in at least one possible world

On the other hand, actuality and the actual world are the result of God's creation and as such not merely something that wouldn't be without God but also something that is good because it is willed by God: The contingent actuality of the world is not merely a *verum* but a *bonum* and hence not merely to be understood against the backdrop of logical possibility but also of the divine will.

Now God's will is good because God wills what is good for his creatures, and because to will what is good for others even when it is costly for oneself is a manifestation of love, God's will is rightly seen as enacted love. But then we cannot understand the actuality of our world in the light of our knowledge of God's will as love without critically distinguishing between the *world as it is* and the *world as it ought to be as creation:* The world in its contingent actuality *could and should be better;* that is, it could and should correspond more closely to the summum bonum of its creator, that is, to the creative love that determines the divine will freely to open up the divine life to what is different or even opposed to it. For it is not the actual state of the world but God's will which determines what the world is, can be, and ought to be as God's creation; and if the world differs from this, then it is better to say that it is *on the way of becoming God's creation* than that it *is* God's creation as it is. In short, it is not the actuality of the world but its possibility as creation which defines what it is.

If Bishop Stephen Tempier had been aware of this he would not have condemned the following proposition in 1277: *quod causa prima non posset plures mundos facere.*[23] Clearly the problem of God's absolute power was a major issue of the Paris condemnations. Theological "authorities wanted everyone to concede that God could do anything whatever short of a logical contradiction,"[24] "thus stressing logical possibility, rather than temporal or physical possibility, as the preeminent type of possibility."[25] However, this left the question of the singularity of the world hanging in the air. Aristotle's arguments for the uniqueness of the world in *De caelo* and *Physics* were no longer convincing: Because the *kosmos* consists of all possible matter, there can be only one world. Now the singularity of the world had to be established independent of any reference to matter, merely in terms of logical noncontradictoriness.

This is precisely what Duns Scotus did in the fourteenth century. Sara L. Uckelman writes, "His theory of modality is rooted in the intellect of God: Anything which can be understood or conceived receives its being as intelligible or understandable in the intellect of God. These intelligible beings make up the various possibilities. Some intelligible beings are not compossible with others; compossibility, understood as logical compossibility, partitions the conceptual space into sets of beings all of which are compossible. One of these sets God actualized, and the others though unactualized are possible."[26]

However, while this argument limited the set of possible worlds to those that could be created because they were characterized by logical compossibility, it did not answer why God created this rather than any another of the set of noncontradictory worlds. It was precisely this to which Thomas had given an answer by arguing that only the possible worlds that correspond to God's good nature and will are *factibile*, and since the summum bonum is one, the *factibile* must also be one. Any argument for a plurality of possible worlds which God could have created must show that for God there would have been another world that is *factibile*, that is, not merely noncontradictory and hence possible but also such that its actuality would have been compatible with the good will and love of God.

It was precisely this which Leibniz attempted to show to be impossible in his *Theodicee*. And just as his arguments were in no way refuted by the facts of the Lisbon earthquake or any other disaster in the world, because they are based not on the goodness of the world but on the goodness of God's creative will, so the singularity of the world cannot be shown by reference to the logically possible but merely by reference to the uniqueness of the creator and the unequivocal definiteness of God's loving will. There may be more than one possible world. But there is only one creation. Hence nothing can be a possible world that is not a part or an aspect of creation, and since God in fact willed this and no other creation, no other possible world could be a *factibile* because it would be incompatible with the will and love of God.

THE ACTUALITY OF THE POSSIBLE

Second, this implies an understanding of God which Nicholas of Cusa two centuries earlier had briefly put, God is the *posse esse absolutum et infinitum*.[27] God is everything that can be (*deum id esse quod esse potest*).[28] For whatever is, must be possible, and whatever is possible, must be a possibility for God: "Nihil enim esse potest, quod deus actu non sit."[29] God is not the totality of the possible bur rather the one without whom nothing would be possible.

In a very similar way Kant argues in *The Only Possible Argument in Support of a Demonstration of the Existence of God* that God is the ground of the possibility of everything: God includes all that is possible or actual. For if anything exists at all, it is impossible that nothing exists whatsoever. But whatever exists is possible, and all possibility is the possibility of something actual, "whether as its determination, or through it as a consequence."[30] "Every possibility presupposes something actual, in and through which everything is given that can be thought."[31] For as Kant put the same point in his *Lectures on the Philosophical Doctrine of Religion*, "every possibility presupposes something actually given, since if everything were merely possible, then the possible itself would have no ground; so this ground of possibility must itself be given not merely as possible but also as actual."[32] This is true with respect to every possibility, and that without which there would be no possibility whatsoever Kant calls "God." Or for Kierkegaard, who summed up this line of thought: God is "the actuality of the possible."[33]

SECULARIZED POSSIBILITY

It was only a matter of time before this theological insight became secularized. In *Being and Time* Heidegger transposes Kierkegaard's theological thesis into a fundamental characteristic of Dasein, as usual without indicating his indebtedness to Kierkegaard. The fundamental locus of possibility is no longer God but Dasein, the finite and contingent enactment of being-in-the-world. As such, Dasein "is always what it can be and how it is its possibility," it is "being-possible."[34] The possibility at stake here is neither "logical possibility" nor "the contingency of something objectively present," that is, something that "is *not yet* real and *not always* necessary."[35] It is rather "the most primordial and the ultimate positive ontological determination of Da-sein."[36] For Dasein "is a being which, as being-in-the-world, is concerned about itself";[37] it "is the possibility of being free *for* its ownmost potentiality of being."[38]

This must be understood in two different respects. On the one hand, as "essentially attuned, Da-sein has always already got itself into definite possibilities," it is "*thrown possibility* throughout."[39] On the other hand, as "understanding, Da-sein projects its being upon possibilities."[40] Understanding "is the mode of being of Da-sein in which it *is* its possibilities as possibilities," and hence "it *is* what it becomes or does not become."[41] Together "attunement and understanding characterize the primordial disclosedness of being-in-the-world. In the mode of 'being attuned' Da-sein 'sees' possibilities in terms of which it is. In the projective disclosure of such possibilities, it is already attuned. The project of its ownmost potentiality of being is delivered over to the fact of thrownness into the there."[42] In this strict sense, Dasein's essence is existence.[43]

However, as 'thrown possibility' the range of possibilities open to it is restricted to Dasein's contingent place in the world, "its potentiality of being belongs essentially to its facticity,"[44] and the possibilities upon which it projects its being "are prefigured by the scope of what can be essentially disclosed to it" at its place in time and locus in the world.[45] Moreover, as "projecting understanding" it is always torn between *inauthentic understanding,* in which it "is lost in its 'world,'" "is dominated by public interpretedness," and understands its possibilities of being in the mode of the *Man,*[46] and *authentic understanding,* "originating from its own self as such."[47] But the most "eminent possibility of Da-sein," which it has to assert over against its falling prey to the world of the *Man,* is death. "As a potentiality of being, Da-sein is unable to bypass the possibility of death. Death is the possibility of the absolute impossibility of Da-sein. Thus *death* reveals itself as the *ownmost nonrelational possibility not to be bypassed.*"[48] That is to say, Dasein's being-toward-the-end is the metapossibility that governs all its other possibilities because it is "the possibility of the absolute impossibility of Da-sein." Dasein's understanding is authentic when and insofar as it takes this ultimate possibility not to be bypassed into account in projecting its being upon possibilities.

The being-possible, which Dasein is, is thus utterly determined by its contingency (thrownness) and finitude (being-toward-death). The eternal "actuality of the possible" in Kierkegaard is thus completely temporalized and finitized: There is possibility *"only insofar as Da-sein is and as long as it is."*[49] Whereas Husserl thought that the empirical *I* will die but the transcendental *I* will not die, Heidegger leaves no room for hope: "The fact that there are 'eternal truths' will not be adequately proven until it is successfully demonstrated that Da-sein has been and will be for all eternity. As long as this proof is lacking, the statement remains a fantasical assertion which does not gain in legitimacy by being generally 'believed' by the philosophers."[50] "The contention that there are 'eternal truths,' as well as the confusion of the phenomenally based 'ideality' of Das-sein with an idealized absolute subject, belong to the remnants of Christian theology within the philosophical problematic that have not yet been radically eliminated. 'There is' being—not beings—only insofar as truth is. And truth *is* only because and as long as Da-sein is."[51] For truth is "the disclosedness of Da-sein"[52] as a thrown project, a finite and factical being-possible, which will come to an end. The truth about our life is that we shall die.

LIMITED POSSIBILITIES

Heidegger has no philosophical use for Kierkegaard's dialectics of the eternal in his account of possibility. But in trying to avoid the paradoxical presence of the eternal in the temporal by excluding the eternal, he also severely limits his account of possibility. Not only does he restrict all possibility to being in an active verbal sense, that is, the enactment of possibilities in the practice of existence. He also delimits the scope of possibility by the dual factors of thrownness and project to the finite possibilities that constitute the being-possible of a concrete Dasein that is mine. The thrown project of my Dasein defines what is, and what is not, possible for me.

But this gives undue weight to the limits of my existential situation. The possibilities upon which Dasein projects its being are always and only the possibilities disclosed to it in its factical *There*. They are rooted in the thrownness of Dasein and determined by its concrete situation in the world. This captures the utter contingency of human life. However, it does not allow for anything *radically* new to occur but only for other possibilities in the series of worldly possibilities of this particular being-in-the-world, which is governed and determined by the ultimate possibility of its being-toward-death.

Heidegger's account of existential possibility fails to be true to the breaking in of the radical new in a life. It cannot account for a novelty that occasions a complete change of direction, a conversion that is not merely the continuation of a series of worldly acts by another, or an addition of another possibility to the series of worldly possibilities, but inaugurates a completely new series, that is, opens up possibilities that are not rooted in Dasein's existential situation but are played into its way in such a surprising and unexpected manner that they radically alter the course of its existence. A Dasein to which this happens not merely exists differently in its world, but rather exists in a different world; it does not simply continue to exist in its worldly way, but is changed in its way of existing in a way that requires it to draw a sharp distinction between its old and new ways of existing, its old world and its new, its old life and its new life.

Heidegger's analytic of Dasein in *Being and Time* has no reflective resources to allow for this. It knows only one structure of being-in-the-world, and only one world in which Dasein exists. This is what his philosophical project of a fundamental ontology seeks to unfold, and this is why he couldn't solve the problem of theology's relation to philosophy and the sciences in a satisfactory way.[53] He saw that the solution proposed in "Phenomenology and Theology" (phenomenology is ontology and addresses the whole; theology is a positive science and addresses the particular phenomenon of faith) did not work. But he could not identify the reason for this because of his monistic and closed understanding of Dasein's being-in-the-world: He had no analytic means to differentiate conceptually between different worlds, or between, on the one hand, possibilities rooted in Dasein's thrownness and, on the other, possibilities played into Dasein's way, which do not merely express or manifest what is already a possibility of Dasein's factical potentiality but rather *enlarge and augment* its possibilities in unexpected and unforeseeable ways by enforcing and strengthening some of its possibilities while turning others into impossible possibilities. By tying possibility to the potentiality of Dasein's factical being-in-the-world, Heidegger fails to be true to the power and potentiality of the possible of fundamentally changing Dasein's way of being-in-the-world. Heidegger's monistic view of the structure of being-in-the-world does not allow for the possibility of other, "nonworldly" (e.g., eschatological) ways of being. He has no conceptual resource to account for the radically new, or to distinguish between *other possibilities of being-in-the-world* and the *possibility of being-in-another-world*, or to differentiate between totalities or wholes in such a way that more than one totality of being-in-the-world becomes a meaningful possibility.

As long as we start from the ontological structure of Dasein this will be impossible to show. But the fact that this structure exists is itself dependent on conditions without which it would not be possible. The fact and structure of Dasein is not self-explicatory or self-grounding. On the contrary, it is a necessary part of the understanding, which Dasein always already is, that it understands itself as a *thrown project,* that is, a contingent and limited set of possibilities of a contingent potentiality, which might not have been. Dasein is not necessary, and not everything possible in a formal sense (i.e., not self-contradictory) is a real existential possibility of Dasein. It is what it can be only because it can be what is played into its way. It depends on being opened up to possibilities, which are not its own creation, and on being empowered to make these possibilities its own potentiality, which it cannot do out of its own potency. It is, as Bernhard Waldenfels has made clear, a *responsive* structure, i.e. a structure whose character and existence depends on something prior to itself to which it responds in becoming what it is.[54]

The two sides of Dasein's existence, its passive side of being always already attuned to the possibilities of its world and its active side of its understanding projection onto the possibilities which it is, are thus conditioned by something prior to Dasein's twofold structure of passivity and activity to which it responds in enacting its contingent attunement and limited understanding. Dasein's activity and passivity are possibilities that depend on a prior and more fundamental passivity: the passivity of being enabled to be Dasein. The "thrown possibility" of Dasein is itself a response to a passivity, which constitutes its potency as Dasein and cannot meaningfully be explained as being constituted by this potency. The very fact of Dasein manifests a gap in Heidegger's analytic of Dasein that opens up the possibility of other interpretations.

From this gap one must start in order to salvage the irreducible diversity, potency, and creativity of the possible from Heidegger's neo-Aristotelian attempt to construe the possible uniformly in terms of the factical potentiality of Dasein's contingent being-in-the-world in the attuned projecting practice of its existence. Dasein is not merely what it can be (being-possible); it is more than it can be (more than possible). Why and in which way can be seen if we pay attention to aspects of phenomena, which Heidegger underestimated or unduly ignored such as their character as sign-events, the creative potentiality of the possible, or the priority of creative passivity over Dasein's activity.

DIFFERENTIATED POSSIBILITY: PHENOMENA AS SIGN-EVENTS

Phenomena, according to Heidegger, are "what shows itself from itself,"[55] *"what shows itself in itself,* what is manifest."[56] This does not necessarily mean that they show themselves as they are in themselves, for the "possibility . . . exists that they can show themselves as they are *not* in themselves."[57] But whether they show what they are in themselves or what they are not in themselves, they are "self-showings," that is, sign-events.

As sign-events, phenomena are characterized by the four semiotic dimensions of sign-events: the relation between sign and other signs (the syntactic dimension), the relation between sign and signified (the semantic dimension), the relation between sign and interpreter (the pragmatic dimension), and the relation between sign and media or bearer of signs (the material or medial dimension) (fig. 1). That is to say, every phenomenon is *one among* or *together with* others (*with-structure*); every phenomenon discloses itself *as* something (*as-structure*); all phenomena are phenomena *for someone* (*for-structure*); and all mediate their as- and for-structures through natural or cultural media, bearers, or vehicles (*through-structure*). In this sense, phenomena are four-dimensional sign-processes in which a material medium (*through-structure*) is understood or used by (a group of) interpreters (*for-structure*) as a sign among signs (*with-structure*) to signify something as something (*as-structure*).

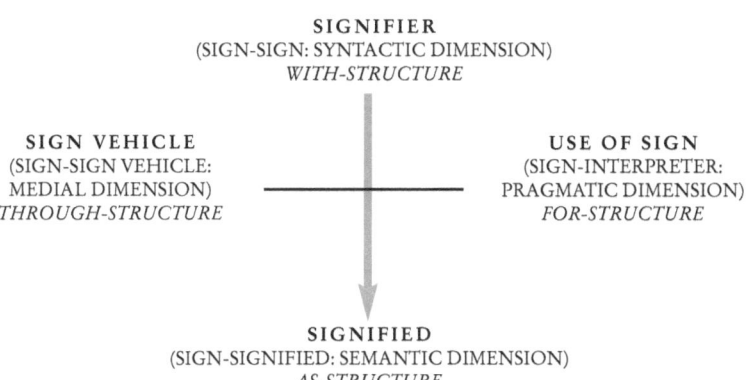

SIGNIFIER
(SIGN-SIGN: SYNTACTIC DIMENSION)
WITH-STRUCTURE

SIGN VEHICLE   USE OF SIGN
(SIGN-SIGN VEHICLE: (SIGN-INTERPRETER:
MEDIAL DIMENSION)   PRAGMATIC DIMENSION)
THROUGH-STRUCTURE   *FOR-STRUCTURE*

SIGNIFIED
(SIGN-SIGNIFIED: SEMANTIC DIMENSION)
AS-STRUCTURE

The semiotic structure of phenomena involves a differentiated concept of possibility and actuality. As sign-processes, phenomena have *four horizons of possibility* and *three dimensions of actuality*. That is to say, they are what they are by selecting from four dimensions of possibility (possible interpretive communities; the experienceable; possible signifiers; the signifiable), and do so by combining three dimensions of actuality (Society, Nature, Culture) (fig. 2).[58]

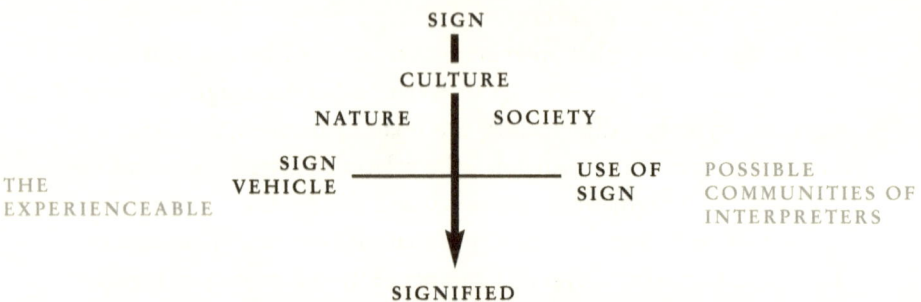

In order for a sign-event to take place, there must be something that is used as a sign (media: through-structure), its use as a sign among signs to signify something (sign: with-structure), and someone who uses or interprets it as a sign (interpreter: for-structure). The *media* are actual *natural entities* (beings, systems, structures, or sets of events: Nature); the *users* or *interpreters* are actual *social entities* (systems, agents, groups, or organizations: Society); and *signs* as part of a system of signs are actual *cultural entities* (beings, systems, structures, sets of events: Culture). Cultural entities differ from natural ones precisely in opening up a realm of the possible by distinguishing between signifier and signified, the totality of possible signifiers and the totality of that which can be signified.

Therefore the concept of possibility has to be differentiated along the four dimensions of a sign-event, and in this respect possibility is irreducibly plural and diverse. Thus the media (sign-vehicle or bearer) belong to the *totality of what can be experienced* by us (the experienceable), the user or interpreter is a concrete token of the *totality of possible (communities of) interpreters,* the sign is one of the *totalities of possible signifiers,* and what is signified is a token of the *totality of what can be signified* (the signifiable).

In light of this Heidegger's strict ontological distinction between possibilities of objective presences (beings, things, events) and existential possibilities of Dasein cannot be sustained. This distinction is an abstract conceptual opposition of different aspects of multidimensional sign-events or phenomena, namely, their through-structure (objective presence) and their for-structure (Dasein). While it is true that phenomena occur and are interpreted as signs only within the practices of concrete interpreters, their existence in the world is not the sole condition of the possibility of such interpretations. What is also needed beyond the for-structure of phenomena (Dasein) is the condition of the possibility of natural sign-vehicles (possible media) and of cultural systems of signs (possible signs), and implied in them also is the condition of the totality of the signifiable.

RADICAL POSSIBILITY: REVERSING THE REAL AND THE IDEAL

The multidimensional structure of phenomena as sign-events constitutes what I shall call the *ontological plasticity of phenomena*.[59] Phenomena can rightfully be described in more than one true and adequate way. They allow for a plurality of possible descriptions. This is not only true of the individual sign-event but also of the totality of phenomena.

To see this, consider the difference between an empirical (scientific) and a theological account of Christian discourse. English-speaking Christians use the monosyllable "god" (media) in worship practices as the title term "God" (sign) to refer to God (signified) (fig. 3).

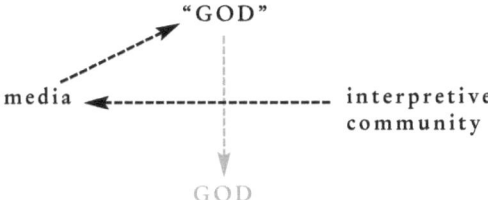

This semiotic fact can be understood in different ways. In an empirical or scientific perspective what is *real* about it are the historical and empirical realities of (a) the interpretive Christian community, (b) the media they use, and (c) the cultural artifacts, which they create by using these media. On the other hand, that to which Christians refer by using their signs in this way is taken to be at best *ideal* or merely imaginative. Their usage constitutes a realm of meaning that is not part of the causal realities of our empirical and historical world and hence not a real but an ideal sphere of human life. In this perspective, to be "real" is to be part of the causal nexus of our world that can be described in empirical terms. What is real makes a difference to our lives that can (in principle at least) be experienced by us. Spheres of meaning, on the other hand, are called "ideal" because they are related to our lives not in causal but in logical, linguistic or semiotic terms. More exactly, whereas acts of meaning constitution are part of the causal nexus of our world and hence part of what is real, the content of meaning thus constituted is ideal and to be explained not in causal but interpretive terms (fig. 4).

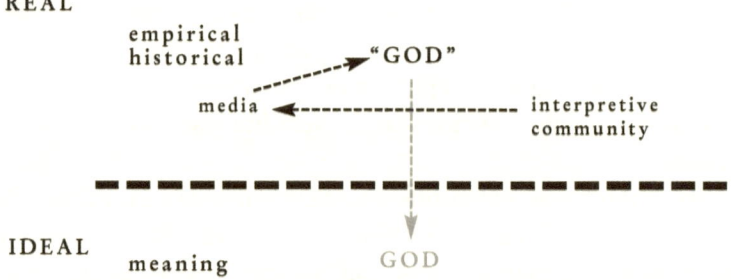

In this view theology in all its manifold variety is a kind of ideology, that is, the study of a particular realm of meaning constituted by the semiotic cultural practice of a particular religious community or tradition. However, this misses the point of the theological self-understanding of those who live the Christian faith. They understand their doing theology as a form of *fides quaerens intellectum,* that is, as a culturally situated and methodically disciplined intellectual attempt to inquire into the diverse and distinct realities, actualities, and possibilities of faith in its historical and global variety and plurality with the aim of improving the communal and individual life of faith in the contemporary situation. Theology thus understood studies exactly the same realities as the philological and linguistic disciplines and the empirical and historical sciences with exactly the same methods but *from a different perspective, with a different purpose,* and *in a different horizon.* Its aim is not merely theoretical, but practical; it seeks not merely to understand Christian life and its meaning practices in a historical and empirical perspective, but aims at changing and improving the actual practice of Christian life in the contemporary world to become a better and more adequate human life *coram deo.* It does so in a theological perspective that reverses the distinction between the real and the ideal in such a way that what is called merely "ideal" in a philosophical perspective is taken to be the true reality in terms of which all empirical and historical "realities" have to be understood.

This change of perspective is all-pervasive in Christian life and thought, and it has been a constant source of confusion in the history of the West. It has been spelled out in many different ways, including the contrast between (Platonic or German) idealism and (Aristotelian or empirical) realism. In order to avoid confusion, it is better to replace the real/ideal distinction by the distinction between *creator* and *creation* in the theological perspective, that is, by the distinction between *creative actuality* or *divine creativity,* on the one hand, and *created reality,* on the other (fig. 5).

Created Reality

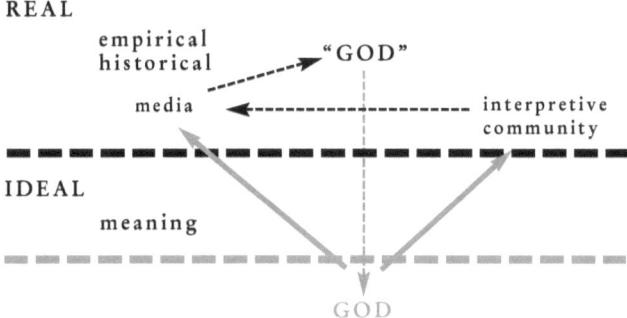

Divine Creativity

The point of this distinction is not to draw a contrast within the realm of the real (there are not realities that are created and others that are not), nor is creativity understood to be merely the meaning of the term *creativity* and thus refer to something that is conceptually ideal but not real. Rather, creativity is used to signify that without which it would not be possible to draw a distinction between the real and the ideal because without it there would not be anything real or ideal. It is neither one of the natural realities of our world nor merely a cultural meaning construction (which, no doubt, the term and the meanings constituted by its use also are) but rather is used to refer to that without which referring to it or anything else would not be possible. That is to say, the distinction between *divine creativity* and *created reality* is not a descriptive distinction within the perspective on the world in terms of the distinction between the real and the ideal but an *orienting distinction* that implies a different perspective on everything: Everything real and ideal is to be distinguished as a *created reality* from the fundamental *creativity* without which it would not have been, whereas this *creativity* cannot be identified among that which is actually or possibly real, or actually or possibly ideal. Rather, it is beyond that distinction in the precise sense that it must not be identified with anything real or ideal whereas everything real or ideal *analytically* implies it *when seen from the perspective of creativity as created reality*.

This fundamental change of perspective permeates all Christian life of faith and its theological reflection and is worked out in different ways in the different areas of theological doctrine. For example, if God's creative activity is the basic reality, then *creation* is to be understood as *God making creatures make themselves* not only in the realm of nature but also in the world of culture and society. There is nothing actual or possible that is not dependent on the prior actuality of God's creative activity in nature, culture and society (fig. 6).

CREATION: *God makes creatures make themselves*

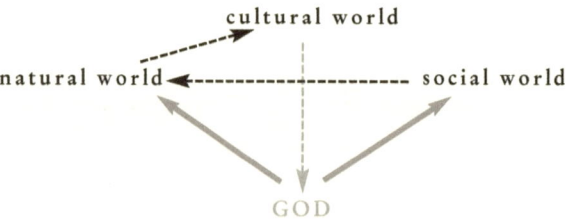

The same shift to the prior activity of God is true with respect to *revelation*. In a general sense revelation is understood as God making his divine will and intention for Israel in particular and humanity in general accessible and understood through people of his own choosing (prophets) (fig. 7).

REVELATION: *God makes creatures understand God's will*

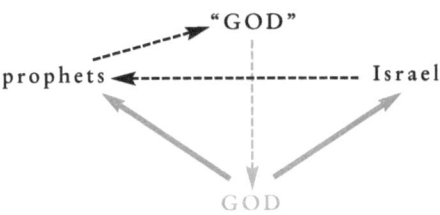

In a specific Christian sense, this structure of revelation is seen and confessed by Christians to be embodied in a concrete and ultimate way in the life, teaching, and death of Jesus whom Christians understand as Christ because in him they see disclosed the ultimate character and reality of God as saving and redeeming love (fig. 8).

DIVINE SELF-REVELATION: *God makes creatures understand God's attitude toward all humankind as love*

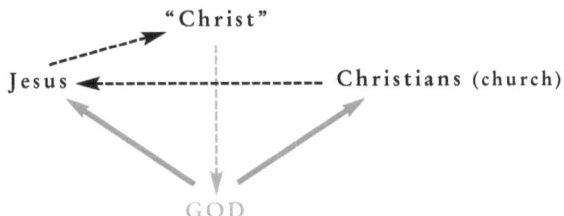

Because Jesus Christ was seen as the disclosure or revelation of the divine reality of God's love for humankind, Christians inscribed this structure in the very idea of God and thereby transformed Jesus's notion of God into the Trinitarian understanding of God as Father, Son, and Spirit in mainline Christianity (fig. 9).

TRINITY: *Active in created reality as Son and Spirit communicating creative love*

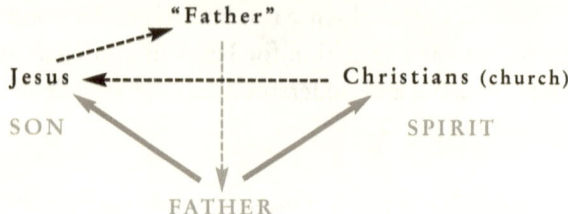

The same self-referential semiotic complexity characterizes the Christian understanding of the *gospel*. Its dynamic nature and reality was spelled out in Protestant dogmatics in terms of exactly the same structure (fig. 10).

GOSPEL

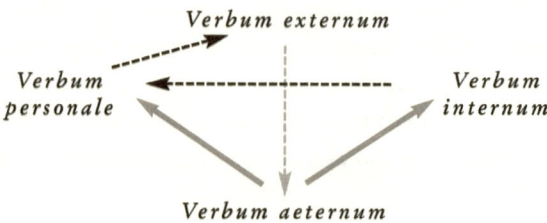

Since the gospel manifests a divine reality, the *communication* of the gospel is similarly understood to be not merely a human but also a divine activity. *Incarnation, communication,* and *inspiration* are therefore seen as the basic creative activities of the triune God of Love who is what he does and becomes what he is by doing what he is (fig. 11).

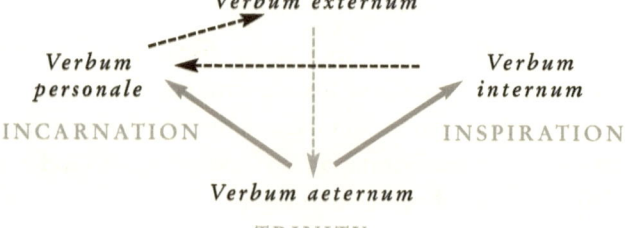

As these examples show—and they could easily be multiplied—Christian theology is not an arbitrary interpretation of (some) empirical and historical religious realities or experiences. It rather is a *total and comprehensive re-vision* of our world in its threefold dimension of reality and fourfold dimension of possibility in a *radically theological perspective*. In this all-encompassing interpretive perspective the common order of the real and the ideal is turned upside down. The ideal is not construed on the basis of the real understood in empirical and historical terms but rather everything actual and possible is understood in terms of God's creative activity. This is the fundamental reality that grounds all other possibility and actuality. Hence the basic orienting distinction in Christian life and thought is not the distinction between the real and the ideal but rather that between *creative* and *created reality* and, with respect to the latter, between *old life* and *new life*. Christian theology is reality depicting, but it describes and contemplates the realities of our world from the perspective of divine creative reality disclosed in Christ as love.

Unless this radical shift of perspective is clearly grasped and theology not mistakenly taken to be a merely arbitrary and subjectivist redescription of empirical or historical realities, the point and potentiality of Christian life and thought will not be accessible and understood. Theological accounts of human life do not add an "ideological" dimension to empirical and historical reality "as it truly is" but put everything in a new and different perspective: They say more about the world not by adding a supernatural dimension to the natural but by describing the natural from a perspective that allows us to see and say more than is manifest in the limited horizons of empirical and historical studies, or a philosophy of a worldly way of existing. Philosophy offers an ontological account of worldly existence, theology an ontological account of eschatological existence. Both are not partial perspectives on our life and world but total and comprehensive perspectives on the same. The sameness of their respective reference ranges can be shown by the mutual translatability of their accounts of phenomena between the two perspectives. They can use the same language, but they use it in different ways and according to different grammars, the grammar of existing in the world and the grammar of

living in creation. The mutual translatability of theological and philosophical views does not overcome the indeterminacy of translation.
On the contrary, it underlines the irreducible and radical difference of
the two perspectives, standpoints, and horizons.

THE NEW: RETRIEVING THE CREATIVE POTENCY
OF THE POSSIBLE

The possibility of radically distinct comprehensive views of the same
totality of phenomena is not extrinsic to the world and an impossible
view from nowhere but intrinsic to the very nature of phenomena as
sign-events. It constitutes what I have called the ontological plasticity
of phenomena. There is not only one ontological structure of being-
in-the-world, which determines everything that is, or isn't, possible
for us. Phenomena are intrinsically multidimensional events, which
can rightly be understood in different perspectives, from different
points of view and within different horizons. There is not one basic
structure or point of view that defines the horizon of everything.
Each structure can be further specified, and possibilities can be described relative to each level of specification. But there is not one
structure that integrates all other structures. Rather, different perspectives are possible, and indeed the case.

Thus, the theological perspective on everything is not based on a
monist philosophical foundation that grounds or enables it. Rather,
theology and philosophy can be construed as different total perspectives on everything, including the other perspective and themselves.
Each occurs in the horizon of the other but neither of them constitutes the more basic or 'true' horizon of the phenomena of our world.
They mutually allow to thematize each other, but they do so within
different horizons and from different perspectives on the totality of
phenomena.[60]

The difference between the two total perspectives can be spelled
out in many different ways. With respect to the understanding of the
possible, the theological perspective has the important critical function of drawing attention to, and being true to, the—slow or sudden,

developing or revolutionary, slowly dawning or life-shattering— break-in of the radically new in human life and reality, the radical change of the permanently changing world in its entirety occasioned by the rupture of the ordinary by the break-in of the extraordinary. The contingent actuality of a life does not determine the range of that which is possible for it: there is more to a life than what *it can be by and from itself.*

Thus, the theological emphasis on the divine actuality of the possible is not merely a version of the insight that every actuality is full of possibilities, or that there is no possibility without actuality, or that even that which perishes remains possible because *pura potentia* permits being and non-being at the same time so that "every potency is at the one and the same time a potency of its opposite."[61] It rather expresses the surprising discovery that something becomes possible to a life, which was not even a possibility of this life before this event. There is more to a given actual life (and indeed to every actual reality) than the totality of possibilities by which it can be defined at any given time, or by the totality of possibilities constituted by the totality of its finite temporal actuality. The break-in of the new shows that it is not the actual which defines what is possible for it but the possible which shows the actual to be more than it can be, or not be, because of what it actually is.

In a theological perspective, human life is not merely the thrown project of a Heideggerian analysis of Dasein but the addressee and playing field of possibilities, which have the creative potential and potency to change life radically and totally. The break-in of divine creativity re-creates a life as a "new life" and radically reorients it in faith's new perspective on everything. This new perspective is grounded in God's judgment about this life, which faith acknowledges as the fundamental truth about it; and faith cannot do so without understanding its own actuality to be part of the very actuality of the possible, which it acknowledges. Thus the possibility of faith is one (but not the only one) of the new possibilities that have been impossible for a life before but now become possible for it—not, however, as one of its *de re* possibilities ("For this life, it is possible that . . .") but as a possibility of divine creativity ("This is made possible by

God") expressed in the divine judgment about the ultimate (eschato-logical) truth of this life. In this sense, the new possibility of a life of faith is not an internal possibility of this life but an external possibility played into its way by God's creative presence who makes this life participate in a different and more comprehensive possibility: the divine creativity of the possible. This not only creates new possibilities for a life, that is, makes possible what has been impossible before,[62] nor does it merely end old actualities and replace what has been the case before by something new while leaving the old actuality a possibility. Rather, it creates new possibilities which make possible what has been impossible before and at the same time make impossible what has been possible before if and insofar as it is incompatible with the newly created total or comprehensive possibility.

Thus the break-in of divine creativity that constitutes faith opens up a radically new view on everything, including itself. It creates a new possibility beyond the actual and what is possible or impossible on the basis of it, which is characterized by three features.

1. It is a comprehensive or total possibility of the *whole life*, not merely a partial aspect of or within it. That is to say, it does not merely add another possibility to the set of possibilities that define the totality of the possible states of a life, but rather puts this whole series into a new perspective and frame of reference. It is an operator that determines the character of the whole series and does not merely add a further element to the series: A human life in its entirety now becomes a life of faith, that is, a life that is continuously being changed from its own life orientation of nonfaith (ignoring God's presence: sinner) to the life orientation of faith (acknowledging God's presence by acknowledging both this presence and the possibility of acknowledging it as God's gift: saved sinner).

2. It is not a possibility of the life whose possibility it *becomes* by making it the life of a saved sinner. Rather, it is a *possibility of the divine creativity* that places this human life with all its actualities and possibilities in a new frame of reference. This new frame is not accessible from within this life as such but can only be acknowledged as an actual possibility for it in the light of the break-in of

divine creativity that discloses the decisive truth about this life to be that it is made true by God. In this sense, faith is not a possibility of human life to be actualized by us but rather a way of participating in the possibilities of God that is made possible by God—"faith participates in the possibilities of God"[63]—and to make this possibility actual is one of the possibilities of God.

3. As such, it is an *eschatological* (i.e., definitive and ultimate) possibility of the whole of this life and, as such, not one of its *de re* possibilities but of the divine operation of transforming it from a life of nonfaith into a life of faith. It becomes *manifest* in the break-in of God's creative presence that makes this life become what God judges it to be: the life of a sinner saved and made true by the redeeming and justifying love of God. And it *becomes* a possibility of this life only because and insofar as this life is the field of operation of God's creative presence: It is a possibility of divine creativity in which a human life is made to participate by being given the gift of being opened to God's presence by God's presence. But this possibility always remains a *divine* possibility and never becomes a possibility of human life that could be exercised without explicitly referring to God's creative presence.

God's presence is the creative presence of divine love. But "love without possibilities is no love. Rather, love is full of creative possibilities."[64] It is these possibilities which faith experiences as being played into its way by the break-in of God's creative presence into a life. This break-in is more than one event among others. It is a break-in of creativity that creates creative possibilities that are radically new and cannot be reduced to a potentiality of an abstract specter of "human life as such." There is no such life but only life lived in concrete ways. And the two concrete ways that define the totality of a life in the light of the break-in of the divine creativity of love are *nonfaith* and *faith*. Any attempt to identify nonfaith or faith as phenomenal realities in human life independent of the perspective of faith is bound to fail because it misconstrues the grammar of faith in Christian life and theology. Nonfaith and faith are not descriptive concepts of empirical or historical realities that can come in degrees but orienting distinctions that are intrinsic to the perspective and practice of faith. In order to explicate their meaning one has to refer to God "in the midst of the struggle between nothingness and possibility"[65] and understand the life of faith as the risky and daring life of love and hope in the creative future of divine possibility that will overcome the remnants and ruins of nothingness in which humanity still lives. But this is a topic for another occasion.

NOTES

1. Aristotle, *Met.* VI, 1026 a, 31.

2. Christian Wolff, *Philosophia Rationalis Sive Logica, Methodo Scientifica Pertractata et ad Usum Scientiarum Atque Vitae Aptata: Praemittitur Discursus Praeliminaris de Philosophia in Genere*, Editio Tertia Emendatior cum privilegiis ed. (Frankfurt and Leipzig, 1740), Caput II. De philosophia in genere, §29 (p. 13).

3. Martin Heidegger, *Being and Time: A Translation of Sein und Zeit*, trans. Joan Stambaugh, SUNY Series in Contemporary Continental Philosophy (Albany: State University of New York Press, 1996), 34. Original emphasis.

4. Eberhard Jüngel, "The World as Possibility and Actuality: The Ontology of the Doctrine of Justification," in *Theological Essays*, ed. J. B. Webster (Edinburgh: T & T Clark, 1989), 95–123, 123.

5. Ibid., 112.

6. Cf. Richard Kearney, *The God Who May Be: A Hermeneutics of Religion*, Indiana Series in the Philosophy of Religion (Bloomington: Indiana University Press, 2001). His brief sketch of the "Metaphysics of the Possible" (83–84) and of some "Post-Metaphysical Readings of the Possible" such as Husserl, Bloch, Heidegger, and Derrida (84–100) points to a task that needs to be taken up but is not performed in a satisfactory manner in his book. This is also borne out by the contributions in J. P. Manoussakis, *After God: Richard Kearney and the Religious Turn in Continental Philosophy*, Perspectives in Continental Philosophy (New York: Fordham University Press, 2006).

7. In the twelfth and thirteenth centuries, *vera/falsa, bona/mala*, etc., were not understood as modalities. Cf. William Shirwood, *Introductiones in Logicam = Einführung in Die Logik*, ed. Hartmut Brands and Christoph Kann, Philosophische Bibliothek (Hamburg: F. Meiner, 1995), 33.

8. Cf. Th. Buchheim, C. H. Corneille, and K. Lorenz, eds., *Potentialität und Possibilität: Modalaussagen in der Geschichte der Metaphysik* (Stuttgart: Frommann-Holzboog, 2001); C. Herberichs and S. Reichlin, eds., *Kein Zu-*

fall: Konzeptionen von Kontingenz in der mittelalterlichen Literatur (Göttingen: Vandenhoeck & Ruprecht, 2010).

9. Arthur O. Lovejoy, *The Great Chain of Being: A Study of the History of an Idea* (Cambridge, MA: Harvard University Press, 1936).

10. More precisely, and in alethic terms: necessary propositions are always true; possible propositions are sometimes true and sometimes false; impossible propositions are always false.

11. Cf. P. Schulthess, "Kontingenz: Begriffsanalytisches und Grundlegende Positionen in der Philosophie im Mittelalter," in Herberichs and Reichlin, *Kein Zufall*, 50–78.

12. Petrus Damianus, *De divina omnipotentia*, ed. A. Cantin (Paris: Cerf, 1972), 412.

13. S. Hieronymi, *Vita III*, in *Patrologia Latina Database* (1845), ed. J. P. Migne (Ann Arbor, MI: ProQuest Info. and the Learning Co., 1995), vol. 22, 597B.

14. Aristotle, *De int. 9*, 19a22–27.

15. Damianus, *De divina omnipotentia*, 412.414.

16. *De divinatione*, II, 41, 86.

17. Tertullian, *De carne Christi*, III, PL 2, 801b.

18. Cf. S. L. Uckelman, *Modalities in Medieval Logic*, ILLC Dissertation Series Ds-2009-04 (Amsterdam: Institute for Logic, Language and Computation, Universiteit van Amsterdam, 2009), esp. chaps. 1, 2, and 3.

19. Praeterea, super illud I Cor. I, *stultam fecit Deus sapientiam huius mundi*, dicit Glossa, *sapientiam huius mundi fecit Deus stultam, ostendendo possibile, quod illa impossibile iudicabat.* Unde videtur quod non sit aliquid iudicandum possibile vel impossibile secundum inferiores causas, prout sapientia huius mundi iudicat; sed secundum potentiam divinam. Si igitur Deus sit omnipotens, omnia erunt possibilia. Nihil ergo impossibile. Sublato autem impossibili, tollitur necessarium, nam quod necesse est esse, impossibile est non esse. Nihil ergo erit necessarium in rebus, si Deus est omnipotens. Hoc autem est impossibile. Ergo Deus non est omnipotens.

20. Respondeo dicendum quod communiter confitentur omnes Deum esse omnipotentem. Sed rationem omnipotentiae assignare videtur difficile. Dubium enim potest esse quid comprehendatur sub ista distributione, cum dicitur omnia posse Deum. Sed si quis recte consideret, cum potentia dicatur ad possibilia, cum Deus omnia posse dicitur, nihil rectius intelligitur quam quod possit omnia possibilia, et ob hoc omnipotens dicatur. Possibile autem dicitur dupliciter, secundum philosophum, in V Metaphys. Uno modo, per respectum ad aliquam potentiam, sicut quod subditur humanae potentiae, dicitur esse possibile homini. Non autem potest dici quod Deus dicatur omnipotens, quia potest omnia quae sunt possibilia naturae creatae, quia divina potentia in plura extenditur. Si autem dicatur quod Deus sit omnipotens, quia

potest omnia quae sunt possibilia suae potentiae, erit circulatio in manifesta-
tione omnipotentiae, hoc enim non erit aliud quam dicere quod Deus est omnipotens, quia potest omnia quae potest. Relinquitur igitur quod Deus dicatur omnipotens, quia potest omnia possibilia absolute, quod est alter modus
dicendi possibile. Dicitur autem aliquid possibile vel impossibile absolute, ex
habitudine terminorum, possibile quidem, quia praedicatum non repugnat
subiecto, ut Socratem sedere; impossibile vero absolute, quia praedicatum repugnat subiecto, ut hominem esse asinum. Est autem considerandum quod,
cum unumquodque agens agat sibi simile, unicuique potentiae activae corre-
spondet possibile ut obiectum proprium, secundum rationem illius actus in
quo fundatur potentia activa, sicut potentia calefactiva refertur, ut ad proprium obiectum, ad esse calefactibile. Esse autem divinum, super quod ratio
divinae potentiae fundatur, est esse infinitum, non limitatum ad aliquod
genus entis, sed praehabens in se totius esse perfectionem. Unde quidquid
potest habere rationem entis, continetur sub possibilibus absolutis, respectu
quorum Deus dicitur omnipotens. Nihil autem opponitur rationi entis, nisi
non ens. Hoc igitur repugnat rationi possibilis absoluti, quod subditur divinae omnipotentiae, quod implicat in se esse et non esse simul. Hoc enim
omnipotentiae non subditur, non propter defectum divinae potentiae; sed
quia non potest habere rationem factibilis neque possibilis. Quaecumque
igitur contradictionem non implicant, sub illis possibilibus continentur,
respectu quorum dicitur Deus omnipotens. Ea vero quae contradictionem
implicant, sub divina omnipotentia non continentur, quia non possunt habere
possibilium rationem. Unde convenientius dicitur quod non possunt fieri,
quam quod Deus non potest ea facere. Neque hoc est contra verbum Angeli
dicentis, *non erit impossibile apud Deum omne verbum*. Id enim quod contradictionem implicat, verbum esse non potest, quia nullus intellectus potest
illud concipere.

   21. Ad quartum dicendum quod possibile absolutum non dicitur neque
secundum causas superiores, neque secundum causas inferiores sed secundum seipsum. Possibile vero quod dicitur secundum aliquam potentiam,
nominatur possibile secundum proximam causam. Unde ea quae immediate
nata sunt fieri a Deo solo, ut creare, iustificare, et huiusmodi, dicuntur possibilia secundum causam superiorem, quae autem nata sunt fieri a causis in-
ferioribus, dicuntur possibilia secundum causas inferiores. Nam secundum
conditionem causae proximae, effectus habet contingentiam vel necessitatem,
ut supra dictum est. In hoc autem reputatur stulta mundi sapientia, quod ea
quae sunt impossibilia naturae, etiam Deo impossibilia iudicabat. Et sic
patet quod omnipotentia Dei impossibilitatem et necessitatem a rebus non
excludit.

   22. Thomas Aquinas, *Summa theologiae*, q. 25, a. 3 crp.

23. (*Sic et Non*), art. 34, David Piché, ed., *La condemnation parisienne de 1277* (Paris: J. Vrin, 1999), 90.

24. Edward Grant, *The Foundations of Modern Science in the Middle Ages: Their Religious, Institutional, and Intellectual Contexts*, Cambridge History of Science (New York: Cambridge University Press, 1996), 78–79.

25. Sara L. Uckelman, "Logic and the Condemnations of 1277," *Journal of Philosophical Logic* 39, no. 2 (2010): 201–27 (216).

26. Ibid., 222.

27. *De visione Dei*, c. 15, n. 62 (Op. Omn. XII, 30).

28. Nicholas of Cusa, *Trialogus de Possest* 8, 2 (Paris: J. Vrin, 2006), 29.

29. Ibid., 6–7.

30. I. Kant, *Vorkritische Schriften II: 1757–1777*, 79: "Alle Möglichkeit ist in irgend etwas Wirklichen gegeben, entweder in demselben als eine Bestimmung, oder durch dasselbe als eine Folge."

31. I. Kant, *AA* II, 83: "Alle Möglichkeit setzt etwas Wirkliches voraus, worin und wodurch alles Denkliche gegeben ist."

32. Immanuel Kant, "Lectures on the Philosophical Doctrine of Religion," in *Religion and Rational Theology*, ed. Allen W. Wood and George Di Giovanni, Cambridge Edition of the Works of Immanuel Kant (New York: Cambridge University Press, 1996), 335–452 (377).

33. Kierkegaard, *Journal AA* 22 (1837), in *SK Skrifter*, vol. 17 (Copenhagen: Gads Forlag, 2000), 41.21. This is very different from R. Kearney's thesis that "God neither is nor is not but may be." Kearney, *The God Who May Be*, 1.

34. Heidegger, *Being and Time*, 143.

35. Ibid. Original emphasis.

36. Ibid., 143–44.

37. Ibid., 143.

38. Ibid., 144.

39. Ibid. Original emphasis.

40. Ibid., 148.

41. Ibid., 145. Original emphasis.

42. Ibid., 148.

43. Ibid., 42.231.

44. Ibid., 145.

45. Ibid., 146.

46. Ibid., 222.

47. Ibid., 146.

48. Ibid., 250–51. Original emphasis.

49. Ibid., 226; original emphasis. What Heidegger here writes of truth ("'There is' truth only insofar as Da-sein is and as long as it is") is also true of

possibility. Without Dasein there is no possibility, and Dasein is finite and will come to an end—not only each ontic instantiation of it (you, me, we, they), but the ontological structure as such.

50. Ibid., 227.

51. Ibid., 229. Original emphasis.

52. Ibid., 223.

53. In a way satisfactory to Heidegger himself. He was aware that this wasn't the case in his 1927 paper "Phenomenology and Theology" when he wrote to Bultmann on October 10, 1928, that he didn't want to publish it because the borderline between philosophy and theology was "noch nicht scharf und prinzipiell genug gezogen. . . . Was keine genügende Durcharbeitung erfährt, ist *der* Charakter der Theologie, der sie in gewisser formaler Weise der Philosophie insofern gleichstellt, als sie auch auf das Ganze geht, aber ontisch." He explains this further in a letter of December 18, 1928, by pointing out that his "Fragestellung im Vortrag ist bezüglich der Theologie als Wissenschaft nicht nur zu eng, sondern unhaltbar. Die Positivität der Theologie, die ich zwar glaube getroffen zu haben, ist etwas anderes als die der Wissenschaften. Theologie steht in einer ganz anderen Weise als die Philosophie außerhalb der Wissenschaften. Aber darüber ein andermal." He never got around to clarifying it. He was clear about what theology is not but not about what it is. As he put it in a letter to Elisabeth Blochmann of August 8, 1928: "Zwar bin ich persönlich überzeugt, dass Theologie *keine* Wissenschaft ist—aber ich bin heute noch nicht im Stande, das *wirklich zu zeigen* und zwar so, dass dabei die große geistesgeschichtliche Funktion der Theologie *positiv* begriffen ist." He never got around to showing this.

54. B. Waldenfels, *Ordnung im Zwielicht* (Frankfurt: Suhrkamp, 1987); *Der Stachel des Fremden* (Frankfurt: Suhrkamp, 1990); *Antwortregister* (Frankfurt: Suhrkamp, 1994); *Grenzen der Normalisierung: Studien zur Phänomenologie des Fremden* 2 (Frankfurt: Suhrkamp, 1998); *Sinnschwellen: Studien zur Phänomenologie des Fremden* 3 (Frankfurt: Suhrkamp, 1999); *Bruchlinien der Erfahrung: Phänomenologie, Psychoanalyse, Phänomenotechnik* (Frankfurt: Suhrkamp, 2002); "Die Macht der Ereignisse," in *Ereignis auf Französisch*, ed. M. Rölli (Munich: Verlag, 2004), 447–58; *Phänomenologie der Aufmerksamkeit* (Frankfurt: Suhrkamp, 2004); *Schattenrisse der Moral* (Frankfurt: Suhrkamp, 2006).

55. Heidegger, *Being and Time*, 34.

56. Ibid., 28.

57. Ibid. Original emphasis.

58. Cf. I. U. Dalferth, *Die Wirklichkeit des Möglichen: Hermeneutische Religionsphilosophie* (Tübingen: Mohr Siebeck, 2003), 19–22.

59. Cf. I. U. Dalferth, *Radikale Theologie* (Leipzig: Evangelische Verlagsanstalt, 2010).

60. Cf. I. U. Dalferth, *Theology and Philosophy* (Eugene, OR: Wipf & Stock, 2002).

61. Aristotle, *Met.* VIII (theta), 8, 1050 f.

62. This aspect is underlined in Richard Kearney's interpretation of Mark 10:27: "For humans it is impossible, but not for God; because for God everything is possible." Kearney, *The God Who May Be*, 80 ff.

63. Eberhard Jüngel, *God as the Mystery of the World: On the Foundation of the Theology of the Crucified One in the Dispute between Theism and Atheism* (Grand Rapids, MI: Eerdmans, 1983), 310.

64. Ibid., 339.

65. Ibid., 217.

Chapter Five

CAN WE TALK THEOLOGICALLY?
Thomas Aquinas and Nicholas of Cusa on the Possibility of
a Theological Understanding of Islam

PIM VALKENBERG

One of the most interesting aspects of comparing the premodern and
the postmodern situation is that there seem to be interesting analogies
between them. In the Middle Ages, scholars from different cultures
and religions were able to talk with one another because they shared
a common philosophical background. Yet, even though some Christians tried to approach Judaism not as blindness or heresy but as a
partner in faith, most Christians in the West—including Thomas
Aquinas—were not able or willing to communicate at a theological
level with Islam. In the postmodern situation after 9/11, religion has
become more relevant than ever since the beginnings of modernity,
but still most Christians in the West are not able or willing to take
Islam as a religion seriously. Some of them flatly deny that Islam is a
religion but attack it as a political system that seeks to conquer the
world.[1] The Evangelical Christian leader Pat Robertson is reported to
have said in a TV show that he hosted in 2007, "Ladies and gentlemen,
we have to recognize that Islam is not a religion. It is a worldwide political movement meant on domination of the world. And it is meant
to subjugate all people under Islamic law." Similarly, a Dutch right-
wing politician recently said to an American public, "Let no one fool

you about Islam being a religion. Sure, it has a god and a hereafter, and 72 virgins. But in its essence Islam is a political ideology. It is a system that lays down detailed rules for society and the life of every person. Islam wants to dictate every aspect of life. Islam means 'submission.' Islam is not compatible with freedom and democracy, because what it strives for is sharia. If you want to compare Islam to anything, compare it to communism or national-socialism, these are all totalitarian ideologies." These contemporary voices are willing to recognize that Islam has the phenomenological likeness of a religion— it has a god and an idea about the hereafter—but they are not willing to take it seriously as a religion because of their insistence that it is a political phenomenon. Such a view holds true for most scholarly approaches to Islam as well. Most scholars are content to approach Islam as a political, sociological, or historical phenomenon. Of course, they see that Islam claims to be a religion first, but that is not their field, so they are not able to approach Islam theologically. But if we cannot talk at the level of what Muslims say motivates them deeply to live their lives as people devoted to God, how can we hope to really understand them and to live together in this postmodern era?

In this chapter I discuss two medieval Christian approaches to Islam, represented by Thomas Aquinas (thirteenth century) and Nicholas of Cusa (fifteenth century). In addition to discussing the limits of their theological conversation with Islam, I want to explore whether these approaches may still be relevant for us today.

THOMAS AQUINAS AND THE LIMITS OF THEOLOGICAL CONVERSATION WITH ISLAM: THE *SUMMA CONTRA GENTILES*

It makes no sense to idealize or romanticize the Middle Ages as a period of vigorous religious life, splendid philosophical and theological conversations, or peaceful coexistence, for example, in Al-Andalus. This would be a myth, the "myth of Toledo" (Mariano Delgado), as much as the myth of the Dark Ages as the era of the Crusades, a time of cruelty and fanaticism. Also, it makes no sense to try to find answers to our modern questions in that period. If we were interested in Aquinas as a champion of dialogue or even as one who had a basic respect for other religions, we would be disappointed. Yet it is true that the Middle Ages saw deep relationships between philosophers and theologians from the three monotheistic traditions who were motivated by similar concerns. This leads some theologians and Islamicists, for instance, Roger Arnaldez, to say that there was a "community of thinking" in the Middle Ages that may teach us some lessons today.[2] It has been argued that the heritage of the Greek philosophers offered an idiom that expressed both a basic problem for the three Abrahamic religions and a ground for resolving or at least understanding the problem. The basic problem is commonly phrased as the relation between faith and reason, or, more historically, between the worldview that was believed to lay behind the words in the Sacred Scriptures revealed by God as authoritative and the worldview that was presented by the Greek philosophers—often in Arabic translation—apparently without appealing to such a revealed authority. Aquinas was well aware of the fact that he could not learn from Jewish or Muslim philosophers about the Christian understanding of revelation, but he could learn from them about this Greek worldview insofar as it did not require a specific appeal to revelation. For this reason, as Harry Wolfson and David Burrell have made clear, the communication between Muslims, Jews, and Christians in the Middle Ages largely succeeded on the terms of a philosophical theology.[3]

The awareness of the levels of communication that are possible between different groups determines the very structure of Thomas Aquinas's *Summa contra gentiles* (1258–64). A traditional theory even says that this theological work was written at the request of Raymond of Peñaforte with a view to the conversion of Muslims in Spain and North Africa.[4] This theory is quite unlikely since Aquinas barely shows an awareness of contemporary Muslims as addressees of his arguments, but the fact remains that apologetic motifs are predominant in this book: as the original Latin title of the book says, it wants to defend the truth of the Catholic faith against the errors of the unbelievers (*de veritate Catholicae fidei contra errores infidelium*). This defense is probably directed not so much against Muslims in Spain or Africa as against classical Greek philosophical worldviews that were transmitted by Arab philosophers.[5] This would explain why Aquinas is not willing or able to perceive Islam as a religion, since Islamic points of view were mainly presented to him through the philosophical writings of Arabs. It would also explain why he lumps Muslims (perceived as "Mohammedans") and pagans together as people who do not accept any of the books that Christians would consider authoritative, while Jews at least accept part of these books. So the acceptance of authoritative sources determines the mode of defense, and it also explains why it is sometimes hard to defend your faith against those with whom you share no sources.

This is what Aquinas says in the second chapter of his *Summa contra gentiles*:

> It is difficult [to proceed against errors] because some of them, such as the Mohammedans and the pagans, do not agree with us in accepting the authority of any Scripture, by which they may be convinced of their error. Thus, against the Jews we are able to argue by means of the Old Testament, while against heretics we are able to argue by means of the New Testament. But the Mohammedans and the pagans accept neither the one nor the other. We must, therefore, have recourse to the natural reason, to which all men are forced to give their assent. However, it is true, in divine matters the natural reason has its failings.[6]

This well-known quotation deserves closer examination. First, it is remarkable that Aquinas uses the word *Mohammedans*, not so much because we now know that it betrays a Christian bias against the religion of Islam,[7] but because most scholars during the Middle Ages used the word *Saraceni*. Even before Muslims identified their religion as Islam, John of Damascus, who grew up at the Umayyad court shortly after the new religion came into power there, referred to the adherents of this new religion as "Ishmaelites," "Hagarenes," and "Saracenes." These three words refer to the stories about Abraham, his wives Sarah and Hagar, and his sons Isaac and Ishmael. So John of

Damascus seems to give an endorsement of the Abrahamic heritage of the three religions concerned, albeit in a negative vein. The word Σαρασκενοι in Greek is associated with Sarah who sent Hagar and Ishmael destitute and without possessions into the desert. So, according to John of Damascus, *Saracenes* means "those who have been sent away empty by Sarah."[8] In fact, the term *Saraceni* probably comes from the Arabic word *Sharqiyyūn,* which simply means "people from the East, Orientals." That Aquinas refers to Muhammad by name, however, seems to suggest a religious connotation, albeit again a negative rather than a positive one. This assumption is confirmed when Aquinas mentions Muhammad once again, in chapter 6, where he opposes the way in which Christians come to faith to the way in which Muhammad led his people to faith. In this long quotation, Aquinas in fact gives a summary of the polemical tradition that began with John of Damascus and that included Muhammad as seducer and as imposter, polygamy and other sexual pleasures, and spreading of the word through violence. Aquinas says:

> He [Muhammad] seduced the people by promises of carnal pleasure to which the concupiscence of the flesh goads us. His teaching also contained precepts that were in conformity with his promises, and he gave free rein to carnal pleasure. In all this, as is not unexpected, he was obeyed by carnal men. As for proofs of the truth of his doctrine, he brought forward only such as could be grasped by the natural ability of anyone with a very modest wisdom. Indeed, the truths that he taught he mingled with many fables and with doctrines of the greatest falsity. He did not bring forth any signs produced in a supernatural way, which alone fittingly gives witness to divine inspiration; for a visible action that can be only divine reveals an invisibly inspired teacher of truth. On the contrary, Mohammed said that he was sent in the power of his arms—which are signs not lacking even to robbers and tyrants. What is more, no wise men, men trained in things divine and human, believed in him from the beginning. Those who believed in him were brutal men and desert wanderers, utterly ignorant of all divine teaching, through whose numbers Mohammed forced others to become his

followers by the violence of his arms. Nor do divine pronounce-
ments on the part of preceding prophets offer him any witness. On
the contrary, he perverts almost all the testimonies of the Old and
New Testaments by making them into fabrications of his own, as
can be seen by anyone who examines his law. It was, therefore, a
shrewd decision on his part to forbid his followers to read the Old
and New Testaments, lest these books convict him of falsity. It is
thus clear that those who place any faith in his words believe fool-
ishly.[9]

It is clear that the reference to the prophet Muhammad serves
Aquinas as a black foil to the light of Christ. Yet a second aspect of
the second chapter of *Summa contra gentiles* shows that this apologetic strategy will only work when Aquinas is able to find some common ground for his defense of the Catholic faith against the errors
of unbelievers. He can only convince others of the truth of what he
wants to tell them if they accept the content or—if there is no common content—the medium of communication. So Aquinas's point
here is that with heretics we share the Christian scriptures and with
the Jews we share at least the book that Christians read as the Old
Testament. But with Muslims we do not share any common content
except the fact that we are all human beings. For Aquinas, a human
being is an *animal rationale,* and therefore Muslims should at least
accept rationality. The idea of a common philosophical heritage discussed earlier can now be translated as a minimum requirement for
agreeing on what counts as reasoning. There is not only a philosophical ground for this, but it is important for the Christian tradition
of apologetics as well, since it has been derived from what St. Peter
says in the New Testament: "Always be ready to give an explanation
to anyone who asks you for a reason for your hope."[10] So "giving
reasons" is not only what we do as human beings, but for Christians
it is also a special task in explaining their faith. However, as Aquinas
says at the end of the quotation, natural reason is a limited instrument
when we are talking about faith. We are not really talking at the level
of believers but at the level of human beings.

This medieval discussion has an interesting late modern parallel. "A Common Word" is a document published by 138 Muslim religious leaders and scholars in Amman, Jordan, in 2007. It is an indirect reply to Pope Benedict XVI's Regensburg address of September 2006 in which he quoted the Byzantine emperor Manuel II Paleologos as follows: "Show me just what Mohammed brought that was new, and there you will find things only evil and inhuman, such as his command to spread by the sword the faith he preached." In the edited version of this address on the Vatican website, Pope Benedict adds an interesting footnote:

> In the Muslim world, this quotation has unfortunately been taken as an expression of my personal position, thus arousing understandable indignation. I hope that the reader of my text can see immediately that this sentence does not express my personal view of the Qur'an, for which I have the respect due to the holy book of a great religion. In quoting the text of the Emperor Manuel II, I intended solely to draw out the essential relationship between faith and reason. On this point I am in agreement with Manuel II, but without endorsing his polemic.[11]

Pope Benedict was right in the fact that the main point of his address was to emphasize the rational nature of the Christian faith, in line with the intellectualism of Thomas Aquinas and more or less against what is perceived as the voluntarism of Duns Scotus, starkly represented in Islam by Ibn Hazm according to whom God is not bound by his Word and can therefore act according to his goodwill, completely arbitrarily.

One month after this Regensburg address, a group of thirty-eight Muslim scholars reacted with an open letter to the pope in which they pointed out, among many other things, that mainstream Islam is just as intellectualistic as Thomism and that Ibn Hazm represents a minority position. They pointed out that the pope made a number of mistakes in his view on Islam and that he might want to choose theological authorities on Islam that would be acceptable to Muslims if he really wanted to engage in dialogue with Islam. A year later, the same group, together with one hundred others, sent the document "A Common Word" to all Christian leaders in an effort to open a new worldwide dialogue between Christians and Muslims. The history of this document and its reception among Christians is a fascinating story that might well influence the relations between Christians and Muslims in the twenty-first century, but at this moment I want to point out only that the Vatican did not immediately react to this document, while many Protestants reacted immediately and very favorably, for instance, the declaration by a number of scholars from Yale University.[12] Jean-Louis Tauran, who had recently become the new president of the Pontifical Council for Interreligious Dialogue, is quoted as saying that it is difficult to come to a theological dialogue with Muslims, because "Muslims do not accept that one can question the Quran, because it was written, they say, by dictation from God. With such an absolute interpretation, it is difficult to discuss the contents of faith."[13] My point here is that the Vatican reaction seemed to suggest that a theological dialogue with the Muslims behind "A Common Word" would be difficult and that therefore there could not be any common theological ground between Catholics and Muslims. A few months later, in a presentation of his work as president of the Pontifical Council for Interreligious Dialogue, Tauran said that dialogue is both a risk and an opportunity.[14]

In the meantime, Catholics and Muslims established the Catholic-Muslim Forum, made public in a press release at the Vatican in March 2008. The agenda of this forum is very interesting; it shows two theological themes, suggested by the authors of "A Common Word," namely, "Love of God" and "Love of Neighbor," while adding two themes suggested by Pope Benedict and Cardinal Tauran, "Theological and Spiritual Foundations" and "Human Dignity and Mutual Respect." Benedict and Tauran's approach seems to be more cautious than that of their Muslim interlocutors. Instead of addressing theological themes, and in doing so basing the Catholic-Muslim Forum on a common theological ground, they first want to explore the question whether theological and spiritual common points in fact exist and whether we should not rather begin with an agenda that seems to be set by the European Enlightenment: human dignity and mutual respect. Just like Thomas Aquinas, they seem to suggest that as Catholics and Muslims we may have difficulty finding one another on theological common ground and that we might therefore be wiser to take a more philosophical approach. Pope Benedict said the following to the members of the Catholic-Muslim Forum at the end of their first gathering in Rome, on November 7, 2008:

> We should thus work together in promoting genuine respect for the dignity of the human person and fundamental human rights, even though our anthropological visions and our theologies justify this in different ways. There is a great and vast field in which we can act together in defending and promoting the moral values which are part of our common heritage. Only by starting with the recognition of the centrality of the person and the dignity of each human being, respecting and defending life which is the gift of God, and is thus sacred for Christians and Muslims alike—only on the basis of this recognition can we find a common ground for building a more fraternal world, a world in which confrontations and differences are peacefully settled, and the devastating power of ideologies is neutralized.[15]

I find this statement very interesting. It shows that Pope Benedict is rooted in the tradition of the modern Enlightenment and tries to focus on this type of rationality against the threat of religious violence. In his time and age, Aquinas did something similar: he sought the common ground of rational argumentation in his defense of the Catholic faith against Muslim unbelievers.

But Aquinas gives a precise reason for his refusal to talk theologically with Muslims, and that is the relevant aspect of the quotation from the second chapter of the *Summa contra gentiles*. Differently from heretics and Jews, the followers of Muhammad do not recognize the authority of the scriptures, and therefore Christians cannot use these in defending their faith against Muslims. Aquinas is right and not right on this point. Theoretically he is not right, since the Muslim concept of revelation implies that God has revealed God's guidance to a number of messengers in a number of books, and the *Taurat* revealed to Moses and the *Injīl* revealed to Jesus count among them. The Qur'ān mentions acceptance of these books and these prophets many times, and Nicholas of Cusa uses that as one of his arguments to show that Jesus Christ is in fact, according to the Qur'ān, the greatest prophet of all. A number of quotations from the Qur'ān could be given, but the beginning of *surat Al-ʿImrān*, the third surah that discusses the family of Jesus, may suffice. Muhammad is addressed here as follows: "It is He Who has sent down to thee (step by step), in truth, the Book, confirming what went before it; and He sent down the Law (of Moses) and the Gospel (of Jesus)."[16] So in theory Aquinas is wrong, because the Qur'ān accepts the Torah and the Gospel as revelations of God; yet in fact he is right, because in a later theological development Muslims began to expand the notion of *naskh,* according to which a later text in the Qur'ān abrogates the legal power of an earlier text, to include the pre-qur'ānic revelations. Thus developed what Abdulaziz Sachedina calls the "theological doctrine of 'supersession,'" according to which the Qur'ān abrogates earlier revelations.[17] In a polemical move, Muslims began to say that Jews and Christians changed the texts (*tahrīf al-nass*) or the interpretations (*tahrīf al-maʿā ni*) of their scriptures, mainly to exclude allusions to the coming prophet Muhammad.[18] Strange as this may seem to us, it is not so different from the Christian allegation that Jews were blind to the true Christological sense of their scriptures. The effect of this doctrine of falsification is that Muslims hold that there is a decisive difference between the Gospel as God revealed it to Jesus and the Gospel that is handed down in the Christian tradition; consequently, they extol the value of the former, but they do not care to read the latter. So when Aquinas says that Muslims do not accept the authority of the Old and New Testaments, he is—historically speaking—right.

In the quotation above from chapter 6 of the *Summa contra gentiles*, Aquinas reproduces the Christian polemical tradition that we have seen in John of Damascus and that we will encounter again in Nicholas of Cusa: Muhammad did not want his followers to read the Old and New Testaments because if they read them they would find out that Muhammad falsified his so-called revelation by perversely borrowing materials from these books. So, we may conclude, there is a mutual polemical tradition of falsification that withholds theologians from the two traditions from talking theologically. The Sacred Scriptures cannot form the common ground for theological conversation since they have been falsified after having been received as authentic revelation from God—as Muslims say about the Christian scriptures—or since they have been plagiarized from the authentic scriptures by someone who posed as a prophet—as Christians say about the Qur'ān.

This brings us to the second reason that makes a real theological conversation with Islam impossible for Aquinas: the perversity of Muhammad as a prophet. The main opposition that Aquinas wants to make in *Summa contra gentiles* I.6 is between the truth of Christ and the falsity of Muhammad. Truth is central here, because Aquinas wants to show that, although the truth of faith transcends the powers of natural reason, it can be revealed by fitting arguments and confirmed by miracles. In the medieval debates between Jews, Christians, and Muslims about "prophetology," that is, establishing criteria for true prophethood, these two characteristics have always been important: a true prophet should act according to reason, and his prophethood should be confirmed by miracles.[19] On these two points, according to Aquinas, Muhammad fails miserably. Leaving aside for the moment the argument about miracles and even the argument about violence as being contrary to reasonableness—Pope Benedict's point in his Regensburg address—I want to focus on the famous polemical argument about Muhammad's sensual nature. Let me repeat what Aquinas says: "He seduced the people by promises of carnal pleasure to which the concupiscence of the flesh goads us. His teaching also contained precepts that were in conformity with his promises, and he gave free rein to carnal pleasure." Here of course lies another issue that has been used frequently in present-day Western critiques of Islam: polygamy, inequality in relations between men and women, and even Muhammad's supposed abuse of young children.[20] Yet I want to focus on another aspect of this issue that—again—seems to build a barrier against theological conversation: eschatology. Many people are aware that the Qur'ān often speaks about the garden of the future where the believers will recline in the shadow of the trees, eating fruits and drinking wine with big-eyed women beside them.[21] A lot of details about the text and the interpretation of these garden visions are quite uncertain, but for the West it has always been a source of derision and a proof for the sensual nature of Islam. And, to be honest, there seems to be quite a distance between Aquinas's description of *visio beata* as the final end of human beings in heaven and drinking wine on benches. I mention this because this image of Paradise is the one element of Islamic theology that Aquinas often mentions.[22] More precisely, Aquinas sees Christ's words, "at the resurrection they neither marry nor are given in marriage but are like the angels in heaven" (Matt. 22:30), as being directed not only against the Sadducees but also against the Saracenes.[23] Again, for Aquinas, the character of human beings as "rational animals" is at stake here. He refuses to believe in a final union with God in which bodily pleasures would be more important than spiritual and rational relationships. In our final bliss we will be spiritualized, not reverting to animal pleasures. For Nicholas of Cusa, this will be the point where he can no longer maintain his willingness to take Islam seriously as a theological tradition.

ANSWERING OBJECTIONS FROM MUSLIMS: THE REASONS FOR OUR FAITH

It seems that we have to conclude that there is no space for a theological approach to Islam in Aquinas, due to a polemical tradition that stresses the idea that Islam cannot be a true religion because it denies the truth of the revealed scriptures, is based on a pseudo-prophet who falsified his scripture, and does not have a rational and spiritual view on the future life. Yet, despite the unfriendly remarks on Muhammad, one cannot say that Aquinas capitalizes on this polemical method; he is not interested in attacking others but in defending his own faith, and in the first chapters of the *Summa contra gentiles* he explains how he intends to do so. If we cannot discuss proper theological sources because the adversaries do not accept their authority, we can only base our defense on human reason. Aquinas shows that he is aware that in matters of faith reason does not bring us very far, and we should not try to base our faith on it; but we can at least show that the reasons brought forward against our faith do not hold, since there is but one truth and therefore faith and reason cannot contradict one another. If we cannot demonstrate our faith, we can at least show that it is a reasonable faith.

This conviction about the rational nature of faith returns in a short work, written about 1266, that brings Aquinas closest to what we might call a theological dialogue with Islam. This work is titled *De rationibus fidei*, which might be translated as "The Reasons for Our Faith," or maybe "Giving Account of Our Faith," as it refers to the text in the first letter of Peter that Christians considered the great urge to apologetics: "Always be ready to give an explanation to anyone who asks you for a reason for your hope"(1 Pet. 3:15). Here Aquinas answers a number of questions that have been posed to him by a *cantor* (singer; a liturgical function) from Antioch in present-day Syria. This Christian from the West, possibly a Dominican friar, lived in a city occupied by the Crusaders (until 1267) but with a largely Muslim population. He had encountered some objections against the Christian faith brought forward by the Saraceni but also by Christians of the Eastern rites. In this work, Aquinas employs the method of defending the faith that he announced in his *Summa contra gentiles*: he uses reasoning only in his defense against the Muslims, but in his defense against the Greek and Armenian Christians he appeals to the Christian scriptures.[24] We even find an echo of this in the *cantor*'s request; Aquinas writes, "On these points you request moral and philosophical reasons which the Muslims might consider; for it would be fruitless to cite authorities against persons who do not recognize them."[25] Aquinas mentions three objections of Muslims against the Christian faith in the beginning of his work.

These, then, are the points, which, as you affirm, are attacked and ridiculed by the unbelievers. For the Muslims [Saraceni], as you say, ridicule our claim that Christ is the Son of God, since God does not have a wife; and they think us mad, assuming we profess there are three gods. They also mock our belief that Christ, the Son of God, was crucified for the salvation of the human race, because if God is omnipotent, He could have saved the human race without the suffering of His Son; He could also have so constructed man that he could not have sinned. They rebuke Christians because daily at the altar they eat their God and because the body of Christ, were it even as big as a mountain, should long since have been consumed.[26]

In this brief summary of the Muslim objections, Aquinas shows more awareness of the theological problems between Islam and Christianity than in the entire *Summa contra gentiles*. The first two objections refer to main points of contention between the two religions: the theology of the Trinity and the divine nature of Christ; and his death at the cross and the necessity of salvation. The Muslim resistance to these two basic Christian doctrines already begins in the Qur'ān since they violate the basic confession of God's unity (*tawhīd*) and of his guarding his prophets and envoys from all evil. The conviction that God does not need any partner and that humans do not need salvation is seen as a rational principle in the Islamic tradition of theology (*kalām*), and therefore the objections that the *cantor* mentions are of a rational nature: Does God need a woman? Could he not create humans without sin? The third objection sounds like a mockery of the Eucharist: How can you eat the body of Christ? Later on, Aquinas adds a fourth point of debate that has become famous among Muslim theologians (*mutakallimūn*) as well: the relation between divine predestination and human acting.

While I cannot enter into an analysis of all the questions discussed in the ten chapters of *De rationibus fidei*, I want to see if Aquinas gives a more theological approach to Islam in this work than in the first chapters of his *Summa contra gentiles*. The beginning of the discussion on the Trinity does not sound promising in this respect: "First . . . consideration should be given to the silly character of the ridicule heaped by Muslims upon our assertion that Christ is the Son of God, as though God is thereby said to have a wife. For since the mockers are carnal, they are incapable of grasping anything except what pertains to flesh and blood. Anyone of intelligence, however, can realize that the process of begetting is not the same in all things, but occurs in each thing according to its own proper characteristics."[27] Aquinas begins polemically with an *argumentum ad hominem* that is reminiscent of the sixth chapter of *Summa contra gentiles*: being carnal people, Muslims can only understand the divine Sonship of Christ as something that involves procreation. This is the same argument that Aquinas used against the Muslim view of the afterlife, and it has been used for centuries before him as a way to disparage the Jewish interpretation of their scriptures: while Jews and Muslims understand their scriptures according to the flesh, Christians understand theirs according to the spirit. We will see how Nicholas of Cusa turns the argument around by saying that we can read the Qur'ān as a warning not to think about the Trinity in terms of family relationships. But Aquinas and Cusanus agree in explaining that divine generation has to be understood in terms of intellectual generation. The best metaphor here is not procreation but the processes of knowing and loving in which Word and Spirit proceed from the Father and Father and Son together, respectively. Aquinas clearly speaks theologically here, but he understands his theological task as explaining his own faith, not as trying to understand the faith of another, even though the other's objections must be understood before a suitable answer can be given. In this case, we may say that Aquinas is able to give an effective answer because the *cantor* has apparently understood the significance of the theological objections of Muslims against the Christian doctrine of Christ's divine Sonship.

Aquinas begins with a similar lashing when he discusses the reason for God to become incarnate: "From a similar mental blindness Muslims are led to ridicule as well the Christian Faith which confesses Christ, the Son of God, died, because they do not grasp the depth of so great a mystery."[28] Yet the reproach seems to be less harsh, as it sounds like Anselm's famous saying to Boso: *nondum considerasti quanti ponderis sit peccatum,* "you have not yet considered the weight of sin."[29] It is true that the two religions look differently at the death on the cross. For Christianity, this is the ultimate consequence of human depravity and human dignity, and it is most of all the way of God's conquering love; for Islam, on the contrary, it is an impossible end for a prophet of God because God would not allow one of his envoys to suffer such an ignominious death. On this issue, Aquinas seems to come closest to a theological debate with Islam when he discusses the question as to how to understand the saying that the Word of God has suffered and died at the cross. He uses the contrast to the person of Muhammad to highlight the specific characteristic of Christ as Word and image of God. Introducing this section, he says, "We undertake the present debate with those who claim to be worshipers of God whether they are Christians, or Muslims or Jews."[30] This quotation suggests enough similarity to allow for a theological debate between those who worship God (*Dei cultores*), and it is significant that he starts to use quotations from scripture here, in particular, the first chapter of St. Paul's letter to the Corinthians where he says, "We proclaim Christ crucified, a stumbling block to Jews and foolishness to Gentiles" (1 Cor. 1:23). Aquinas points to the fact that Christ's death on the cross was in fact the culmination of a life of poverty and lowliness. One can sense here how Aquinas speaks as a mendicant friar who chose the life of preaching and poverty rather than a life in a rich monastery or at a princely court. It is a great defense of the uniqueness of Christ, who, "though he was in the form of God, did not regard equality with God something to be grasped" but emptied himself and became "obedient to death, even death on a cross" (Phil. 2:6–8). And it might have fitted wonderfully with the image of Christ that St. Francis wanted to proclaim to the sultan at Damietta fifty years before, in 1219. But one may wonder if the Crusaders in Antioch were able to proclaim Christ in the same way. Antioch fell to the Egyptian Mamluks in 1268, so Aquinas's answers did not have the time to do much good for the Christians there. This brings us to another city and another siege, and another theologian trying to find out what caused Christians and Muslims to wage war on one another.[31]

NICHOLAS OF CUSA, THE FALL OF
CONSTANTINOPLE, AND THE RELEVANCE OF
CHRISTIAN KNOWLEDGE OF THE QUR'ĀN

The German Nikolaus von Kues (1401–64), born in Bernkastel-Kues along the Mosel River, was not only a scholar of theology, philosophy, canon law, mathematics, and natural sciences but also served the church as a diplomat and cardinal and was involved in attempts to re-unite the Western (Latin) and the Eastern (Greek) Church. In order to facilitate the negotiations on this attempt at reunification, Nicholas visited Constantinople sixteen years before it was conquered by the Ottoman sultan Mehmet II in 1453. It is quite probable that Nicholas gained some knowledge of Islam during his travels, and therefore the fall of Constantinople provoked two reactions from his side. His im-mediate reaction is a book, *De pace fidei*, that contains a fascinating plea for unity and peace between the religions, but later he gives a more theological reaction in a theological reading of the Qur'ān, the *Cribratio Alkorani*. This book contains a very interesting combina-tion of two different hermeneutic strategies: the old polemical tradi-tion that we already met in Aquinas and a new approach to under-stand the Qur'ān from a theological point of view.

Nicholas of Cusa wrote his first reaction, containing a fervent plea for the peace of faith, only a few weeks after the event that the West knew as the Fall of Constantinople. In this fictitious dialogue between representatives of many religions and cultures, Nicholas tests the possibility for a peaceful agreement in one faith.[32] He intro-duces his fiction as follows: "There was a certain man who, having formerly seen the sites in the regions of Constantinople, was inflamed with zeal for God as a result of those deeds that were reported to have been perpetrated at Constantinople most recently and most cruelly by the King of the Turks. Consequently, with many groanings he beseeched the Creator of all, because of His kindness, to restrain the persecution that was raging more fiercely than usual on account of the difference of rite between the [two] religions."[33] This man, in whom we might well recognize Cusanus himself, seems to be convinced that violence between religions can be overcome if religious persons realize that their religious rites are in fact varieties of one basic faith: *una religio in rituum varietate.* This may sound like a modern concept of religious plurality in the manner of William James or Wilfred Cantwell Smith, but Nicholas of Cusa speaks explicitly as a Christian theologian. He is aware of the fact that no human being is able to comprehend God's infinite being, and therefore all human beings seek God in different rites and call him by different names. Yet underneath these differences there is one faith, and as soon as we become aware of this we will be able to live in peace and harmony. In the imaginary story of *De pace fidei,* the king of heaven and earth receives a number of messengers who bring the stories of religious strife and oppression. One of these messengers asks the heavenly king to manifest his face so that the enmity will end and all people realize that "there is only one religion in a variety of rites."[34] The messenger adds that if it is not possible to eliminate the differences of rites, let there at least be one religion and one true worship of God. One may surmise that this one religion will be Christianity, according to which God has manifested himself fully in Jesus Christ, but in the fiction of *De pace fidei* this remains just a possibility because all attention is focused on the different rites in which the one God is sought. In that sense, we may say that this first reaction to the fall of Constantinople clearly is an appeal to dialogue and peaceful conversation in which we try to find what unites us, not resort to strife and warfare in which we seek to articulate what divides us.

This appeal to the peace of faith against religious warfare seems to speak to the pluralist mind-set of many modern liberal Christians. The mood here seems to be totally different from that of Aquinas's defense of faith. We have seen that it is difficult to find openings for real theological conversation with Islam in Aquinas; here we clearly have conversation, but is it a real theological conversation, or is it rather a political utopia? Apparently, Nicholas of Cusa did not consider his work on the peace of faith the last word on Sultan Mehmet's conquest, since he decided to delve more deeply into the Qur'ān and confront the theological differences more thoroughly. Yet precisely this move from an irenic utopian ideal to the gloomy reality of theological differences goes against our preferences. If only Nicholas had begun with his apologetic reflex and continued to grow toward pluralism we could easily embrace him as a hero for contemporary interreligious dialogue. Yet the truth of history tells us that Nicholas began with a "modern" answer that stressed the unity of faith as an instrument of peace but continued to look for a deeper "postmodern" answer that gave more attention to the theological differences than the rosy ideals. Nor is Nicholas an exception: similar stories can be told about earlier scholars who wrote on Islam, such as Riccoldo of Montecroce (1243–1320) and Ramon Llull (1232–1316). So the major lesson that these medieval premodern developments might have for us is that we must grow from the typically modern idea that differences have to be transcended in order to achieve a unity beyond the religions—the leading idea of the pluralist approach in the Christian theology of religions—to the postmodern or postliberal insight that differences do matter and that we can talk theologically only if these differences are taken into account. In the Christian theology of religions, this insight was brought forward by theologians such as Gavin D'Costa and S. Mark Heim,[35] and it was developed further by James Fredericks and Francis Clooney as comparative theology.[36] If comparative theology is the way to further theological conversation between traditions by learning from the deep differences between them,[37] this might be a way that is congenial with some of the basic ideas of Thomas Aquinas and, more specifically, Nicholas of Cusa, who tried to read the Qur'ān as a Christian theologian in order to promote dialogue between Christians and Muslims as a way to diminish violence between them.

NICHOLAS OF CUSA AND HIS *CRIBRATIO ALKORANI*

When Nicholas of Cusa finished his *Cribratio Alkorani* in 1461, he offered the book to Pope Pius II, who apparently wanted to prepare a letter to Sultan Mehmet II in order to convince him of the truth of the Christian faith. The cardinal offers his help to the pope in proving that the sect of Muhammad is in error and has to be eliminated. At the end of his work, he inserts letters to the sultan and the caliph of Baghdad, apparently to give the pope some basic materials readily at hand.[38] But apart from this church-political motif, Nicholas seems to be driven by a desire to understand the *Lex* (Law, or religion) of the Arabs. In the prologue to his work, he tells us that he went to great lengths to get sufficient documentation. He obtained a copy of the Latin translation of the Qur'ān that Peter the Venerable, abbot of Cluny, ordered to be made by Robert of Ketton. This copy of the *Lex sive Doctrina Mahumeti* has been preserved in Cusanus's personal library, and one can even see how he glossed this Latin text of the Qur'ān and produced his famous phrase about "one religion, many rites" in this very context.[39] When he journeyed to Constantinople he tried to find an Arabic version, and—although he could not read that text himself—he discussed some of its topics with a number of friars there. He also read some of the older refutations of Islam by Friars Riccoldo of Montecroce and Thomas Aquinas. As he says in the same prologue, in the end he decided to write his own book, trying to prove the truth of the Gospel from the text of the Qur'ān. This clearly shows that Nicholas wanted to write in the tradition of apologetics: a defense of one's own religion that is often paired with polemical attacks on the religion of Islam.

In this prologue Nicholas of Cusa mentions some of the scholars with whom he collaborated in his project of getting to know the Qur'ān. The most important scholar among them is the Franciscan friar John of Segovia whom Nicholas met during the Council of Basel in 1432. After the fall of Constantinople, John and Nicholas exchanged letters in which they suggested that it might be better to try to meet the challenge posed by the "sect of the Saracenes" by way of peace rather than war.[40] So this exchange may be seen as the driving idea behind Nicholas's book on the peace of faith. Meanwhile, in Rome, Nicholas found a book on Islam that pleased him more than any others he had seen, those written by Thomas Aquinas included. This book was *Against the Law of the Saracens* by Riccoldo of Montecroce, which is preserved in Nicholas's own library and is the main source for his *Cribratio Alkorani*. In a comparison of these works, Jasper Hopkins remarks that they share the same polemical strategy, although there is a difference: unlike Ricoldo, Nicholas "also accentuates the point that God's glory and the Gospel's truth are manifested in and through the Koran. Moreover, through *pia interpretatio* he attempts to put the theologically best interpretation upon various *prima facie* discreditable passages in the Koran, whereas Ricoldo was more likely to remain at the surface level of interpretation."[41] This quotation gives us the two contrasting hermeneutic strategies by Cusanus that I now want to investigate.

After having mentioned these other theologians and their endeavors to approach Islam, Nicholas adds, "But I applied my mind to disclosing, even from the Koran, that the Gospel is true."[42] The phrase "even from the Koran" (*etiam ex Alkorano*) clearly displays the ambivalence in his hermeneutic strategy. On the one hand, if it is possible to demonstrate the truth of the Gospel from the Qur'ān, then this book must contain some truth, and since all truth is from God, God might be said to disclose some kind of truth through the Qur'ān. On the other hand, this truth may be found only in the middle of mendacious and erroneous statements; the very title *Cribratio Alkorani*, "Sifting of the Qur'ān," evokes the image of a gold panner sifting the water of a river in the hope of finding nuggets amid the silt. The criterion for what may count as true gold is, of course, Christ as true revelation of God; if Nicholas finds the truth about Christ in the Qur'ān, it may be seen as an endorsement of the Gospel; but if it does not tell the truth about Christ, it is a lie or a fraud. This is what Nicholas says: "Now, my intention is as follows: having presupposed the Gospel of Christ, to analyze the book of Muhammad and to show that even in it there are contained those [teachings] through which the Gospel would be altogether confirmed, were it in need of confirmation, and that wherever [the Koran] disagrees [with Christ], this [disagreement] has resulted from Muhammad's ignorance and, following [thereupon], from his perverse intent. For whereas Christ sought not His own glory but the glory of God the Father and the salvation of men, Muhammad sought not the glory of God and the salvation of men but rather his own glory."[43]

Here we meet the apologetic tradition that is the default hermeneutic strategy in Cusanus's book. Muhammad is a pseudo-prophet
who seeks his own glory, and while the Qur'ān itself contends that
God is its author, it must be the work of a human being who has acted
under the influence of what Nicholas calls the "god of this world,"
who is none other than the devil.[44] At this point, Nicholas clearly re-
peats the old Christian polemical tradition in which Muhammad is a
deceiver and an instrument of the devil. This tradition, for which John
of Damascus had set the tone in the eighth century, measures the
Qur'ān against the norm of orthodox Christology: wherever this
book denies the truth about the Son of God, it has to have an antidi-
vine origin.[45]

In an interesting shift of perspectives, Cusanus gives the floor to
the Muslims who say that their book basically confirms the mission
of earlier prophets. They say that God sent messengers to all nations,
concluding that "if the variety of laws and of rites is found to be
present in the identity-of-faith that is exhorted within the various nations by the messengers of God, then indeed this [kind of diversity]
cannot at all prevent one who is obedient from obtaining a fitting reward at the hands of the most gracious and most just Judge."[46] Here
we hear the famous words about the one religion in a variety of rites
as a Muslim argument, and indeed this is where Nicholas found it:
"fides una, ritus diversus," he noted in the margin of his copy of the
Qur'ān in the Toletan Collection.[47] Yet he does not accept this argument, because the Qur'ān does not speak the truth concerning Christ.
Since the Qur'ān on the one hand commends the truth of the Jewish
and Christian scriptures but on the other hand deviates from these
scriptures, it possesses inconsistency, and such a thing cannot be
ascribed to God.[48]

PIA INTERPRETATIO AS A NEW
HERMENEUTIC STRATEGY

Next to the old polemical hermeneutical strategy, there are consider-
able traces of a more benevolent strategy in the *Cribratio Alkorani*.

This strategy is mainly derived from the basic idea that the Qur'ān can be read as confirming the Gospel, and this implies that the arguments concerning the authorship of this book begin to shift. In the middle of an argumentation that only the devil could have inspired Muhammad to write the Qur'ān in order to confuse Christians, Nicholas of Cusa mentions the possibility that Muhammad could have read a certain version of the Gospel and that he could have derived some ray of truth from it. So, essentially, the Qur'ān cannot bring anything new but can only be an endorsement of the Gospel.[49] There are two ways of reading the Qur'ān: the reading of the Muslims, which helps them in their worldly desires; and the reading of the wise persons, which confirms the truth of the Gospel. Nicholas's theological reading of the Qur'ān is of course based on such a reading "beyond the intention of the author," obviously not God or the Antichrist but Muhammad. However, the phrasing "praeter intentionem auctoris" could be read to suggest that God may have used the Qur'ān to confirm the Christians in their reading of the Gospel. In a similar way Nicholas suggests in *De pace fidei* that the critique of the Trinity by Jews and Muslims can be read as leading Christians to a better understanding of their own faith. At these moments we may be inclined to read Cusanus as a precursor of modern pluralists, for instance, in a statement such as this: "Suppose we admit . . . that the goal and intent of the book of the Koran is not only not to detract from God the Creator or from Christ or from God's prophets and envoys or from the divine books of the Testament, the Psalter, and the Gospel, but also to give glory to God the Creator, to praise and to bear witness to Christ (the son of the Virgin Mary) above all the prophets, and to confirm and to approve of the Testament and the Gospel. [If so,] then when one reads the Koran with this understanding, assuredly some fruit can be elicited [from it]."[50] However, in the actual text Nicholas of Cusa adds a phrase (printed in italics) that seems to ruin the dialogical possibilities of this text: "But suppose we admit—*as the followers of the Koran claim ([a claim] whose denial all the wise and zealous believe, as was made evident above)*—that the goal and intent of the book of the Koran. . . ." This time the wise people believe that the benevolent lecture of the Qur'ān has to be denied. And yet Cusanus goes on as if this objection had never been phrased, because—after having mentioned some places in which the Qur'ān contradicts the Gospel, which makes such a fruitful lecture difficult—he concludes, "Nevertheless, when all the foregoing [objections] are considered in such a way that they [are viewed as] serving the previously mentioned intent, then some fruit can be elicited [from the Koran]. For example, when someone reads the [record of] Muhammad's life that is written in the Koran, he understands immediately that it was inserted with God's permission in order for there to be known that Muhammad is neither to be compared to, nor preferred to, Christ or Moses or other prophets."[51] Again, the result of this conclusion is highly ambiguous. On the one hand, Cusanus states that a fruitful reading of the Qur'ān is possible despite objections raised, and this possibility rests on the fact that God might not be the author of the Qur'ān but permitted some useful materials to be inserted in it;[52] on the other hand, this fruitful reading does not lead to a pluralistic but to an apologetic conclusion: Muhammad cannot be compared to Christ.

Nicholas does find some places in the Qur'ān where Christ seems to have been put above other prophets. Where the Qur'ān speaks the truth about Christ, God must be its author; where it sounds heretical, Muhammad or the devil may be its author. Christological truth is the criterion here, even though it seems to lead to a somewhat inconsistent approach to authorship.[53] At some places, he even accepts the qur'ānic critique as an occasion for Christians to be more precise in their language: they should refrain from saying "Christ is God" if this seems to imply that Christ is another god but rather speak about Christ as the Son of God, of one substance with the Father, so that he is "the same God as the Father and not another God.[54]" He also admits that the Qur'ān is right in preferring to talk about the Word of God instead of the Son of God, lest some less educated Arabs might understand "Son" in a physical instead of an intellectual sense. If one wants to convey the meaning of intellectual generation, the concept "Word" is better suited than the concept "Son."[55] On this issue, Cusanus echoes what we have heard from Thomas Aquinas in his *De rationibus fidei*.

In the second book of the *Cribratio Alkorani,* Cusanus broaches the topic of the Trinity, and it is here that he uses his famous formula of *pia interpretatio.* This expression has been translated differently. Ludwig Hagemann quite rightly points to the dialogical intent behind this notion, which he tends to translate as "favorable, charitable or benevolent interpretation."[56] Jasper Hopkins objects that this translation does not do justice to the theological intent of Cusanus's interpretation, and he proposes to translate *pia interpretatio* as "devout interpretation."[57] While agreeing with Hopkins's main analysis, I do not particularly like the pietistic resonances of the word *devout,* and therefore I propose to translate *pia interpretatio* as "faithful interpretation," considering that the word *pius* in medieval Latin, like the German *fromm* or the Dutch *vroom,* has the connotation "steadfast in faith."[58] The word *faithful* has the advantage that it indicates the dual bind of any interreligious hermeneutics: it tries to be faithful to one's own tradition in the first place but to give an at least possible interpretation of the others' religious text as well.

The first text in which Cusanus mentions his faithful interpretation of the Qur'ān introduces the second book as follows: "Let me now turn to a clarification of [the doctrine of] the Trinity that we revere in the divinity. And let me show that on a devout [*faithful*] interpretation the Koran does not contradict [the doctrine of] the Trinity in the sense in which we who adhere to the Gospel speak of trinity."[59] Cusanus proceeds in the same way as in the first book: Muslims might think that they confess singularity in God, while Christians confess plurality in God. But according to mystical theology—we might again think of Cusanus's idea of *docta ignorantia* here—there cannot be plurality in God, since God is not one or three or Father or Son or Spirit but transcends all these names.[60] Again, the qur'ānic critique may help Christians remember that God transcends all names.

The second time Nicholas uses the phrase *pia interpretatio* is in his discussion of the motives for the Qur'ān to deny the crucifixion of Christ. Maybe this was because Muhammad thought that it would derogate from the honor of Christ as prophet of God, but if that is the case he did not understand the mystery of the cross. A faithful interpretation of the Qur'ān reveals divine pedagogy here:

Therefore, it is certain that if without an explication of the mysteries [of Christ's death] the Koran had openly affirmed to the Arabs
that Christ was crucified, it would not [thereby] have been magni-
fying Christ in their minds. Therefore, [the Koran,] on a devout
[*faithful*] interpretation [thereof,] aimed to hide from the Arabs
[Christ's] lowly death and to affirm that He was still living and
would come [again]. Now, [the Koran] would not have been able to
teach of Christ's resurrection from the dead through His power to
lay down His life and to take it up again (as He avows in the Gospel) unless it had showed Christ to be not only a man but also
God—[a view] which it supposed to be at odds with [the doctrine
of] God's oneness, which it was preaching. Moreover, it was not
consistent with the Koran's faith to maintain that Christ had already risen from the dead—as will be explained in a moment. So
perhaps these are the reasons that [the Koran] spoke in the way it
did. Nevertheless, [the Koran] makes these [statements] in such
way that the wise can infer that the Gospel is altogether true, as will
be evident.[61]

The last topic broached in book II is the qur'ānic doctrine of
Paradise, another traditional topic where Christian polemics have
been deployed abundantly, as we saw in Aquinas. Again, Nicholas
uses his hermeneutic rule of faithful interpretation, but this time it
does not lead to understanding but instead renews the polemical tradition. He first gives the argument of divine pedagogy that we have
met before: Muhammad had to describe Paradise in terms of carnal
pleasures since he had to address the uncivilized Arabs. But this time
Nicholas does not buy the argument. He seems to be personally disappointed in his reading of the Qur'ān on this point, and therefore the
faithful interpretation suggested by Muslim readers like Ibn Sina does
not work for him.

While I was reading the Koran, I noticed that very often mention is
made of the day of awesome judgment as well as of Paradise and of
Hell. And [this mention is] always [made] in different ways and
through likenesses, since that which has never entered into human

conception cannot be described otherwise than conjecturally, by reference to sensible things, which are images of intelligible things. And because I likewise saw that the Kingdom of Heaven is befigured in the Gospel and in the Old Testament by means of different likenesses, I told myself that this [befiguring in the Koran] could be excused because of the devout [faithful] interpretation by the followers of [that] Book. Moreover, I read in the Koran [the following]: that chastity is praised in the Virgin Mary and in John [the son] of Zecharias and, generally speaking, in all individuals. . . . But subsequently I was taken aback by [the Koran's] so often having made mention of maidens and their breasts and of lustful physical copulation in Paradise. . . . And I was ashamed to read these vile things. And I said to myself: "If Muhammad ascribes to God this book full of vileness, or if he himself wrote [it] and attributes its authority to God, then I am amazed that those wise and chaste and virtuous Arabs, Moors, Egyptians, Persians, Africans, and Turks who are said to be of the law esteem Muhammad as a prophet. [For] his life cannot be emulated by anyone who aspires unto the Kingdom of Heaven, where people do not marry but are like the angels, as Christ has taught.[62]

Nicholas here reproduces one of the traditional themes in Christian polemics against the Qur'ān but at the same time he seems to have been truly shocked by the vulgarisms that he read. Not only does this hardly show Muhammad in a favorable light, but it is a blasphemy to suggest that God would have given laws such as these. And yet in the final paragraph of this chapter, Nicholas once more comes back to his idea of faithful interpretation, and he suggests that God has willed to hide the truth beneath the mire of the carnal images in the Qur'ān: "Nevertheless, God Almighty willed that amid all these filthy and vain things, and things such as are abominable to the wise even among the Arabs, there also be inserted things in which the splendor of the Gospel was so contained as hidden that it would manifest itself to the wise if it were sought for with diligent effort."[63] Two things are noteworthy here. In the first place, not only Christians can apparently give a faithful interpretation of the Qur'ān, but wise men among the

Arabs—Ibn Sina is probably his example—can do so as well. In the second place, by now it is clear that God may use even the Qur'ān to show some hints of the truth for people who understand. Of course, this truth is fully revealed only by Christ, but apparently Muslims also may be guided by a faithful interpretation of the Qur'ān, an interpretation that Nicholas hopes will lead them toward recognizing Christ.

In the third book of his *Cribratio Alkorani*, Nicholas returns to the polemical hermeneutics in which Muhammad is an imposter who made up the book that he ascribed to God. In this book the political situation and the violent nature of Islam are directly addressed: although God commanded him not to use violence,[64] Muhammad used violence to persecute the Christians. Here Nicholas addresses Muhammad directly in a desperate question that suddenly evokes the fall of Constantinople.

> How is it that you manifest yourself to be other [than gracious and gentle] in your deeds and that you render false God's attestation? Why is it that you make your God to be at odds with Himself as often as you have changed your mind? . . . Why, in Christians, do you oppose Christ to such an extent that you persecute those whom you do not deny to be saved through their own law? There were Christians before you. And by means of those who were faithful to Christ, Christ occupied a large part of this world—as a result of the very steadfast obedience, even unto death, of an infinite number of martyrs for God. Why do your followers persecute Christ in order to do away with His acquired people? But we are comforted by the Gospel (against which you offend subsequently to your very many expressions of approval), where Christ says: "Blessed are those who suffer persecution for the sake of justice, for theirs is the Kingdom of Heaven."[65]

The most polemical passage follows in chapter 8, where Nicholas reproaches Muhammad for using religion in order to gain power by the sword. He did not really believe in the law that he said had been received from God, since he did not live according to this law.[66] So there is no basis in the Qur'ān for religious warfare against the Christians; nothing but greed and the will to dominate are the driving forces behind the siege of Constantinople. Nicholas comes back to his basic theological approach when he says that it is ignorance of Christ that makes Muhammad do this, and ignorance of the true Gospel: "If only you had known how to read and write and had studied at least the short canonical epistle of that most beloved disciple of Christ, the evangelist John, then surely you would have been free of laboring on the Koran and would have found repose in that [Johannine] light of truth."[67] Nicholas notes that the Qur'ān says religious plurality is willed by God, so he wonders why Muhammad and his followers act differently from what God commanded them to do. In the end, he addresses the sultan of Babylon (Mehmet II) who also denied his Christian faith in order to become powerful. He summons the sultan to restore the honor of Christ and his mother, like so many emperors of Constantinople before him did. He closes this address to the sultan with an argument that calls the hermeneutic procedure of faithful interpretation to mind for the last time.

> The time is to come (as was stated earlier on the basis of the Koran) when there will be only the faith of Christ. Begin to draw near [to this faith] and all the princes of the earth and of that [Muslim] sect will follow you. Then there will be said: 'Behold, God permitted evil things to be done in order that good things might result.' The faith of the Gospel was despised everywhere by the idolatrous Orientals. The law of the Arabs came as someone unwilling to consent unto the faith [of the Gospel] and it led the Arabs unto the worship of one God; nevertheless, the Gospel was secretly approved [by the Koran]. And now it has pleased God that the approved Gospel, covered over in the Koran by many foolish things, should come to light, even as it was often approved of in [that] same book. In this way, those who previously were the most strongly resistant will be led from the law of the Arabs unto the Gospel—[led] for the glory of the Great God, the King of kings, the Creator and Lord of the universe.[68]

This final passage explains why Nicholas of Cusa wanted to write this book in this context: he hoped to be able to uncover the light of the Gospel from the Qur'ān and in this way convince the sultan to stop the war against the Christians and to seek the peace of faith.

CONCLUSION

It would of course be an anachronism to suggest that we might learn directly from medieval theologians and their approach to Islam. Though some phrases in Nicholas of Cusa may sound surprisingly modern, there is a world of difference between the conditions and the theological presuppositions with which he worked and the modern situation. Yet I think that it is possible to see a faint prefiguration of some of the hermeneutic procedures adopted by modern comparative theologians in the *Cribratio Alkorani*. In his article, "The Role of *Pia Interpretatio* in Nicholas of Cusa's Hermeneutical Approach to the Koran," Hopkins sums up five "exegetical rules" that are applied in this work.[69] They can be summarized as follows: (1) Interpret the Qur'ān in such a way that it is compatible with the Christian Scriptures; (2) try to interpret the Qur'ān in such a way as to render it self-consistent; (3) where the Qur'ān contradicts the Gospel, look for the human author's (Muhammad's) true intention; (4) interpret the Qur'ān as intending to give glory to God without detracting from Christ; and (5) whenever possible, work with the interpretations that the wise among Muslims assign to the Qur'ān.

Theologically speaking, the fourth rule is the most important, since it opens the possibility for a Christian reading of the Qur'ān that does justice to the monotheism that the two religious traditions have in common while not jeopardizing the constitutive role of Christ as God's revealing Word for Christians. In the meantime the fifth rule betrays an awareness that the Qur'ān is the revealing Word of God for Muslims, and that no Christian interpretation that wants to do justice to the religious function of the Qur'ān can bypass the history of Muslim interpretations. These two principles together form the basic principles of a Christian theological reading of the Qur'ān. In his "Sifting of the Qur'ān," Nicholas of Cusa has hidden nuggets of this new theological approach between the abundant remains of the apologetic approach that he could never entirely shake off in the context of his time. It is up to us, living a few centuries later, to sift the insights that guide us to a future of better understanding between Muslims and Christians from between the quicksand that has brought us into such a protracted impasse. It is my contention that a theological understanding of Islam is one of the most important things that we might have learned from the medieval theologians, although they had to work with a knowledge that was so much less than ours. In fact, this places our time in a rather grim prospect: we have so much more knowledge, such superior communication available, and yet the large majority of Christians still settle for a very superficial knowledge of Islam—if they are interested in it at all. Many scholars are able to engage in conversation with Islam, but very few of them are interested in the theological aspects of this conversation, maybe because the obstacles are so enormous and progress seems to be impossible. In hindsight, we can only admire Aquinas and Cusanus for what they were able to attain with their little knowledge of the world of Islam. And we can only be hopeful that Muslim initiatives such as "A Common Word" will encourage us to find new ways to talk theologically across traditional borders.

NOTES

1. The first quotation is from Pat Robertson, founder of the Christian Broadcasting Network and host of the 700 Club, on June 12, 2007, quoted from www.MediaMatters.org, accessed March 3, 2010. The second is from the Dutch politician Geert Wilders in a speech on April 5, 2009, in New York, quoted from www.citizensforaconstitutionalrepublic.com, accessed March 3, 2010.

2. Roger Arnaldez, *A la croisée des trois monotheisms: Une communauté de pensée au Moyen Age* (Paris: Albin Michel, 1993), 8.

3. H. A. Wolfson, *The Philosophy of the Kalam* (Cambridge, MA: Harvard University Press, 1976); David B. Burrell, *Faith and Freedom: An Interfaith Perspective* (Malden, MA: Blackwell, 2004).

4. This theory is based on the testimony of Peter of Marseille, see Marie-Dominique Chenu, *Introduction à la théologie de S. Thomas d'Aquin* (Paris: Vrin, 1950), 247–48.

5. Helmut Hoping, *Weisheit als Wissen des Ursprungs: Philosophie und Theologie in der "Summa contra gentiles" des Thomas von Aquin* (Freiburg: Herder, 1997), 64.

6. Thomas Aquinas, *Summa contra gentiles*, bk I, chap. 2 (*ScG* I.2). Translation *Saint Thomas Aquinas, Summa contra gentiles. Book One: God*, translated with introduction and notes by Anton C. Pegis, FRSC (Notre Dame: University of Notre Dame Press, 1975), 62. The original edition of this translation is from 1955.

7. Muslims do not like the term *Mohammedans* at all, since it would seem to imply that Muhammad has the same place in their religion as Christ has for the Christians. Yet "Mohammedans" was the usual label in the modern period until the second half of the twentieth century.

8. See John of Damascus, *On Heresies*, chap. 100 from his major work, *Fount of Knowledge*. Critical text in R. Le Coz, *Jean Damascène: Écrits sur l'Islam: Présentation, commentaires et traduction*, Sources Chrétiennes 383 (Paris: Cerf, 1992), 41–58. See also Adelbert Davids and Pim Valkenberg, "John of Damascus: The Heresy of the Ishmaelites," in *The Three Rings: Textual Studies in the Historical Trialogue of Judaism, Christianity, and Islam*, ed. Barbara Roggema, Marcel Poorthuis, and Pim Valkenberg. (Leuven: Peeters, 2005), 71–90.

9. Thomas Aquinas, *Summa contra gentiles*, I.6. Translation Pegis, pp. 73–74. This translation uses the older form "Mohammed" for "Muhammad."

10. 1 Pet. 3:15. The *Vulgata* translation has "paratus semper ad satisfactionem omni poscenti ei rationem de ea, quae in nobis est, spe."

11. Quoted from the Papal Archives on the Vatican website: www .vatican.va/holy_father/benedict_xvi/speeches/2006/september/documents/ hf_ben-svi_spe_20060912_university-regensberg_en.html, accessed March 9, 2010.

12. This document, "Loving God and Neighbor Together: A Christian Response to *A Common Word between Us and You*," has recently been published, together with the *Common Word* document itself, in *A Common Word: Muslims and Christians on Loving God and Neighbor*, ed. Miroslav Volf, Ghazi bin Muhammad, and Melissa Yarrington (Grand Rapids, MI: Eerdmans, 2010). Both documents can also be found on the official website www.acommonword.com, accessed March 9, 2010.

13. Quoted from a press release from Zenit.org, dated Paris, October 19, 2007. This article can be found at www.acommonword.com as well.

14. The presentation can be found on the website of "A Common Word" (see above, accessed March 23, 2010) but also on the website of the

Washington National Cathedral, in a section devoted to the Christian-Muslim Summit, March 1–3, 2010, in which Cardinal Tauran was one of the participants: www.nationalcathedral.org/learn/summit2010, accessed January 22, 2010.

15. I quote from the press release published by the Vatican Press Agency. See also the Papal Archives, www.vatican.va/holy_father/benedict _svi/speeches/2008/november/documents/hf_ben-xvi_spe_20081106 _cath-islamic-leaders_en.html, accessed March 28, 2010.

16. Qur'ān 3:3, in the interpretation of Abdullah Yusuf Ali, *The Meaning of the Holy Qur'ān* (Beltsville, MD: Amana Publications, 1427/2006), 126.

17. Abdulaziz Sachedina, "The Qur'ān and Other Religions," in *The Cambridge Companion to the Qur'ān*, ed. Jane Dammen McAuliffe (Cambridge: Cambridge University Press, 2006), 291–309.

18. Jane Dammen McAuliffe, *Qur'ānic Christians: An Analysis of Classical and Modern Exegesis* (Cambridge: Cambridge University Press, 1991), 168.

19. See Roggema, Poorthuis, and Valkenberg, *The Three Rings*, xvi.

20. Among the fiercest critics of Islam on this point is another Dutch politician, Ayaan Hirsi Ali, who now works with the American Enterprise Institute.

21. See, e.g., Qur'ān 37:40–49; 55:46–76.

22. Henk Schoot mentions eight places in which Aquinas contrasts the Christian idea of eternal bliss with the (Jewish and) Muslim idea of an afterlife including physical pleasures: "Christ Crucified Contested: Thomas Aquinas Answering Objections from Jews and Muslims," in Roggema, Poorthuis, and Valkenberg, *The Three Rings*, 141–62 (144).

23. For instance, in his commentary on the final article of faith (*In Symb. Apost.* 11). Also, *Summa contra gentiles* IV.83 (13–14).

24. Schoot, "Christ Crucified Contested," 148–49.

25. The Latin text of *De rationibus fidei* is critically edited as volume XL B of the Leonine edition (Rome, 1968). English translations may be found in *Islamochristiana* 22 (1996): 31–52 (by J. Kenny, OP) and in a small booklet published by the Franciscans of the Immaculate (New Bedford, MA, 2002): *Aquinas on Reasons for Our Faith against the Muslims, Greeks and Armenians*, trans. Fr. Peter Damian Fehlner. This quotation is from Fehlner, p. 21.

26. *De rationibus fidei,* chap. 1; translation Fehlner, p. 20. I have omitted the references to the Qur'ān between brackets in this translation, since they are not part of the original text.

27. Aquinas, *De rationibus fidei*, chap. 3; translation Fehlner, p. 23.

28. Aquinas, *De rationibus fidei*, chap. 5; translation Fehlner, p. 32.

29. Anselm of Canterbury, *Cur Deus homo*, bk I, chap. 21.

30. Aquinas, *De rationibus fidei*, chap. 7: *Suscepimus autem praesentem disputationem ad eos qui se Dei cultores dicunt, sive sunt Christiani, sive Saraceni, sive Iudaei.* Translation Fehlner, p. 47.

31. Part of the text on Nicholas of Cusa has been presented at the second conference of the European Society for Intercultural Theology and Interreligious Studies, "Interreligious Hermeneutics," Salzburg, Austria, April 2009. See Pim Valkenberg, "Sifting the Qur'ān: Two Forms of Interreligious Hermeneutics in Nicholas of Cusa," in *Interreligious Hermeneutics in Pluralistic Europe*, ed. David Cheetham et al. (Amsterdam: Rodopi, 2011), 27–48.

32. See Jasper Hopkins, *Nicholas of Cusa's "De pace fidei" and "Cribratio Alkorani": Translation and Analysis* (Minneapolis: Arthur J. Banning Press, 1990), 3.

33. *De pace fidei* 1.1; translation Hopkins, p. 33.

34. *De pace fidei* 1.6; translation Hopkins, p. 35.

35. See G. D'Costa, ed., *Christian Uniqueness Reconsidered: The Myth of a Pluralistic Theology of Religions* (Maryknoll, NY: Orbis Books, 1990); G. D'Costa, *The Meeting of Religions and the Trinity* (Maryknoll, NY: Orbis Books, 2000); S. Mark Heim, *Salvations: Truth and Difference in Religions* (Maryknoll, NY: Orbis Books, 1995); S. Mark Heim, *The Depth of the Riches: A Trinitarian Theology of Religious Ends* (Grand Rapids, MI: Eerdmans, 2001).

36. James L. Fredericks, *Faith among Faiths: Christian Theology and Non-Christian Religions* (Mahwah, NJ: Paulist Press, 1999); Francis X. Clooney, SJ, *Comparative Theology: Deep Learning across Religious Borders* (Malden, MA: Wiley Blackwell, 2010).

37. See my *Sharing Lights on the Way to God: Muslim-Christian Dialogue and Theology in the Context of Abrahamic Partnership*, Currents of Encounter 26 (Amsterdam: Rodopi, 2006); also "Das Konzept der Offenbaring im Islam aus der Perspektive Komparativer Theologie," in *Komparative Theologie: Interreligiöse Vergleiche als Weg der Religionstheologie*, Beiträge zu einer Theologie der Religionen 7, ed. Reinhold Bernhardt and Klaus von Stosch (Zurich: Theologischer Verlag, 2009), 123–45.

38. For the *Cribratio Alkorani* I have used the critical edition by Ludwig Hagemann, *Nicolai de Cusa Cribratio Alkorani*, Edidit commentariisque illustravit Ludovicus Hagemann, Nicolai de Cusa Opera Omnia VIII (Hamburg: Felix Meiner, 1986). English translation Hopkins, pp. 75–185.

39. See James Biechler, "Interreligious Dialogue," in *Introducing Nicholas of Cusa: A Guide to a Renaissance Man*, ed. Christopher M. Bellitto, Thomas M. Izbicki, and Gerald Christianson (Mahwah, NJ: Paulist Press, 2004), 270–96 (279). Also, Pim Valkenberg, "One Faith, Different Rites: Nicholas of Cusa's New Awareness of Religious Pluralism," in *Understand-*

ing Religious Pluralism: Perspectives from Religious Studies and Theology, ed. Peter C. Phan and Jonathan Ray (Eugene, OR: Pickwick Publications, 2014), 192–208; Pim Valkenberg, *"Una Religio in Rituum Varietate:* Religious Pluralism, the Qur'an, and Nicholas of Cusa," in *Nicholas of Cusa and Islam: Polemic and Dialogue in the Late Middle Ages,* ed. Ian Christopher Levy et al. (Leiden: Brill, 2014) 30–48.

40. See Ludwig Hagemann's introduction in his edition of the *Cribratio Alkorani,* p. x.

41. Hopkins, *Nicholas of Cusa's "De pace fidei" and "Cribratio Alkorani,"* 66.

42. *Cribratio Alkorani* prologue, 4; translation Hopkins, p. 76.

43. *Cribratio Alkorani* prologue, 10; translation Hopkins, pp. 78–79.

44. *Cribratio Alkorani* I 1.23.

45. Norman Daniel, *Islam and the West: The Making of an Image* (Edinburgh, 1960; Oxford: Oneworld, 1993), 13. For John of Damascus, see Davids and Valkenberg, "John of Damascus: The Heresy of the Ishmaelites," 78.

46. *Cribratio Alkorani* I 2.27; translation Hopkins, p. 88.

47. See the edition by Hagemann, p. 223.

48. *Cribratio Alkorani* I 4.32.

49. *Cribratio Alkorani* I 6.40–41.

50. *Cribratio Alkorani* I 7.44; translation Hopkins, p. 96.

51. *Cribratio Alkorani* I 7.44; translation Hopkins, p. 96.

52. *Cum quis legit vitam Mahumeti, quae in Alkorano scribitur* (Hagemann, p. 40) may refer not to the Qur'ān itself but to the volume of the *Corpus Toletanum* that Nicholas had before his eyes when writing the *Cribratio Alkorani.* He frequently refers to the *Liber generationis Mahumet* that contains, among others, a description of the life of the prophet Muhammad.

53. This is not so different from the Christological exegesis of the Psalms and other books of the Hebrew Bible where some places are said to refer explicitly and truly to Christ if they are quoted in the New Testament, even though they may literally refer to David. In Thomas Aquinas, for instance, this leads to a similar inconsistency as to the necessity of Christological exegesis of the Psalms. See Henk Schoot and Pim Valkenberg, "Thomas Aquinas and Judaism," in *Aquinas in Dialogue: Thomas for the Twenty-First Century,* ed. Jim Fodor and Frederick Christian Bauerschmidt (Malden, MA: Blackwell, 2004), 47–66.

54. *Cribratio Alkorani* I 11.57; translation Hopkins, p. 102.

55. *Cribratio Alkorani* I 13.62.

56. See Ludwig Hagemann, *Christentum contra Islam: Eine Geschichte gescheiterter Beziehungen* (Darmstadt: Primus Verlag, 1999), 69. "eine aus christlicher Sicht wohlwollende, gutmütige und weitherzige Auslegung des Korans."

57. Jasper Hopkins, *A Miscellany on Nicholas of Cusa* (Minneapolis: Arthur J. Banning Press, 1994), 51–54.

58. Pim Valkenberg, "Learned Ignorance and Faithful Interpretation of the Qur'an in Nicholas of Cusa (1401–1464)," in *Learned Ignorance: Intellectual Humility among Jews, Christians, and Muslims*, ed. James L. Heft, S.M., Reuven Firestone, and Omid Safi (Oxford: Oxford University Press, 2011), 34–52 (45).

59. *Cribratio Alkorani* II 1.86; translation Hopkins, p. 115.

60. *Cribratio Alkorani* II.1.88: *Tunc certe, cum excedat omnem sensum et omnem intellectum et omne nomen et omne nominabile, nec dicitur unus nec trinus nec bonus nec sapiens nec pater nec filius nec spiritus sanctus et ita de omnibus, quae dici aut cogitari possunt, uti Dionysius Areopagita hoc astruit, quoniam omnia talia nomina excellit et antecedit in infinitum.* A very similar phrase can be found in *De docta ignorantia* I.26; see Valkenberg, "Learned Ignorance and Faithful Interpretation," 46.

61. *Cribratio Alkorani* II 13.124; translation Hopkins, p. 132.

62. *Cribratio Alkorani* II 19.154–55; translation Hopkins, p. 147.

63. *Cribratio Alkorani* II 19.158; translation Hopkins, p. 149.

64. Cusanus refers to the qur'ānic injunction, "Let there be no compulsion in religion," 2:256.

65. *Cribratio Alkorani* III 6.180–81; translation Hopkins, p. 160.

66. *Cribratio Alkorani* III 8.184.

67. *Cribratio Alkorani* III 11.197; translation Hopkins, p. 168.

68. *Cribratio Alkorani* III 17.223; translation Hopkins, p. 181.

69. Hopkins, *A Miscellany on Nicholas of Cusa*, 45–50.

Chapter Six

THE HUMANITY OF THEOLOGY

Aquinian Reflections on the Presumption and Despair
in the Human Claim to Know God

ANSELM K. MIN

PRESUMPTION, DESPAIR, AND HOPE IN THEOLOGY

According to the classical tradition of Aristotle and St. Thomas virtue
lies in the mean. Intellectual virtues are perfections of the intellect,
moral virtues those of appetites or passions, but both kinds consist in
conformity with the rule or measure of right reason. We can deviate
from this measure by either excess or deficiency, by either exceeding
the measure or falling short of it. The idea of virtue as a mean, however, is a little complicated when it is applied to theological virtues
like faith, hope, and charity. While moral and intellectual virtues respectively perfect our passions and our intellect in relation to a created rule or measure as determined by right reason, theological virtues perfect them in relation to an uncreated rule or measure, God
himself in his divine truth, which measures our faith; the immensity
of his omnipotence and loving kindness, which measures our hope;
and his divine goodness, which measures our charity. Still, St. Thomas
distinguishes, as he does on so many occasions, between considering
them "in relation to us" and "in relation to God." In relation to God,
who is infinite, we cannot believe, hope in, or love God too much, as

we are invited to believe, hope in, and love God as God ought to be believed, hoped in, and loved, that is, always more. Unlike the moral and intellectual virtues, the good of theological virtues does not consist in a mean. In relation to us, however, it makes sense to speak of a mean and extremes. Although we cannot approach God as God ought to be approached in his infinity, we should still approach him "according to the measure of our condition [*secundum mensuram nostrae conditionis*]" (I–II, 64, 4).[1] In this "accidental" sense and in relation to us, we can speak of the extremes of presumption and despair in the case of the virtue of hope. We are guilty of presumption when we hope to receive from God "a good in excess of our condition" by "presuming above our capability," and of despair when we fail to "hope for what according to our condition we might hope for" by "despairing of things of which we are capable" (II–II, 17, 5).

In this chapter I want to mix categories. Presumption and despair belong to the category of hope, indicating its excess and its deficiency respectively, whereas theology and its mode of knowing belong to the category of faith. I begin by assuming that it makes sense to ask whether theology can fail by the excess of hope, presumption, and by its deficiency, despair. I claim that many theologies today are guilty of presumption, as many are guilty of despair, in the mode and degree of their claim to know God. Rationalist theologies are presumptuous theologies by claiming to know God "in excess of our condition"; skeptical theologies, whether atheistic or fideistic, are despairing theologies that "despair of things of which we are capable" and fail to "hope for what according to our condition we might hope for."

What does it mean to do theology with hope, and what is the "measure of our condition" by which to distinguish hope from presumption and despair in matters of theology? As a mode of knowing, theology is a relation between the human knower and the divine known. What is legitimate to hope for in the human knowledge of God, then, depends on the nature and limits of human knowledge with regard to God and what it is legitimate to hope for beyond such limits by virtue of the "immensity of God's omnipotence and loving kindness." As a mode of the human knowledge of God as the ultimate end and salvation of human existence, theology uses reason to the limit in its desire to know God insofar as God is knowable through his created effects of nature, and reflects on the content of revelation accepted in faith with regard to what goes beyond that limit insofar as it is revealed in the created effects of grace. Theology is the joint operation of reason and faith.

What, then, does it mean to speak of a hoping theology, a theology of hope, as opposed to presumptuous and despairing theologies? (It should be clear that I am not talking about a theology of hope in Moltmann's political sense but in the sense of a permanent characteristic of the human capacity and desire to know God.) A theology is a genuinely hoping theology if it truly respects the nature and limits of the human knowledge of God and hopes for divine self-revelation through a readiness to believe, that is, through faith, for what goes beyond that limit. This is the "measure of our condition." A theology is presumptuous when it oversteps the nature and limits of human reason—"in excess of our condition"—and seeks to reduce the mystery of God to the dimensions of human rationality; it has no room for hope in God because it already knows God as God can be known in himself. By the same token a theology is despairing when it underestimates the nature and limits of human reason and despairs of the human knowledge of God by denying the possibility of knowing God even within the limits of human reason—"despairing of things of which we are capable" and failing to "hope for what according to our condition we might hope for" by resorting to atheism, agnosticism, and philosophical fideism, or by denying the possibility of using human reason in the elaboration of the revealed content of faith as in theological fideism.

The central question in this chapter, then, is whether a theology is willing to go all the way to the limit of human knowledge, without stopping short, remain open in hope to the beckoning light of revelation, ready to accept it in faith, and then perform its humble human service of making the content of revelation not indeed intrinsically intelligible but at least humanly plausible, without claiming to attain the knowledge of God in his own incomprehensible essence. Is a theology ready to stay true to its humanity, neither overestimating its power to know God and reducing God to its own measure and image and denying its need for revelation nor underestimating its power to know God even within its own limits and its own graced ability to serve the knowledge of God in faith? Is a theology aware of its own humanity, and does it remain faithful to that humanity? Does it remain in the very tensive and precarious middle of true humanity between the presumption to know God in his own essence and the despair of knowing anything of God at all?

I want to do two things here. First, I take the example of the theology of St. Thomas as a model of a theology fully aware of its own humanity and faithful to that humanity despite the temptations to presumption and despair. I present in brief outline the essentials of his theory of the human knowledge of God, its nature, its limits, and its need for revelation, and touch on his hylomorphic theory of human knowledge, his analogical approach to the knowledge of God, and his conception of the relation between reason and faith. This first part largely comprises exegesis of St. Thomas. Second, I present examples of presumptuous rationalism and despairing agnosticism and fideism from our contemporary world: Alvin Plantinga's Reformed epistemology, D. Z. Phillips's Wittgensteinian theory of forms of life, Richard Swinburne's analytic theism, Karl Rahner's transcendental theology, Whitehead's process theism, and the post/phenomenological theologies of Levinas and Marion. I am not going into the examples of obvious atheists, old or new. I reflect on the difficulty and precariousness and at the same time the compelling necessity of preserving the humanity of theology in its tensive human middle as a creature created in the image of the creator and therefore always seeking to imitate the divine exemplar, often presuming to reduce God to its own dimensions, often despairing to know God at all. Kierkegaard once said that human beings are a tensive unity of finite and infinite, temporal and eternal, and that it takes passion to maintain this unity without dissolving it into the aestheticism of the finite or the pantheism of the infinite. Kierkegaard called that passion faith.[2] I would call it hope as well. Theology too is bound by this structural tension of human existence, and it needs to be reminded of its own humanity again and again, especially in our time.

THE NATURE AND LIMITS OF THE HUMAN
KNOWLEDGE OF GOD ACCORDING TO ST. THOMAS

It is essential to know something of the metaphysics of St. Thomas in order to understand his theory of the capacities and limits of the human intellect in relation to God. There are two metaphysical principles that govern his theory of knowledge. The first is that the knower can know only according to the kind of being or nature of the knower or what the knower is. *Quidquid cognoscitur cognoscitur secundum modum cognoscentis.* To know is to act, and to act is to express something of the essence, nature, or mode of being (*modus essendi*) of the agent. An agent can only act according to the kind of being or essence it is. It cannot act or know beyond or otherwise than its essence. The known exists in the knower according to the mode of the knower, not according to its own mode. The apple that I know exists in me, not as a physical apple, but as my concept of apple. What the knower is capable of knowing in this way depends on her mode of being, on her capacity to receive the form of the other into herself and be united with that other, not physically, but immaterially.

The second metaphysical principle is that knowledge requires a certain connaturality or proportion between the modes of being of the knower and the known. The human soul through which we know is the form of a body, and it is "connatural" or "proportionate" to that soul to know material things that have their *esse* only in individuated matter. The senses, one of the two cognitive powers of the human soul, are acts of corporeal organs, and it is connatural to the senses to know singular material things, while it is connatural to the intellect, the other human cognitive power, which is not an act of a corporeal organ, to know natures that have their *esse* only in individual matter but not as they exist in individual matter but as abstracted from such matter through an intellectual operation. Through the intellect we can transcend individuated matter and know the universal. The angels or incorporeal substances do not have their *esse* in matter, and it is proper to them to know natures that do not exist in matter. Still, their nature is not to *be* their own *esse* but only to *have* their *esse,* as is the nature of all created beings in whom essence and existence are really distinct and whose *esse,* therefore, is not subsistent. To know God as the subsistent *esse* itself is not proportionate or connatural to either humans or angels or any other created beings but only to the divine intellect. Indeed, only God knows God. It is not possible for any created intellect to see God on the basis of its own essence unless God unites himself to the created intellect through grace and makes himself intelligible to that intellect (I, 12, 4; I, 84, 7; I, 84, 8; I, 85, 1).

Let's see in some detail how St. Thomas applies this general metaphysics of knowledge to the case of the human knowledge of God. How human beings know depends on what they are. Human beings are souls informing their bodies and their bodies essentially animated and made human by their souls. Human beings are not bodies and souls externally put together but hylomorphic unities where the powers of the soul pervade the body, making it alive precisely as human, not just animal, bodies. The interaction between body and soul, therefore, is more intimate than even internal relations, which still preserve to some extent the independent existence of the things related. Neither the soul nor the body, at least in this world, exists independently of each other. Just as the body is a body only insofar as it is informed by the soul in a relationship of potentiality and actuality, the soul is likewise a human soul only when it informs the body. This hylomorphic composition of the human being also entails that the human intellect too is intrinsically dependent on the body for all its functions. It is because of this essential dependence of the intellect on the body that St. Thomas denies the existence of innate ideas, as he also rejects Plato's theory of Forms and Avicenna's theory of one agent intellect for all human beings, through which somehow the human intellect can attain knowledge independently of the body.

For St. Thomas the human intellect derives all its knowledge from sense experience. Material things must first act on the senses and actualize and specify them to sense this or that object in its singularity by means of the sensible species or forms. Out of these sensible forms received from material things the imagination elaborates generalized images of things from which the human intellect abstracts concepts of things. The human intellect depends on the imagination and the images or phantasms it produces on the basis of sense experience for all phases of its activity, for apprehending concepts, making judgments about things, and the many movements of reasoning from one knowledge to another. The imagination and the images are the permanent foundations and material bases for all human intellectual activities. Without images there is no basis for abstracting concepts of things. Without a conversion to the phantasms or images there is no human intellectual activity, which can indeed transcend the images but only in and through them because the human intellect has no independent source of insight into the essences of things apart from what is given in the senses and their images. The only intuition available for the human intellect is sensible, not intellectual. Human knowledge, for St. Thomas, is literally "fantastic" and is based on phantasms or images, models, and pictures. Long before Kant and our recent talk of models and images, St. Thomas recognized the essential dependence of the human intellect on the images produced by the imagination, the importance of the role that models play in our understanding of things, including God, and the role of the creative imagination in providing impetus for our intellectual activities.[3]

Just as the hylomorphic unity of human nature requires the essential dependence of the human intellect on the senses and the imagination, it also defines the limit of all human knowledge. The human intellect has the power to abstract universals from the concrete particularity of matter. It can abstract universal concepts from individual matter, for example, this flesh and this bone; intelligible matter or mathematical quantities like number, dimension, and figure from sensible matter; and concepts such as being, unity, power, act, and the like from common intelligible matter. That is, the human intellect can abstract and transcend the particularity of matter through the abstraction of concepts of things, the sensibility of matter through the abstraction of mathematical concepts such as quantities and shapes, and the materiality of matter itself through the abstraction of the metaphysical concepts of being, unity, power, act, and so on. The human intellect is capable of these different degrees of abstraction, but by the same token it also presupposes the material of knowledge given in and through the senses and the imagination, without which the active intellect has nothing to work on to produce various concepts and without which it has no object to illuminate and make intelligible by means of its intellectual light (I, 84, 6). The first object of the human intellect is being, truth, goodness, and so on, but in this life it is limited to these only as considered in and abstracted from material things (I, 87, 3).

This is to say that the proper object of human knowledge required by the principle of connaturality or proportion between knower and known is the quiddity or nature concretely given in material things. Just as human nature is a composite of matter and form, so the proportionate object of human knowledge is the composite of matter and form or the form, nature, or quiddity given in the particularity of matter. This does not mean that human beings can know only material things and their essences. It does mean that there is no proper knowledge of immaterial things of which there is no image or phantasm, and that human beings can know nonmaterial things only in comparison to material things or by negating material things. The capacity to abstract from and thereby transcend the particularity of matter makes conceptual knowledge as well as mathematical and metaphysical knowledge possible, but these forms of intellectual knowledge are results of abstractions from materiality, not demonstrations or promises of intellectual intuitions into the essences of things apart from their materiality. The human soul, as Aristotle once said, is indeed "somehow all things [*quoddammodo omnia*]" and open to all things, but is so only as subject to material conditions as an essentially hylomorphic being. This is the nature and limits of all human knowledge and also defines the humanity of theology, its nature and its limits.

The two principles of Thomistic knowledge, the principle of the human mode of the knower and the principle of proportion between the knower and the known, mean that the human intellect cannot fully or perfectly understand immaterial substances in the present state of life because these are disproportionate to the human mind, which has no images or phantasms of immaterial substances from which to abstract their nature so as to understand them (I, 88, 1).

Through the quiddity of material things, no matter how hard we may try to abstract from material things, we can never arrive at anything akin to immaterial substances in their positive, essential, inner reality (I, 88, 2). This does not mean we can know nothing about angels. We can know them indirectly by negating materiality, and by their relation to material things. Created immaterial substances do not belong to the same natural genus as material substances, but they do belong to the same logical genus in the sense that they too belong to the category of finite substances in which there is a real distinction between their essence and their existence. This gives us some positive knowledge of angels as finite creatures, although not according to their specific nature. God, however, is above all genera and species, which makes it impossible to know God even in the way and to the degree that we can know finite immaterial substances (I, 88, 2 ad 4).

This does not mean that God is in himself unknown or unknowable. God is infinitely knowable of himself and to himself but not to us because of the weakness of the human intellect, which in the present state has a natural aptitude only for material objects and can know God only through material effects (I, 86, 2). This defect will be removed in the state of glory, in which we will indeed see the essence of God himself but without comprehending him to the full extent of his infinite knowability (I, 86, 2).

Over against those who are tempted to argue that the knowledge of God is self-evident or that God is the first object known by the human mind, St. Thomas insists that in the present state of life our intellect has trouble understanding even created immaterial substances, and still more the essence of the uncreated divine substance. The first object of human knowledge is the quiddity of a material thing, and we know all other things including God only through, by means of, and in comparison to material things. There is a sense in which we know God as the first object of human knowledge, and the sense is that we do see and judge all things in light of the first truth inasmuch as the light of the human mind itself is nothing else than the impression of the first truth on it. This means that God is the first object of human knowledge only in the indirect sense of the light or horizon of all human knowledge, the medium *by which* we understand all things,

not that God is the first direct object of human knowledge, just as the
light of our intellect is not the direct object it understands but only
the medium *by which* it understands all other things. As such, God in
himself remains the incomprehensible horizon of all human knowledge. Likewise, the existence of truth in general is self-evident, but the
existence of the first truth is not self-evident to the human intellect.
Our mind may also be the image of God, but it is hardly a perfect
image, which the Son alone is. An imperfect image does not give us a
perfect knowledge of its exemplar (I, 88, 3; I, 2, 1).

St. Thomas does not deny that we have some general, confused
knowledge of God implanted in our very nature as our ultimate happiness. It is our nature to seek happiness and do so because it has
some natural inkling of what it is, but this is hardly to know that God
exists, any more than knowing that someone is coming is the same as
knowing that it is Peter who is coming. With regard to our ultimate
happiness, some identify it with wealth, others with pleasure, still
others with many other things. God does constitute the ultimate happiness of human nature, but this does not make God self-evident
(I, 2, 1).

It is crucial to recall the important distinction St. Thomas makes
between what is self-evident (*per se notum*) in itself (*secundum se*) but
not to us (*quoad nos*) and what is self-evident both in itself and to us.
We can say that those propositions are self-evident when the predicate is included in the concept (*ratio*) of the subject, but such propositions become self-evident to us only if we know what the subject
and predicate are, that is, only if we know the essence of the subject
and predicate (*quid sit*). Thus the proposition that God exists is self-
evident in itself because the predicate is the same as the subject, because God is his own *esse,* but because we do not know what God is
(*quid sit*), God's existence is not self-evident to us but is in need of
demonstration by means of things that are better known to us, that is,
by God's effects. For St. Thomas the knowledge that God is his own
esse, that in God essence and existence coincide, is itself a knowledge
of God known through his created effects, not a positive knowledge
of God's essence in itself. To know with Anselm that God is "that
than which nothing greater can be thought" is hardly to know the

divine essence in itself in its positive, essential, inner reality. If we "see" the divine essence, we will also "see" why God's existence necessarily follows from that essence, but we do not "see" that essence. Here below we are not gifted with a knowledge of God that is self-evident or intuitive into the divine essence in itself (I, 2, 1).

This has a far-reaching consequence on our knowledge of God. Here again, St. Thomas lays down an important principle: Just as whatever is known is known according to the mode of the knower, so "everything is named by us according to our knowledge of it" (I, 13, prologue). Names or words are signs of our conceptions and understandings of things. What kind of a name we can give to God thus depends on what we can understand of God. Insofar as in this life we cannot see the essence of God, do not understand the essence of God in itself, and possess no conception of the divine essence as such, we have no words or names with which to describe God's essence. God remains incomprehensible and thus unnameable as far as his essence itself is concerned. This does not mean that we can know or say nothing about God. Not at all. We can still know and name God from creatures, the only source of our knowledge of God, affirming what God must be as the creative cause of the very being of all created things, then negating and purifying that affirmation of what belongs to the imperfection of creatures, and then again affirming the pure perfections of God by way of excellence. In this case we should also remember that our names do not express the divine essence in itself, even though they do really refer to the reality of God as known by created effects. We can know and name God as much as created effects can reveal God.

That we can know and name God only from material creatures whose knowledge alone is connatural and proportionate to us as human beings also imposes limitations on the names we attribute to God. Because of the essential distinction between existence and essence in all finite beings, subsistent finite beings are compounds of essence and existence while their forms or essences are not things subsistent in themselves but only the constitutive principles of their being, that is, those *by which* things are what they are. In order to refer to a complete subsistent thing, then, we can only use concrete names taken from compound things, and in order to refer to simple forms we can only use abstract names taken from principles of being. Although God is simple, not compound, and his essence is subsistent, not a principle of being, we can only use concrete names to refer to his substance and perfection and abstract names based on forms to express her simplicity. The language of material objects is the only language available to hylomorphic beings. We have to remember that neither concrete nor abstract names express God's essence (I, 13, 1).

This raises an important question. If our names do not express God's essence, just what do they express? When we name God as good, does it only mean that God is not evil or that God is the cause of goodness, without being good in himself? St. Thomas gives a twofold answer to this question. Negative names, like simplicity and immutability, and names signifying relations to creatures, like creator and redeemer, do not signify his substance or essence at all but only the distance of the creature from God or the relations of creatures to God. Divine simplicity means the distance of the creature as a compound being from God, while being creator or redeemer means the dependence of the creatures on God for their existence or redemption. For St. Thomas, to say that God is living does not mean the mere negation that God is not an inanimate being, and to say that God is good does not mean that God is only the cause of the good in created things. There are three reasons for disputing these interpretations. They do not explain why some names are more appropriate to God than others. If to say that God is good means no more than that God is the cause of goodness, why not also say that God is a body since God is also the cause of bodies? This would also deprive all names applied to God of their primary meaning, like calling medicine healthy because it is the cause of health. Nor is this our intention when we say that God is living; we certainly mean more than that God is the cause of our life or that God is not a dead thing.

What, then, do the positive names signify? For St. Thomas, the names express God only in the way that the human intellect can know him, but the human intellect can know him only insofar as creatures represent him. Now, God possesses all the perfections of creatures in himself, and every creature represents God and is like God to the extent that it possesses some perfection, but it does not represent God as something of the same species or genus. God is above all species and all genera. It only represents God "as the excelling principle [*sicut excellens principium*] of whose form the effects fall short, although they derive some kind of likeness thereto" (I, 13, 2). Those names do signify the divine substance but only imperfectly as created effects represent the divine substance only imperfectly. Thus when we say God is good, it does not mean either that God is not evil or that God is the cause of goodness. It means that whatever good we attribute to creatures preexists in God according to a higher mode (*secundum modum altiorem*), in a more eminent mode (*eminentiori modo*) than can be understood or signified. It is because God is good in himself that he can cause goodness in things, not the other way around. Those absolute, positive names do signify God himself, his essence, but do so only imperfectly.

This is an important point to remember. That we do not see God's essence in this life is not to say that we do not know God himself at all. We do know God himself, God's essence indeed, but only as imperfectly as created effects can reveal that essence. It still remains true, then, that "in this life we cannot know God's essence as it is in itself but know it as it is represented in the perfections of creatures" (I, 13, 2 ad 3). Our names signify God only in a similar way, as our naming only follows our understanding. *The proper distinction, then, is not between knowing God in his essence and knowing God in his effects but between knowing God's essence in itself and knowing God's essence as revealed in creatures.* In both instances we do know something of God's essence, in one case in itself, in the other as known through its effects. This is crucial to remember. Philosophers and theologians often distinguish, as I have been doing so far, between knowing God in his essence and knowing God in his effects, but this is a misleading shorthand for the proper distinction between knowing God's essence as knowable in itself and knowing God's essence as knowable through its effects. In both instances it is God himself, who God really is, that is, his own essence, that is known, the only question being whether that essence is known in itself or through something other than itself, its created effects. Even the created effects reveal something of God himself, who God really is, God's own essence; all agents produce something similar to themselves (*omne agens agit simile sibi*). The distinction only reminds us of the infinite distance between God and creatures.

For St. Thomas, we know God only as the cause of the perfections of creatures, which exist in God in a more eminent way. The human intellect apprehends the perfections as they exist in creatures and signifies them through words precisely as it apprehends them. Here it is crucial to distinguish between two things, the signified perfections themselves (*res significata*) such as goodness, life, knowledge, and love and the mode of signifying (*modus significandi*). As far as the signified perfections are concerned, these apply primarily (*per prius*) and more properly (*magis proprie*) to God than to creatures, but as regards the mode of signification, they properly apply to creatures, not to God. Names that include the imperfect mode of participating in divine perfections as part of their signification, such as stone, which signifies a material being, apply to God only metaphorically. Pure perfections or names that signify the perfections themselves absolutely, that is, without including a reference to the finite mode of participating in the divine perfections, such as being, good, and life, apply to God properly. Names that contain materiality in their very meaning apply to God only metaphorically, but names that contain materiality only in the mode of signification but not in the perfections signified can apply to God properly, like knowledge, life, and goodness (I, 13, 3).

This distinction between perfections signified and the mode of signification is crucial to understanding St. Thomas's conception of analogical predication. First of all, is univocal predication possible between God and creatures? The answer is no. All agents produce effects similar to themselves, but where the effects do not equal the power of the agent there is a difference in the way perfections exist in the cause and in the way they exist in the effects, that is, in their modes of signification. They exist in the cause in a united and identical way but in the effects in a divided and manifold way (*divisim et multipliciter*). In the case of the creative relation between God and creatures, the perfections preexist in God in a united and simple way (*unite et simpliciter*) but in creatures in a divided and multiple way. Thus when a name expressing a perfection is applied to creatures, it signifies that perfection as something distinct from other perfections. For example, when we call a human being wise, we signify that wisdom as something distinct from her essence, her power, her existence, and other perfections such as good, beautiful, and just. When we apply wisdom to God, however, we do not signify anything distinct from God's essence, existence, or other perfections. This also means that names applied to creatures not only circumscribe but also comprehend the reality signified, whereas names applied to God leave the reality signified as uncomprehended and as transcending their finite mode of signification. That is to say, it is impossible to apply names univocally or in the same way to God and creatures.

This does not mean that names are applied to God and creatures in a purely equivocal sense. This would make any knowledge of God from creatures simply impossible as well as expose any inference to the fallacy of equivocation.

This leaves only analogical predication or naming according to proportion, relation, or order. We can talk about the relation of many to one, as when we speak of healthy medicine and healthy urine in relation to the health of a body, or about the relation of one to another, as when we speak of healthy medicine and a healthy animal where the medicine is the cause of the health of the animal. In the same way we can predicate names of God and creatures analogically because God is the cause of creatures and because creatures are ordered to God as to a principle and cause, in which all the perfections of creatures pre-exist excellently. This mode of community of perfections is the middle point between pure equivocation and simple univocation. The meaning or *ratio* of the name is not one as in univocation or totally different as in equivocation. The name is applied in different ways according to the multiplicity of relations to some one thing in the way that health is predicated of urine as a sign of health and of medicine as its cause (I, 13, 5).

Let me now summarize the three moments of analogical predication. The first moment is the moment of causality. All agents produce something similar to themselves as they express something of themselves in their actions. Insofar as creation expresses something of God, we can predicate created perfections of God as their cause, knowing that such perfections preexist in God. Short of the intuition into the essence of God in itself, this way of causality is the only way of theological predication. The second moment is the moment of negation. The infinite distance between finite beings and God as the cause of their being means that we cannot predicate created perfections of God without denying their materiality and their finite mode of signification. Once these created perfections have been purified of their materiality and finitude, they can, as pure perfections, apply to God in a more eminent mode, although we can neither conceptualize nor visualize the divine mode in which these perfections properly belong to God, where they exist in a united and simple way, not in the way of division and multiplicity proper to finite beings.

It is essential to remember that analogical predication involves all three moments. Without the moment of causality, there is no ground for predicating anything of God. No affirmation would be possible about God. Without the moment of negation and purification predication becomes mythological and ideological, a mere projection of human ideals and aspirations, exactly as Feuerbach reduces all theology to anthropology. Without the moment of eminence we reduce God to a merely supreme being, one object among others who happens to be the highest, without infinite qualitative ontological difference.[4] Often analogy is understood only as similarity, without negation and eminence, and therefore as univocity in disguise. No wonder that it is often dismissed as the "invention of the Anti-Christ" (Barth) trying to reconstruct God out of the similarities with the creature and ultimately to reduce God to a creature, a most disastrous misunderstanding. Analogical predication involves not only affirmation but also negation and eminence. Only the three moments together constitute analogical predication. Just as without negation and eminence analogical predication is reduced to univocity, so without affirmation and eminence it is reduced to equivocity.

Analogical predication is a movement of the human mind trying to reach God in a way faithful to its own humanity. Short of self-evidence and intuition into the essence of God in itself, the human knower is left only with the way of moving toward God from finite effects, whether effects of nature or effects of grace. Revelation is no guarantee of an insight into the divine essence in itself. Because effects do reveal something of the cause and finite effects something of the infinite cause, it is possible for human reason to affirm truths about God's existence and the kind of being she is to the extent she is knowable through her created effects. However, precisely because the human mind is limited to the essences of material things as objects of its proper knowledge, it can know God only analogically, not univocally, by negating and purifying its knowledge of God of all material and finite imperfections, and by affirming what it knows of God in a more excellent way without really or properly knowing what it is saying but also stretching itself beyond its natural capacity in the hope of attaining to a being who remains incomprehensible, who can be indicated only as something pointed to without ever being attained.[5]

THE PRESUMPTION AND DESPAIR IN
CONTEMPORARY CLAIMS TO KNOW GOD

Theology is an exercise in claiming to know many things of God, and there are at least five ways, according to my interpretation of St. Thomas, that theology can betray its own humanity by violating the nature and limits of the human knowledge of God.

(1) The first way for theology to betray its humanity is by despairing even of what human reason is capable of and falling into theological tribalism. By "theological tribalism," I mean the tendency to limit access to the knowledge of God to a particular group, that is, those who share the same faith or the same basic belief or the same form of life or the same horizon. While I am not a rationalist in the sense of someone who believes that human reason is in no way conditioned by any sort of interests, perspectives, or form of life, because human reason is indeed so conditioned, I do not believe that this conditioning is absolute or fixed either. My view is much more dialectical

in this regard in the sense that those limiting conditions, communal, economic, political, cultural, or religious, are themselves always exposed and open to changes and that these changes are not just communal, economic, political, cultural, or religious, but also ontological. Among the ontological challenges of life common to all human life regardless of their basic beliefs, subjective horizons, collective ideologies, and common forms of life is the experience of contingency, that nothing is its own existence, that its own essence does not guarantee its own security of being, that our essence as human beings is totally dependent on conditions beyond our control, that all life, all existence in the world is thoroughly transitory and contingent. This sense of the contingency of existence is common to all cultures, although it is interpreted differently. It does provide a common search for a source, ground, and fulfillment of our contingent existence that transcend such transitoriness, for a being who is not a being like us, a being whose essence is to be, a being indeed whose essence we cannot see or comprehend in this world, a being to whom we can only point to as to an ever receding goal, like the finger pointing at the moon without ever reaching or becoming the moon. Our human reason may indeed be very conditioned and even want to remain conditioned and fixed in that state, but it is always exposed to the contingency of being that shakes it up, like the power of Derrida's *différance* that contaminates and disturbs every identity secure of itself.

It is one thing to say that "basic beliefs" (Alvin Plantinga) and "forms of life" (D. Z. Phillips) and even what St. Thomas calls the "light of faith" do sensitize us to God and make us more willing to appreciate and to believe in God, but it is another thing to reduce the reality of God to the validity or authenticity of our basic beliefs and forms of life, as though God is meaningful and relevant only to a certain group who happens to share such basic beliefs and forms of life. This would be theological tribalism that contradicts the very idea of God who is creator of all things in the totality of their being (*esse*) and therefore absolutely relevant to all beings regardless of their particularity, regardless of whether or not they explicitly recognize God as such. God is the immanent teleological source of all created beings enabling them to be, goading them on to transcend themselves, to grope for the source of their being under many different circumstances and in the form of many different religions and forms of life. If God is indeed the one in whom we live, move, and have our being, his relevance cannot be limited to a particular basic belief or form of life. The search for God may be conditioned, even facilitated by basic beliefs and forms of life, and certainly differently expressed in different cultures, but it is not rooted in these beliefs, forms of life, or cultures. It is rooted in the very contingency of existence common to all human beings and indeed to all finite beings as such.[6]

St. Thomas is saying that it is the proper glory of human reason to know and indeed demonstrate the existence and the usual attributes of God. Human reason works better under the light of faith, and there is a basic harmony of the light of nature, the light of faith, and the light of glory, but he is also saying that the light of nature or natural reason is not so specifically tied to the light of faith that only the believing Christians can demonstrate the existence of God. In principle the possibility of knowing God is open to all precisely because all are creatures and experience the nothingness and contingency of their own being as well as their need of an ontological ground and ultimate end, which they do not possess in themselves, although they will do so in many diverse ways.[7]

(2) In addition to despairing of its own capacity to affirm the existence of God on the basis of causality, especially the universal experience of contingency of existence, which constitutes the first moment of analogical predication, theology can betray its own humanity by way of presumption, making such affirmations human reason is indeed capable of but identifying them with the reality of God as such without making the necessary distinction between our human affirmations about God and the divine reality such affirmations are about, between our human concepts of God and the reality of God of which they are concepts. This is a distinction between subjectivity and objectivity, which in some sense applies to all objects: no object is simply reducible to human subjectivity. For obvious reasons it applies all the more to the distinction between our affirmations about God and the reality of God such affirmations are about.

It is crucial to realize that what natural reason "sees" in its demonstrations of the existence and attributes of God is the intelligible necessity of affirming, on the basis of the causal inference from finite creatures, that God exists and that God is the infinite fullness of being responsible for the perfections exemplified in created beings. While natural reason "sees" the intelligible necessity of making these affirmations about God, its conclusion is at the same time the paradoxical one that the divine essence in itself, the infinite fullness of being itself, is precisely something which human reason "cannot" see but in which it can only believe in this world. The intelligible necessity seen by natural reason is that of affirming the truth of the various propositions about God, not the intrinsic intelligibility of the divine realities such propositions are about. Human reason knows that it is necessary to affirm that God exists and that he is infinite, and in this sense sees the necessity of affirming these propositions, but this does not mean that human reason "sees" the actual reality of God existing as an infinite being, which remains an object of faith, not reason. From the effects of God we know that the proposition "that God is" is true, but we do not see that God "is" in the sense of his act of existing (*actus essendi*) (I, 3, 4 ad 2).

This is an important distinction often forgotten by contemporary philosophers and theologians. For many, it seems as though when we make true affirmations about God, these affirmations are all there is about God and that these affirmations are the divine realities themselves, failing to make the crucial distinction between our human affirmations about God and the transcendent reality of God such affirmations are about, and thus reducing these divine realities to our human propositions and concepts, which, as Marion points out, become finite idols which we can manipulate: "As idol, the concept arranges a presence of the divine without distance, in a god who reflects back to us our experience or thought, with enough familiarity that we always master its play."[8] We forget that "God is above everything we can say or think about God" (I, 1, 9), as St. Thomas reminds us again and again. The high point of natural reason is to see that it cannot see the essence of God in itself. The dynamic of so-called natural theology is precisely a dynamic of self-negation and self-transcendence, crying out for completion by faith. Faith is an internal necessity of natural reason itself inherent in the very depth of its own thoroughly natural movement toward something that at the same time transcends its nature.

(3) The third way for theology to betray its own humanity is by insisting on univocal knowledge of God and finite beings and violating the second moment of analogical predication, the moment of distinguishing between the reality signified and the mode of signification and negating the imperfect mode of signification when applying the signified reality to the divine reality. This insistence on univocal predication in principle denies that there might be an essential disproportion between human beings and God, that there might be realities of which human language cannot univocally be predicated. It is a reduction of God to the dimension of human reason, a case of anthropocentrism pure and simple.

This rationalist anthropocentrism can occur in two different ways, explicitly and implicitly. It occurs explicitly when thinkers try to reduce God to his relations to the world and apply a univocal metaphysical rule to both God and the world. For Whitehead, "God is not to be treated as an exception to all metaphysical principles, invoked to save their collapse. He is their chief exemplification."[9] God is the coeternal correlative of the world, not a transcendent creator of the world out of nothing. In the case of Hegel, all things are governed by the dialectic of identity and difference, and God too is subject to the same dialectic in relation to the world to the point that "God is not God without the world."[10] The content of theology is to be "sublated" and reduced to philosophy, that is, dialectical reason, and there is no sense of God's transcendent incomprehensibility. The nature of God is already known. "Mystery" exists only for "representation" and "understanding" but not for "reason."[11] For both Hegel and Whitehead, God may indeed be a supreme being, but he is not an ontologically infinite being transcending all genera and species.

Such anthropocentrism occurs implicitly in many progressive theologies, from liberation theology to feminist theology to postmodern theology, all of which are interested in developing new images or models of God by projecting the prevailing ideals of humanity, be they liberal or conservative. We project our latest ideals into God without negation and eminence, and the result is an image or concept of God who acts as would the most decent human being by contemporary standards, someone who cares and suffers with us, understands us like an intimate friend, governs us with persuasion, not coercion or power, respects us in our autonomy and originality, is related to us as we are related to him, struggling like us by doing the best he can under the circumstances. In short, God acts like the model chairperson of a democratic committee who prefers consultation to domination, multiplicity to unity, participation to sovereignty, equality to distinction, solidarity to independence, relationality to substantiality, and community to isolation. My problem with this is not so much that these are contemporary ideals of human existence, although some are problematic, as that they are projected into God without negation and eminence.

Often we reconstruct the concept of God by projecting our newest aspirations and hopes and then use that very concept of God as justification of what we want to do. So Jürgen Moltmann, for example, reconstructs the concept of God from monotheism to Trinitarianism on the ground that monotheism is the source of oppressive totalitarianism and exhorts us to think in terms of community because the triune God is a community of love. Monotheism is "monarchism," which encourages domination and hierarchy in human relations and "legitimates dependence, helplessness and servitude." We must therefore overcome monarchism in favor of a Trinitarian doctrine of God, which, moreover, "must be developed as the true theological doctrine of freedom." Such a theology of freedom "must for its part point towards a community of men and women without supremacy and without subjection."[12] We project our latest human values into God, and then use that reconstructed God to support what we advocate in the world and to criticize what we do not like in the world. I must say that contemporary theologians are doing their very best to prove Feuerbach absolutely right.

There are two things that are problematic with this procedure. One is the simple projection of our human values onto God without the moment of negation and purification, purification of the human or finite mode of signification. It is a purely univocal predication of divine names, reducing God to a glorified friend, lover, or very democratic manager of the universe without pointing to the infinite ontological difference between the divine reality signified and its human mode of signification. God becomes a merely supreme being, fundamentally one being among beings, indeed the God of ontotheology. This is a simple reduction of theology to anthropology.

The other thing that is problematic is that it applies a purely anthropological criterion to the critique of traditional concepts of God. On this view monotheism is monolatry, based on the worship of the one, and leads to oppression of difference and multiplicity. Power is oppressive and must be discredited as a theological category. Transcendence is bad because it is indifferent to human suffering. I can go on and on. Adherents of this position want to dismiss monotheism, omnipotence, and transcendence because of their oppressive anthropological consequences, but this is simply naive, uncritical, and misinformed. They do not realize that there is not a single category that has not been abused to oppress human beings, including God, love, friendship, compassion, weakness, powerlessness, tolerance, reciprocity, relationality, gift, hospitality, novelty, promise, certainly freedom and democracy, and, yes, even justice.

This involves not only the fallacy of arguing from accidental bad consequences but also the reduction of theological and metaphysical categories to the anthropological and sociological. When classical theology talked about power, it was not primarily a sociological but a metaphysical concept, meaning the power or capacity to be, to act, to realize potentialities (including all the ideals of the modern and postmodern West), each according to its nature or essence, something that stands for the positive perfections such as truth, goodness, beauty. God's power to be or to let be is not primarily the sociological power to dominate others. For Aquinas, divine omnipotence is best (*maxime*) shown in God's power to forgive, have mercy, and lead creatures to a participation in his own infinite good (I, 25, 3). Why would God want to dominate others? Are others competitors with God on the same level, like the United States trying to dominate the world? God's power to be, the *ipsum esse per se subsistens*, is the name of a being who calls beings out of nothingness and enables them to share in the various perfections of existence despite their fundamental nothingness. It is a gracious power to let finite beings be and be themselves with their own essences or intrinsic principles of being. We must remember that a finite being cannot truly let another being be, still less be itself. We all know how difficult it is to let one another be because we thoroughly depend on and need one another for what we want, and yet others are not always behaving in a way we want them to. We are constantly involved in a struggle for power, finding it difficult to let others be. This is the pathos of finite existence. God is not another finite being who has to struggle with other finite beings in an ongoing power struggle to get what he wants. Only the infinite power of God can let beings be and be themselves. One can go on to critique many other modern and postmodern sociological critiques of traditional conceptions of God.

These critiques of tradition are at bottom anthropocentric and anthropomorphic in their fundamental presuppositions, violating the second moment of negation in analogical predication. The moment of negation is a standing warning about all our anthropomorphic, anthropocentric, ideological, reductionist, idolatrous, and therefore ontotheological tendencies that remain constant temptations for theologians. It reminds us that God does remain above all we can say or understand in our human mode of understanding. It is especially relevant today when not only individual theologians but also the collective reason or theology of many religious groups tend to reduce God to their own projections and fanatical ideologies and abuse the name of God in the struggle for power in the world, often justifying unspeakable violence in God's name. Before we claim to have God on our side in an ideological struggle, it is critical to remember that God's judgments are not human judgments, that God's ways are not human ways, which does not mean that God is indifferent to the morality of human actions, individual or collective. The moment of negation calls all of us to critical self-reflection on the morality of our own behavior and deters us from the all too great eagerness to identify our cause with that of God in our individual and collective struggles against others. The true Godness of God calls for a moment of negation and purification in all our attempts to name God.

(4) The fourth way in which theology betrays its humanity is to deny the third moment of analogical predication, the moment of eminence. Theology does this either by claiming an insight into the essence of God or by using the negation of human subjectivity as the criterion of God's transcendence. The first is rather frequent in much analytic discussion of divine attributes. For example, Richard Swinburne argues that we can rationally justify the trinity of God because love seems to require three, not two, borrowing from Richard of St. Victor.[13] This is a direct projection of human love into the interiority of God with little realization of the radical difference between the way finite, dependent, needy human beings love one another and the way the divine persons love one another who at the same time share the numerically identical divine nature.

With some justification I think it is possible to include some aspects of Rahner's transcendental Christology in the category of contemporary theologies that claim an intuition into the essence of God with a complacency and a confidence not disturbed by any analogical reservation of negation and elevation, making a direct argument about what God must be simply on the basis of human arguments. For example, Rahner is well known for trying to show "why precisely the *Logos* of God became man, and why he alone can become man."[14] In dismissing what he thinks is the widespread classical notion that any one of the three divine persons could have become incarnate, he argues that the Word "alone" can become incarnate because the Word is the internal self-expression of God, which alone makes any external self-expression of God possible. It seems as though the logic of internal self-expression in God is so intuitive and self-evident as to necessitate the conclusion that the Word "alone" could have become incarnate. It is revealing to compare Rahner to St. Thomas, who similarly believes that the processions of the immanent Trinity provide the reasons (*rationes*) for creation (I, 45, 6) but who does not thereby deduce the conclusion that the Word "alone" could have become incarnate.

Rather, the Incarnation of the Son was "most fitting (*convenientissimum*), although the Incarnation of another person would have been possible, given God's incomprehensible essence, power, and will.[15]

Others base their denial of certain doctrines like divine simplicity and omnipotence on an implicit denial of the radical transcendence of God's being. Some deny divine simplicity because they cannot conceive or visualize how all the different attributes of God can be only distinct in meaning but identical in reality. Others deny divine omnipotence because, in addition to the seeming scandal of the worship of "power," they cannot "see" how it is compatible with the existence of so much evil in the world. They do not recognize that the doctrine of simplicity is merely the negation of finitude, that God is not composed of distinct principles of being such as essence and existence, form and matter, substance and accidents, species and genera, as finite beings are in their varying ways. It is a statement about God's ontological transcendence, not a claim to an insight into how God could be ontologically simple. We are not invited to conceptualize, still less visualize, God's simplicity, because God is beyond all human concepts and images. We are invited to believe in what we cannot see, God's utter transcendence, rather than reduce God's reality to what we can conceptualize or visualize. Nor do they realize that the attribute of omnipotence is not an empirical concept of being able to do "everything" into which we can have an insight and from which we can then deduce certain things about what God should have done if God were indeed omnipotent. It is likewise a sign of God's transcendence and an invitation to hope that despite all the evils in the world all finite beings are ultimately under the directing providence of God the creator even though we do not "see" the hand of God in every event.[16]

On the other hand, recent European phenomenology, such as that of Emmanuel Levinas and Jean-Luc Marion, use the criterion of the negation of human subjectivity as the positive criterion of the reality of God. For both of them, God is the one whose disproportionate reality can only be experienced as overturning, rupturing, shattering, contradicting, and overwhelming human subjectivity, its human horizon, its conditions of experience, and thus as a negation of the tendency of representational, ontotheological consciousness to reduce all things including God to its own horizon and its own unity of consciousness. This places the eminence or disproportionate reality of God in the mode of negation, not in negating the human mode of signification as in St. Thomas, but in contradicting the reductionist selfishness of human subjectivity and human experience. While there is something to be said in its favor, it is, like all phenomenology, still tied to the criterion of human experience. Whether affirming human subjectivity in its will to power as in ontotheology or negating that subjectivity in the name of the disproportionate reality of God and saturated phenomena, human subjectivity still remains the criterion, positive in the case of ontotheology, negative in the case of Levinas and Marion, but still the criterion nevertheless. They still measure God in relation to human experience rather than measure the human in relation to God. Is it really the case that God is God because he overwhelms our subjectivity, or is it rather the case that God overwhelms our subjectivity because God is God? And if God overwhelms our subjectivity because God is God, then who is God such that God so overwhelms us? This leads us to the metaphysical realm beyond the intrinsic anthropocentrism of phenomenology. God is God with a reality of his own, beyond all things we can say, irreducible to human predication, affirmative or negative, a reality we can only believe at a level beyond negation, without claiming an intuition into its own essence.[17]

(5) The fifth and last way in which theology betrays its own humanity is the failure to maintain the tension between affirmation required by the incarnational character of the Christian faith and the transcendent character of the God who remains transcendent despite the incarnation or between the transcendence of God and the incarnational character of the God who remains incarnate despite his transcendence. This is indeed the heart of the problem for Christian theology in the matter of naming God. Denial of the incarnational character will be a denial of the Christian character of theology; denial of the transcendent character will be a denial of the theological character of that theology. The history of theology has proven how difficult it is to preserve the tension between incarnation and transcendence, and it is proving very difficult today as well. This is all the more

reason, I believe, to hold the three moments of analogical predication of divine names, affirmation, negation, and elevation in mutual tension without either neglecting or absolutizing any one moment.

The three moments of analogical predication apply to both philosophical or natural theology and systematic theology. Systematic theology, church dogmatics, or dogmatic theology, however this is called, tries to elaborate the content of revelation accepted in faith. Theological reason does not have the privilege of an insight into the essence of God but is subject to all the weaknesses of human reason in relation to the reality of God. Knowing something through faith and revelation is still knowledge of God known through the effects of God, not an intuition into the divine essence itself. Theological reason, therefore, can be guilty of all the preceding errors whereby it betrays its own humanity. It can only affirm, negate, and believe, not do otherwise.

Thus far I have simply assumed that St. Thomas is right. Whether we agree with him, and even whether we agree with my categorization of many contemporary theologies on the scale of despair and arrogance, perhaps many of us will agree that contemporary theologies do need a more self-critical reflection about the nature and limits of the human knowledge of God they involve and must ask themselves whether they are faithful to the challenging limits of human knowledge. I am not advocating a revival of the Kantian critique of pure reason, which I consider a variety of despairing reason in relation to our knowledge of God. I do agree with Kant that you cannot affirm the reality of God in a univocal way; God and creatures do not belong to the same species or genus, God transcending all genera and species. I disagree with him in that human reason can affirm God in an analogical way, by way of negation and eminence. I do agree with him that when we try to affirm God in a univocal way, human reason produces "transcendental illusions," which I take to be in fact the product of anthropocentric projection. As in all things human, so in theology, it is always difficult to preserve the human middle, where virtue lies, between the extremes of despair and arrogance, claiming to know too little of God and presuming to know too much of God. The greatness of St. Thomas lies in discerning the appropriate limits of the human knowledge of God and remaining faithful to those limits. His theology was a theology aware of its own humanity and faithful to that humanity. And we should not forget that his fidelity to the humanity of theology is simply the other side of his rarely trumpeted but nonetheless radical sense of awe before the transcendent mystery of God, which is what theology is about and which he tried to preserve precisely through negation and eminence.

NOTES

1. References in parentheses in the text are to the *Summa theologiae*, Leonine edition of 1888, available online at www.unav.es/filosofia/alarcon/amicis/ctopera.html. Unless indicated otherwise, the translations are from Thomas Aquinas, *Summa theologica*, 5 vols., trans. Fathers of the English Dominican Province (London, 1911, rev. 1920; Benziger, 1948; Allen, TX: Christian Classics, 1981).

2. Søren Kierkegaard, *Concluding Unscientific Postscript*, trans. David F. Swenson and Walter Lowrie (Princeton: Princeton University Press, 1941), 74–84, 176–78.

3. On the role of the phantasm in intellectual knowledge in St. Thomas, see further George P. Klubertanz, *The Philosophy of Human Nature* (New York: Appleton-Century-Crofts, 1953), 167–94.

4. Nicholas of Cusa: "the theology of negation is so necessary to the theology of affirmation that without it God would not be worshiped as the infinite God but as creature; and such worship is idolatry, for it gives to an image that which belongs only to truth itself." "On Learned Ignorance," in *Selected Spiritual Writings*, trans. H. Lawrence Bond (New York: Paulist Press, 1997), 126.

5. On the problem of the predication of divine names, see further my *Paths to the Triune God: An Encounter between Aquinas and Recent Theologies* (Notre Dame: University of Notre Dame Press, 2005), 168–74; and "Speaking of the Unknowable God: The Dilemmas of the Christian Discourse about God," in *Whose God? Which Tradition? The Nature of Belief in God*, ed. D. Z. Phillips (Burlington, VT: Ashgate, 2008), 35–48. For a thorough textual discussion of St. Thomas on analogical predication of divine names, see John F. Wippel, *The Metaphysical Thought of Thomas Aquinas: From Finite to Uncreated Being* (Washington, DC: Catholic University of America Press, 2000), 543–71. On the role of reason in the elaboration of theology, which I could not go into for lack of space, see my *Paths to the Triune God*, chap. 1.

6. For my critique of D. Z. Phillips on this point, see my "D. Z. Phillips on the Grammar of God," *International Journal for Philosophy of Religion* 63, nos. 1–3 (February 2008): 131–46.

7. On the possibility of salvation for non-Christians and that of religious pluralism on the basis of St. Thomas, see my *Paths to the Triune God*, chaps. 2 and 3.

8. Jean-Luc Marion, *The Idol and Distance* (New York: Fordham University Press, 2001), 9.

9. Alfred North Whitehead, *Process and Reality*, Corrected ed., ed. David Ray Griffin and Donald W. Sherburne (New York: Free Press, 1978), 343.

10. Georg Wilhelm Friedrich Hegel, *Lectures on the Philosophy of Religion*, vol. 1, *Introduction and the Concept of Religion*, ed. Peter C. Hodgson (Berkeley: University of California Press, 1984), 308.

11. G. W. F. Hegel, *Lectures on the Philosophy of Religion*, 1-vol. ed., *The Lectures of 1827*, ed. Peter C. Hodgson (Berkeley: University of California Press, 1988), 422–23.

12. Jürgen Moltmann, *The Trinity and the Kingdom* (San Francisco: HarperCollins, 1991), 192 ff.

13. Richard Swinburne, *The Christian God* (Oxford: Clarendon Press, 1994), 190.

14. Karl Rahner, *Foundations of Christian Faith: An Introduction to the Idea of Christianity* (New York: Seabury Press, 1978), 223.

15. See my *Paths to the Triune God*, 82–89.

16. In a very thoughtful essay Karen Kilby argues that there are "genuinely reticent and apophatic aspects" (414) to St. Thomas's Trinitarian theology, especially his doctrines of the divine processions, of the divine persons as subsistent relations, and of the relation between the divine persons and the divine essence. These doctrines have more to do with "the limits of theology" or "dead-ends of theology" (414) than with what we can "grasp," "make sense of," gain "insight" into, "understand," or "imagine" (420). In this inability the principle of divine simplicity plays a decisive role. I think her conclusion is entirely correct, but her implicit assumption that such doctrines were meant to be "grasped," "understood," or "imagined" but then were found incapable of being so grasped, understood, intuited, and imagined seems entirely wrong as far as St. Thomas is concerned. They were not meant to be grasped univocally by human reason in the first place but only analogically. See Karen Kilby, "Aquinas, the Trinity and the Limits of Understanding," *International Journal of Systematic Theology* 7, no. 4 (October 2005): 414–27.

17. See my essay, "Naming the Unnamable God: Levinas, Derrida, Marion," *International Journal for Philosophy of Religion* 60, nos. 1–3 (December 2006): 99–116.

BIBLIOGRAPHY

Adams, Marilyn McCord. *Christ and Horrors: The Coherence of Christology*. Current Issues in Theology. New York: Cambridge University Press, 2006.

———. *Horrendous Evils and the Goodness of God*. Ithaca, NY: Cornell University Press, 1999.

———. *What Sort of Human Nature? Medieval Philosophy and the Systematics of Christology*. Aquinas Lecture 1999. Milwaukee, WI: Marquette University Press, 1999.

Aelred. *Spiritual Friendship*. Translated by Mary Eugenia Laker. Cistercian Fathers. Kalamazoo, MI: Cistercian Publications, 1974.

Ali, Abdullah Yusuf. *The Meaning of the Holy Qur'ān*. 11th ed. Beltsville, MD: Amana Publications, 1427/2006.

Althoff, Gerd. "Friendship and the Political Order." In *Friendship in Medieval Europe*, edited by Julian Haseldine, 91–105. Gloucestershire: Sutton Publishing, 1999.

Aquinas, Thomas. *De rationibus fidei*. Translated by Fr. Peter Damian Fehlner. In *Aquinas on Reasons for Our Faith against the Muslims, Greeks and Armenians*. New Bedford, MA: Franciscans of the Immaculate, 2002.

———. *Saint Thomas Aquinas, Summa contra gentiles. Book One: God*. Translated with Introduction and Notes by Anton C. Pegis, FRSC. Notre Dame, IN: University of Notre Dame Press, 1975.

———. *Summa contra gentiles*. 5 vols. Notre Dame, IN: University of Notre Dame Press, 1975.

———. *Summa theologica*. Translated by Fathers of the English Dominican Province. 5 vols. London, 1911, rev. 1920; Benziger, 1948; Allen, TX: Christian Classics, 1948.

Arnaldez, Roger. *A la croisée des trois monotheisms: Une communauté de pensée au Moyen Age.* Paris: Albin Michel, 1993.

Arnold II of Villers (?). *Alice the Leper: Life of St Alice of Schaerbeek.* Translated by Martinus Cawley. Lafayette, OR: Guadalupe Translations, 2000.

Attridge, Harold W., Joseph Cumming, Emilie M. Townes, and Miroslav Volf. "Loving God and Neighbor Together: A Christian Response to a Common Word between Us and You." In *A Common Word: Muslims and Christians on Loving God and Neighbor*, edited by Miroslav Volf, Ghazi bin Muhammad, and Melissa Yarrington, 51–78. Grand Rapids, MI: Eerdmans, 2010.

Auerbach, Erich. *Mimesis: The Representation of Reality in Western Literature.* Translated by Willard R. Trask. Princeton, NJ: Princeton University Press, 1953, 2003.

Barton, John. "Historical-Critical Approaches." In *The Cambridge Companion to Biblical Interpretation*, edited by John Barton, 9–20. New York: Cambridge University Press, 1998.

Bell, Rudolph M. *Holy Anorexia.* Chicago: University of Chicago Press, 1985.

Benedict XVI. "Faith, Reason and the University: Memories and Reflections." September 12, 2006, www.vatican.va/holy_father/benedict_xvi /speeches/2006/september/documents/hf_ben-xvi_spe_20060912 _university-regensburg_en.html. Accessed March 9, 2010.

Biechler, James. "Interreligious Dialogue." In *Introducing Nicholas of Cusa: A Guide to a Renaissance Man*, edited by Christopher M. Bellitto, Thomas M. Izbicki, and Gerald Christianson, 270–96. Mahwah, NJ: Paulist Press, 2004.

Blundell, Mary Whitlock. *Helping Friends and Harming Enemies: A Study in Sophocles and Greek Ethics.* New York: Cambridge University Press, 1989.

Brett, Mark G. *Biblical Criticism in Crisis? The Impact of the Canonical Approach on Old Testament Studies.* New York: Cambridge University Press, 1991.

Browe, Peter. *Die eucharistischen Wunder des Mittelalters.* Breslau: Müller & Seiffert, 1938.

Buchheim, Th., C. H. Corneille, and K. Lorenz, eds. *Potentialität und Possibilität: Modalaussagen in der Geschichte der Metaphysik.* Stuttgart: Frommann-Holzboog, 2001.

Bunzel, B., B. Schmidl-Mohl, A. Grundböck, and G. Wollenek. "Does Changing the Heart Mean Changing Personality? A Retrospective Inquiry on 47 Heart Transplant Patients." *Quality of Life Research* 1 (1992): 251–56.

Burrell, David B. *Faith and Freedom: An Interfaith Perspective.* Malden, MA: Blackwell, 2004.

Bynum, Caroline Walker. *Holy Feast and Holy Fast: The Religious Significance of Food to Medieval Women.* Berkeley: University of California Press, 1987.

———. "Material Continuity, Personal Survival, and the Resurrection of the Body: A Scholastic Discussion in Its Medieval and Modern Contexts." In *Fragmentation and Redemption: Essays on Gender and the Human Body in Medieval Religion,* 239–97. New York: Zone, 1991.

———. *The Resurrection of the Body in Western Christianity, 200–1336.* New York: Columbia University Press, 1995.

Cabassut, André. "Coeurs, changement des." In *Dictionnaire de spiritualité ascétique et mystique, doctrine et histoire.* 17 vols. Paris: Beauchesne, 1932–95.

Cadbury, Henry Joel. "The Peril of Archaizing Ourselves." *Interpretation* 3, no. 3 (July 1949): 331–37.

Castelnuovo-Tedesco, Pietro. "Transplantation: Psychological Implications of Changes in Body Image." In *Psychonephrology 1: Psychological Factors in Hemodialysis and Transplantation,* edited by Norman B. Levy, 219–25. New York: Plenum, 1981.

Catherine of Siena. *The Letters of Catherine of Siena.* Translated by Suzanne Noffke. 4 vols. Medieval and Renaissance Texts and Studies. Tempe: Arizona Center for Medieval and Renaissance Studies, 2000.

Chaucer, Geoffrey. "Troilus and Criseyde." In *The Riverside Chaucer,* edited by Larry Dean Benson, II.925–31. Boston, MA: Houghton Mifflin, 1987.

Chenu, Marie-Dominique. *Introduction à la théologie de S. Thomas D'Aquin.* Paris: J. Vrin, 1950.

Chrétien de Troyes. *Yvain, or the Knight with the Lion.* Translated by Ruth Harwood Cline. Athens: University of Georgia Press, 1975.

Clooney, Francis X. *Comparative Theology: Deep Learning across Religious Borders.* Malden, MA: Wiley-Blackwell, 2010.

Cohen, Esther. "Towards a History of European Physical Sensibility: Pain in the Later Middle Ages." *Science in Context* 8 (1995): 47–74.

Cunningham, Bert Joseph. *The Morality of Organic Transplantation.* Washington, DC: Catholic University of America Press, 1944.

D'Costa, Gavin. *The Meeting of Religions and the Trinity.* Maryknoll, NY: Orbis Books, 2000.

———, ed. *Christian Uniqueness Reconsidered: The Myth of a Pluralistic Theology of Religions.* Maryknoll, NY: Orbis Books, 1990.

Dalferth, I. U. *Radikale Theologie.* Leipzig: Evangelische Verlagsanstalt, 2010.

———. *Theology and Philosophy*. Eugene, OR: Wipf & Stock, 2002.

———. *Die Wirklichkeit des Möglichen: Hermeneutische Religionsphiloso-phie*. Tübingen: Mohr Siebeck, 2003.

Damianus, Petrus. *De Divina Omnipotentia*. Edited by A. Cantin. Paris: Cerf, 1972.

Daniel, Norman. *Islam and the West: The Making of an Image*. Edinburgh, 1960; Oxford: Oneworld, 1993.

Davids, Adelbert, and Pim Valkenberg. "John of Damascus: The Heresy of the Ishmaelites." In *The Three Rings: Textual Studies in the Historical Trialogue of Judaism, Christianity, and Islam*, edited by Barbara Rog-gema, Marcel Poorthuis, and Pim Valkenberg, 71–90. Leuven: Peeters, 2005.

Doniger, Wendy. "Transplanting Myths of Organ Transplants." In *Organ Transplantation: Meanings and Realities*, edited by Stuart J. Youngner, Renée C. Fox, and Laurence J. O'Connell, 194–220. Madison: University of Wisconsin Press, 1996.

Doueihi, Milad. *A Perverse History of the Human Heart*. Cambridge, MA: Harvard University Press, 1997.

Edwards, O. C. "Historical-Critical Method's Failure of Nerve and a Pre-scription for a Tonic: A Review of Some Recent Literature." *Anglican Theological Review* 59, no. 2 (April 1977): 115–34.

Fiedler, Leslie A. "Why Organ Transplant Programs Do Not Succeed." In *Organ Transplantation: Meanings and Realities*, edited by Stuart J. Youngner, Renée C. Fox, and Laurence J. O'Connell, 56–65. Madison: University of Wisconsin Press, 1996.

Fitzgerald, John T. "Friendship in the Greek World Prior to Aristotle." In *Greco-Roman Perspectives on Friendship*, SBL Resources for Biblical Study 34, edited by John T. Fitzgerald, 13–34. Atlanta, GA: Scholars Press, 1997.

Fowl, Stephen E., ed. *The Theological Interpretation of Scripture: Classic and Contemporary Readings*. Malden, MA: Blackwell, 1997.

Fox, Renée C. "Afterthoughts: Continuing Reflections on Organ Transplan-tation." In *Organ Transplantation: Meanings and Realities*, edited by Stuart J. Youngner, Renée C. Fox, and Laurence J. O'Connell, 252–72. Madison: University of Wisconsin Press, 1996.

Fox, Renée C., and Judith P. Swazey. *Spare Parts: Organ Replacement in American Society*. New York: Oxford University Press, 1992.

Fredericks, James L. *Faith among Faiths: Christian Theology and Non-Christian Religions*. Mahwah, NJ: Paulist Press, 1999.

Garfinkel, Stephen. "Applied Peshat: Historical-Critical Method and Reli-gious Meaning." *Journal of the Ancient Near Eastern Society* 22 (1993): 19–28.

Goswin of Bossut. *Send Me God: The Lives of Ida the Compassionate of Nivelles, Nun of La Ramée, Arnulf, Lay Brother of Villers, and Abundus, Monk of Villers*. Translated by Martinus Cawley. Turnhout: Brepols, 2003.

Grant, Edward. *The Foundations of Modern Science in the Middle Ages: Their Religious, Institutional, and Intellectual Contexts*. Cambridge History of Science. New York: Cambridge University Press, 1996.

Hagemann, Ludwig. *Christentum contra Islam: Eine Geschichte gescheiterter Beziehungen*. Darmstadt: Primus Verlag, 1999.

Hegel, Georg Wilhelm Friedrich. *Lectures on the Philosophy of Religion*. Edited by Peter C. Hodgson. One-volume edition, the Lectures of 1827. Berkeley: University of California Press, 1988.

———. *Lectures on the Philosophy of Religion*. Vol. 1: *Introduction and the Concept of Religion*. Edited by Peter C. Hodgson. Berkeley: University of California Press, 1984.

Heidegger, Martin. *Being and Time: A Translation of Sein und Zeit*. Translated by Joan Stambaugh. SUNY Series in Contemporary Continental Philosophy. Albany: State University of New York Press, 1996.

Heim, S. Mark. *The Depth of the Riches: A Trinitarian Theology of Religious Ends*. Grand Rapids, MI: Eerdmans, 2001.

———. *Salvations: Truth and Difference in Religion*. Maryknoll, NY: Orbis Books, 1995.

Herberichs, C., and S. Reichlin, eds. *Kein Zufall: Konzeptionen von Kontingenz in der mittelalterlichen Literatur*. Göttingen: Vandenhoeck & Ruprecht, 2010.

Hieronymi, S. *Vita III*. In *Patrologia Latina Database*, edited by J. P. Migne. Ann Arbor, MI: ProQuest Info. & the Learning Co., [1845] 1995.

Hoping, Helmut. *Weisheit als Wissen des Ursprungs: Philosophie und Theologie in der "Summa contra gentiles" des Thomas von Aquin*. Freiburg: Herder, 1997.

Hopkins, Jasper. *A Miscellany on Nicholas of Cusa*. Minneapolis, MN: Arthur J. Banning Press, 1994.

———. *Nicholas of Cusa's "De pace fidei" and "Cribratio Alkorani": Translation and Analysis*. Minneapolis, MN: Arthur J. Banning Press, 1990.

Inspector, Y., I. Kutz, and D. David. "Another Person's Heart: Magical and Rational Thinking in the Psychological Adaptation to Heart Transplantation." *Israel Journal of Psychiatry and Related Sciences* 41, no. 3 (2004): 161–73.

Jakemes. *Le Roman du Castelain de Couci et de la Dame de Fayel*. Edited by Maurice Delbouille. Paris: Société des anciens textes français, 1936.

Johannes O.P. of Magdeburg. *The Life of Margaret the Lame*. Translated by Gertrud Jaron Lewis and Tilman Lewis. In *Living Saints of the*

Thirteenth Century, edited by Anneke B. Mulder-Bakker, 313–96. Turnhout: Brepols, 2011.

John of Damascus. "On Heresies." In *Jean Damascène, Écrits sur l'Islam*, edited by R. Le Coz, 41–58. Sources Chrétiennes 383. Paris: Cerf, 1992.

Johnston, Alan F. "The Historical-Critical Method: Egyptian Gold or Pagan Precipice?" *Journal of the Evangelical Theological Society* 26, no. 1 (March 1983): 3–15.

Jonas, Hans. "Philosophical Reflections on Experimenting with Human Subjects." In *Experimentation with Human Subjects*, edited by Paul A. Freund, 1–31. New York: George Braziller, 1970.

Julian of Norwich. *Revelations of Divine Love*. Translated by Clifton Wolters. Baltimore, MD: Penguin Books, 1966.

Jüngel, Eberhard. *God as the Mystery of the World: On the Foundation of the Theology of the Crucified One in the Dispute between Theism and Atheism*. Translated by Darrel L. Guder. Grand Rapids, MI: Eerdmans, 1983.

———. "The World as Possibility and Actuality: The Ontology of the Doctrine of Justification." In *Theological Essays*, edited by J. B. Webster, 95–123. Edinburgh: T & T Clark, 1989.

Kant, Immanuel. "Lectures on the Philosophical Doctrine of Religion." In *Religion and Rational Theology*. Translated by Allen W. Wood. Cambridge Edition of the Works of Immanuel Kant, edited by Paul Guyer and Allen W. Wood, 335–452. New York: Cambridge University Press, 1996.

Kearney, Richard. *The God Who May Be: A Hermeneutics of Religion*. Indiana Series in the Philosophy of Religion. Bloomington: Indiana University Press, 2001.

Kelly, David, and Walter E. Wiest. "Christian Perspectives." In *New Harvest: Transplanting Body Parts and Reaping the Benefits*, edited by C. D. Keyes and Walter E. Wiest, 161–77. Clifton, NJ: Humana Press, 1991.

Kent, Bonnie. "Habits and Virtues (Ia IIae, Qq. 49–70)." In *The Ethics of Aquinas*, edited by Stephen J. Pope, 116–30. Washington, DC: Georgetown University Press, 2002.

Keyes, C. Don. "Body and Self-Identity." In *New Harvest: Transplanting Body Parts and Reaping the Benefits*, edited by C. D. Keyes and Walter E. Wiest, 161–77. Clifton, NJ: Humana Press, 1991.

Kierkegaard, Søren. *Concluding Unscientific Postscript*. Translated by David F. Swenson and Walter Lowrie. Princeton, NJ: Princeton University Press, 1941.

———. *SK Skrifter*. Vol. 17. Copenhagen: Gads Forlag, 2000.

Kilby, Karen. "Aquinas, the Trinity and the Limits of Understanding." *International Journal of Systematic Theology* 7, no. 4 (October 2005): 414–27.

Klubertanz, George P. *The Philosophy of Human Nature*. New York: Appleton-Century-Crofts, 1953.

LaCugna, Catherine Mowry. *God for Us: The Trinity and Christian Life*. San Francisco: HarperCollins, 1991.

Lamberts, Jef. "Liturgie et spiritualité de l'Eucharistie au XIIIe siècle." In *Fête-Dieu (1246–1996): Actes du Colloque de Liège, 12–14 septembre 1996*, edited by André Haquin, 81–95. Louvain-la-Neuve: Université Catholique de Louvain, 1999.

Le Goff, Jacques. *The Birth of Purgatory*. Translated by Arthur Goldhammer. Chicago: University of Chicago Press, 1984.

Lee, John Yong. "Religious Doubt and Theological Virtues: A Thomistic Regulative Epistemology." PhD diss., Claremont Graduate University, 2006.

Levenson, Jon D. "The Bible: Unexamined Commitments of Criticism." *First Things* 30 (February 1993): 24–33.

Linnemann, Eta. *Historical Criticism of the Bible: Methodology or Ideology?* Translated by Robert W. Yarbrough. Grand Rapids, MI: Baker, 1990.

Lock, Margaret. "Transcending Mortality: Organ Transplants and the Practice of Contradictions." *Medical Anthropology Quarterly* 9, no. 3 (1995): 390–93.

Longstaff, Thomas R. W., and Page A. Thomas. *The Synoptic Problem: A Bibliography, 1716–1988*. Macon, GA: Mercer University Press, 1988.

Lovejoy, Arthur O. *The Great Chain of Being: A Study of the History of an Idea*. Cambridge, MA: Harvard University Press, 1936.

Lubac, Henri de. *Medieval Exegesis: The Four Senses of Scripture*. Translated by Mark Sebanc. Grand Rapids, MI: Eerdmans, 1998.

MacFarquhar, Larissa. "The Kindest Cut." *New Yorker* (July 27, 2009): 38–51.

Mai, François M. "Graft and Donor Denial in Heart Transplant Recipients." *American Journal of Psychiatry* 143 (1986): 1159–61.

Maier, Gerhard. "Concrete Alternatives to the Historical-Critical Method." *Evangelical Review of Theology* 6, no. 1 (April 1982): 23–36.

———. *The End of the Historical-Critical Method*. Translated by Edwin W. Levernz and Rudolf F. Norden. St. Louis: Concordia, 1977.

"Man with Suicide Victim's Heart Takes Own Life." Associated Press, April 6, 2008, www.msnbc.msn.com/id/23984857/. Accessed April 12, 2010.

Manoussakis, J. P. *After God: Richard Kearney and the Religious Turn in Continental Philosophy*. Perspectives in Continental Philosophy. New York: Fordham University Press, 2006.

Marion, Jean-Luc. *The Idol and Distance: Five Studies*. New York: Fordham University Press, 2001.

Marriott, McKim. "Hindu Transactions: Diversity without Dualism." In *Transaction and Meaning: Directions in the Anthropology of Exchange and Symbolic Behavior*, edited by Bruce Kapferer, 109–42. Philadelphia: Institute for the Study of Human Issues, 1976.

Martin, James P. "Toward a Post-Critical Paradigm." *New Testament Studies* 33, no. 3 (July 1987): 370–85.

McAuliffe, Jane Dammen. *Qur'anic Christians: An Analysis of Classical and Modern Exegesis*. Cambridge: Cambridge University Press, 1991.

McCown, Chester C. "The Current Plight of Biblical Scholarship." *Journal of Biblical Literature* 75, no. 1 (March 1956): 12–18.

McEvoy, James. "The Theory of Friendship in the Latin Middle Ages: Hermeneutics, Contextualization, and the Transmission and Reception of Ancient Texts and Ideas, from c. AD 375 to c. 1500." In *Friendship in Medieval Europe*, edited by Julian Haseldine, 3–44. Gloucestershire: Sutton Publishing, 1999.

McGuire, Brian Patrick. "Purgatory, the Communion of Saints, and Medieval Change." *Viator* 20 (1989): 61–84.

Mews, Constant J. *The Lost Love Letters of Heloise and Abelard: Perceptions of Dialogue in Twelfth-Century France*. New York: St. Martin's, 1999.

Min, Anselm K. "D. Z. Phillips on the Grammar of God." *International Journal for Philosophy of Religion* 63, nos. 1–3 (February 2008): 131–46.

———. "Naming the Unnamable God: Levinas, Derrida, Marion." *International Journal for Philosophy of Religion* 60, nos. 1–3 (December 2006): 99–116.

———. *Paths to the Triune God: An Encounter between Aquinas and Recent Theologies*. Notre Dame, IN: University of Notre Dame Press, 2005.

———. "Speaking of the Unknowable God: The Dilemmas of the Christian Discourse about God." In *Whose God? Which Tradition? The Nature of Belief in God*, edited by D. Z. Phillips, 35–48. Burlington, VT: Ashgate, 2008.

Moltmann, Jürgen. *The Trinity and the Kingdom*. San Francisco, CA: HarperCollins, 1991.

Mulder-Bakker, Anneke B. *Lives of the Anchoresses: The Rise of the Urban Recluse in Medieval Europe*. Translated by Myra Heerspink Scholz. Philadelphia: University of Pennsylvania Press, 2005.

Nancy, Jean-Luc. *Being Singular Plural*. Translated by Robert D. Richardson and Anne E. O'Byrne. Stanford, CA: Stanford University Press, 2000.

———. *Être singulier pluriel*. Paris: Galilée, 1996.

———. "The Intruder." In *Corpus*, translated by Richard A. Rand, 161–70. New York: Fordham University Press, 2008.

———. *L'Intrus*. Paris: Galilée, 2000.

Neuhaus, Richard John, ed. *Biblical Interpretation in Crisis: The Ratzinger Conference on Bible and Church*. Grand Rapids, MI: Eerdmans, 1989.

Newman, Barbara. "Charles Williams and the Companions of the Co-Inherence." *Spiritus* 9 (2009): 1–26.

Nicholas of Cusa. *De Docta Ignorantia*. Edited by Martin Flach. Strassburg, France: Martin Flach, 1489.

———. *De visione Dei*. Edited by E. Hoffmann. Vol. 12, Nicolai de Cusa Opera Omnia. Leipzig: F. Meiner, 1932.

———. *A Miscellany on Nicholas of Cusa*. Edited by Jasper Hopkins. Minneapolis, MN: Arthur J. Banning Press, 1994.

———. *Nicolai de Cusa "Cribratio Alkorani."* Translated by Ludwig Hagemann. Edited by Ludwig Hagemann. Nicolai de Cusa Opera Omnia VIII. Hamburg: F. Meiner, 1986.

———. "On Learned Ignorance." In *Selected Spiritual Writings.* Translated by H. Lawrence Bond, 85–206. New York: Paulist Press, 1997.

———. *Trialogus de Possest* 8, 2. Paris: J. Vrin, 2006.

Nicholson, Ernest W. *The Pentateuch in the Twentieth Century: The Legacy of Julius Wellhausen*. Oxford: Clarendon Press, 1998.

Pearsall, Paul, Gary E. R. Schwartz, and Linda G. S. Russek. "Changes in Heart Transplant Recipients That Parallel the Personalities of Their Donors." *Integrative Medicine* 2 (1999): 65–72.

Piché, David, ed. *La Condemnation parisienne de 1277*. Paris: J. Vrin, 1999.

Preus, Robert D. "May the Lutheran Church Legitimately Use the Historical-Critical Method?" *Affirm* (Spring 1973): 31–35.

Rahner, Karl. *Foundations of Christian Faith: An Introduction to the Idea of Christianity*. New York: Seabury Press, 1978.

Ranke, Leopold. "Preface: Histories of the Latin and Germanic Nations from 1494–1514." In *The Varieties of History: From Voltaire to the Present*, edited by Fritz Richard Stern, 54–62. Cleveland: Meridian Books, 1956.

Raymond of Capua. *Die Legenda Maior (Vita Catharinae Senensis) des Raimund von Capua*. 2 vols. Edited by Jörg Jungmayr. Berlin: Weidler, 2004.

———. *The Life of Catherine of Siena*. Translated by Conleth Kearns. Wilmington, DE: Michael Glazier, 1980.

Read, Piers Paul. *Alive: The Story of the Andes Survivors*. Philadelphia: Lippincott, 1974.

Richardson, Ruth. "Fearful Symmetry: Corpses for Anatomy, Organs for Transplantation?" In *Organ Transplantation: Meanings and Realities*, edited by Stuart J. Youngner, Renée C. Fox, and Laurence J. O'Connell, 66–100. Madison: University of Wisconsin Press, 1996.

Richard of St. Victor. *La Trinite.* Translated by S. J. Gaston Salet. Paris: Cerf, 1959.

"Robertson: 'Islam Is Not a Religion. It Is a Worldwide Political Movement Meant on Domination.'" Media Matters, June 12, 2007, www.Media Matters.org. Accessed March 3, 2010.

Roggema, Barbara, Marcel Poorthuis, and Pim Valkenberg, eds. *The Three Rings: Textual Studies in the Historical Trialogue of Judaism, Christianity, and Islam.* Leuven: Peeters, 2005.

Rohde, Joachim. *Rediscovering the Teaching of the Evangelists.* Translated by Dorothea M. Barton. New ed. London: SCM Press, 1968.

The Romance of Flamenca. Edited and translated by E. D. Blodgett. New York: Garland, 1995.

Sachedina, Abdulaziz. "The Qur'ān and Other Religions." In *The Cambridge Companion to the Qur'ān,* edited by Jane Dammen McAuliffe, 291–309. Cambridge: Cambridge University Press, 2006.

Sanders, E. P. *Jesus and Judaism.* Philadelphia: Fortress Press, 1985.

Schelbert, Georg. "Defaming the Historical-Critical Method." Translated by Linda Maloney. In *Church in Anguish,* edited by Hans Küng and Leonard Swidler, 106–24. San Francisco: Harper & Row, 1987.

Schoot, Henk. "Christ Crucified Contested: Thomas Aquinas Answering Objections from Jews and Muslims." In *The Three Rings: Textual Studies in the Historical Trialogue of Judaism, Christianity, and Islam,* edited by Barbara Roggema, Marcel Poorthuis and Pim Valkenberg, 141–62. Leuven: Peeters, 2005.

Schoot, Henk, and Pim Valkenberg. "Thomas Aquinas and Judaism." In *Aquinas in Dialogue: Thomas for the Twenty-First Century,* edited by James Fodor and Frederick Christian Bauerschmidt, 47–66. Malden, MA: Blackwell, 2004.

Schulthess, P. "Kontingenz: Begriffsanalytisches und Grundlegende Positionen in der Philosophie im Mittelalter." In *Kein Zufall: Konzeptionen von Kontingenz in der mittelalterlichen Literatur,* edited by C. Herberichs and S. Reichlin, 50–78. Göttingen: Vandenhoeck & Ruprecht, 2010.

Schweitzer, Albert. *The Quest of the Historical Jesus: A Critical Study of Its Progress from Reimarus to Wrede.* Translated by W. Montgomery. New York: Macmillan, 1959.

Scott, E. F. "The Limitations of the Historical Method." In *Studies in Early Christianity,* edited by Shirley Jackson Case, 3–18. New York: Century Co., 1928.

Selzer, Richard. "Whither Thou Goest." In *Imagine a Woman and Other Tales,* 3–28. New York: Random House, 1990.

Shirwood, William. *Introductiones in Logicam = Einführung in Die Logik.* Edited by Hartmut Brands and Christoph Kann. Philosophische Bibliothek. Hamburg: F. Meiner, 1995.

Slattery, Dennis Patrick. *The Wounded Body: Remembering the Markings of Flesh.* Albany: State University of New York Press, 2000.

Smalley, Beryl. *The Study of the Bible in the Middle Ages.* Oxford: Clarendon Press, 1941.

Steinmetz, David. "The Superiority of Pre-Critical Exegesis." *Theology Today* 37, no. 1 (April 1980): 27–38.

Streeter, Burnett Hillman. *The Four Gospels: A Study of Origins, Treating of the Manuscript Tradition, Sources, Authorship, and Dates.* 4th ed. London: Macmillan, 1930.

Swartley, Willard M. "Beyond the Historical-Critical Method." In *Essays on Biblical Interpretation: Anabaptist-Mennonite Perspectives,* 237–64. Elkhart, IN: Institute of Mennonite Studies, 1984.

Swinburne, Richard. *The Christian God.* Oxford: Clarendon Press, 1994.

Sylvia, Claire, and William Novak. *A Change of Heart: A Memoir.* Boston: Little, Brown, 1997.

Tertullian. *De carne Christi liber.* Translated by Ernest Evans. London: SPCK, 1956.

Thomas of Cantimpré. "Life of Lutgard of Aywières." Translated by Margot H. King and Barbara Newman. In *Thomas of Cantimpré: The Collected Saints' Lives,* edited by Barbara Newman, 207–96, Turnhout: Brepols, 2008.

Thompson, John Lee. *Reading the Bible with the Dead: What You Can Learn from the History of Exegesis That You Can't Learn from Exegesis Alone.* Grand Rapids, MI: Eerdmans, 2007.

Troeltsch, Ernst. "Historical and Dogmatic Method in Theology." In *Religion in History,* edited by James Luther Adams and Walter F. Bense, 11–32. Minneapolis, MN: Fortress Press, 1991.

Uckelman, Sara L. "Logic and the Condemnations of 1277." *Journal of Philosophical Logic* 39, no. 2 (2010): 201–27.

———. *Modalities in Medieval Logic.* ILLC Dissertation Series Ds-2009-04. Amsterdam: Institute for Logic, Language and Computation, Universiteit van Amsterdam, 2009.

Valkenberg, Pim. "Das Konzept der Offenbaring im Islam aus der Perspektive Komparativer Theologie." In *Komparative Theologie: Interreligiöse Vergleiche als Weg der Religionstheologie,* edited by Reinhold Bernhardt and Klaus von Stosch, 123–45. Beiträge zu einer Theologie der Religionen 7. Zurich: Theologischer Verlag, 2009.

———. "Nicholas of Cusa and the Relation between Learned Ignorance and a Faithful Christian Interpretation of the Qur'ān." In *Jaarboek 2006*, edited by Henk J. M. Schoot, 35–61. Utrecht: Thomas Instituut, 2006.

———. "One Faith, Different Rites: Nicholas of Cusa's New Awareness of Religious Pluralism." In *Understanding Religious Pluralism: Perspectives from Religious Studies and Theology,* edited by Peter C. Phan and Jonathan Ray, 192–208. Eugene, OR: Pickwick Publications, 2014.

———. *Sharing Lights on the Way to God: Muslim-Christian Dialogue and Theology in the Context of Abrahamic Partnership.* Currents of Encounter 2. Amsterdam: Rodopi, 2006.

———. "Sifting the Qur'ān: Two Forms of Interreligious Hermeneutics in Nicholas of Cusa." In *Interreligious Hermeneutics in Pluralistic Europe*, edited by David Cheetham et al., 27–48. Amsterdam: Rodopi, 2011.

———. "*Una Religio in Rituum Varietate:* Religious Pluralism, the Qur'an, and Nicholas of Cusa." In *Nicholas of Cusa and Islam: Polemic and Dialogue in the Late Middle Ages,* edited by Ian Christopher Levy et al., 30–48. Leiden: Brill, 2014.

Vincensini, Jean-Jacques. "Figure de l'imaginaire et figure du discours: Le motif du 'Coeur Mangé' dans la narration médiévale." In *Le "Cuer" au Moyen Age: Réalité et Sénéfiance,* 439–59. Aix-en-Provence: Centre Universitaire d'Études et de Recherches Médiévales d'Aix, 1991.

Volf, Miroslav. *The End of Memory: Remembering Rightly in a Violent World.* Grand Rapids, MI: Eerdmans, 2006.

Waldenfels, B. *Antwortregister.* Frankfurt: Suhrkamp, 1994.

———. *Bruchlinien der Erfahrung: Phänomenologie, Psychoanalyse, Phänomenotechnik.* Frankfurt: Suhrkamp, 2002.

———. *Grenzen der Normalisierung.* Studien zur Phänomenologie des Fremden 2. Frankfurt: Suhrkamp, 1998.

———. "Die Macht der Ereignisse." In *Ereignis auf Französisch*, edited by M. Rölli, 447–58. Munich: Verlag, 2004.

———. *Ordnung im Zwielicht.* Frankfurt: Suhrkamp, 1987.

———. *Phänomenologie der Aufmerksamkeit.* Frankfurt: Suhrkamp, 2004.

———. *Schattenrisse der Moral.* Frankfurt: Suhrkamp, 2006.

———. *Sinnschwellen.* Studien zur Phänomenologie des Fremden 3. Frankfurt: Suhrkamp, 1999.

———. *Der Stachel des Fremden.* Frankfurt: Suhrkamp, 1990.

Webb, Heather. *The Medieval Heart.* New Haven, CT: Yale University Press, 2010.

Weber, Nancy. *Brokenhearted.* New York: Dutton, 1989.

Whitehead, Alfred North. *Process and Reality.* Edited by David Ray Griffin and Donald W. Sherburne. Corrected ed. New York: Free Press, 1978.

Whybray, R. N. *The Making of the Pentateuch: A Methodological Study.* Sheffield: JSOT, 1987.

Wilders, Geert. "Geert Wilders on Islam." *Citizens for a Constitutional Republic,* April 5, 2009, www.citizensforaconstitutionalrepublic.com /wilders4-5-09.html. Accessed March 3, 2010.

Williams, Charles. *Descent into Hell.* Grand Rapids, MI: Eerdmans, [1937] 1980.

——. *The Descent of the Dove: A Short History of the Holy Spirit in the Church.* Grand Rapids, MI: Eerdmans, [1939] 1974.

Wippel, John F. *The Metaphysical Thought of Thomas Aquinas: From Finite Being to Uncreated Being.* Washington, DC: Catholic University of America Press, 2000.

Wolff, Christian. *Philosophia Rationalis Sive Logica, Methodo Scientifica Pertractata et ad Usum Scientiarum Atque Vitae Aptata: Praemittitur Discursus Praeliminaris de Philosophia in Genere.* Editio Tertia Emendatior cum privilegiis ed. Frankfurt and Leipzig, 1740.

Wolfson, H. A. *The Philosophy of the Kalam.* Cambridge, MA: Harvard University Press, 1976.

Yalof, Ina L. *Life and Death: The Story of a Hospital.* New York: Random House, 1988.

Youngner, Stuart J. "Some Must Die." In *Organ Transplantation: Meanings and Realities,* edited by Stuart J. Youngner, Renée C. Fox, and Laurence J. O'Connell, 32–55. Madison: University of Wisconsin Press, 1996.

Youngner, Stuart J., Martha Allen, Edward T. Bartlett, Helmut F. Cascorbi, Toni Hau, David L. Jackson, Mary B. Mahowald, and Barbara J. Martin. "Psychosocial and Ethical Implications of Organ Retrieval." *New England Journal of Medicine* 313 (August 1, 1985): 321–24.

Zaleski, Carol. *Otherworld Journeys: Accounts of Near-Death Experience in Medieval and Modern Times.* New York: Oxford University Press, 1987.

CONTRIBUTORS

MARILYN MCCORD ADAMS, formerly Regius Professor of Divinity at the University of Oxford, is Visiting Professor at Rutgers University and Honorary Professor at Australian Catholic University. She also served as Pitkin Professor of Historical Theology at Yale University and chair of the Department of Philosophy at UCLA. Among the six books she has written on William Ockham, Christology, the problem of evil, and the Eucharist are *Horrendous Evils and the Goodness of God* (Cornell, 2000) and *Christ and Horrors: The Coherence of Christology* (Cambridge, 2006). In addition, she has translated William Ockham and Paul of Venice and edited two volumes on John Duns Scotus and the problem of evil. Adams has also published more than eighty journal articles. She was the 1999 Aquinas Lecturer at Marquette University.

INGOLF U. DALFERTH is Danforth Professor of Philosophy of Religion at Claremont Graduate University. He has taught at the Universities of Tübingen, Durham, Cambridge, Frankfurt, and, most recently, Zurich. He served as president of the European Society of Philosophy of Religion as well as of the German Society for Philosophy of Religion. He is editor of *Theologische Literaturzeitung* and series editor of Hermeneutische Untersuchungen zur Theologie and Religion in Philosophy and Theology for Mohr Siebeck. Dalferth's major areas of research and teaching are hermeneutics, systematic theology, ecumenical theology, analytical and phenomenological philosophy of religion, religion and emotion, altruism, trust, and evil. In addition to publishing numerous articles and eighteen edited volumes, he has written eighteen books in German and English, including most recently *Malum: Theologische Hermeneutik des Boesen* (Mohr Siebeck, 2010) and *Selbstlose Leidenschaften, Christlicher Glaube, und menschliche Passionen* (Mohr Siebeck, 2013).

KEVIN MADIGAN is Winn Professor of Ecclesiastical History at Harvard Divinity School, where he has taught since 2000. A specialist in medieval Christianity, he also regularly teaches courses on the Holocaust. In addition to numerous articles, he is the author of *Resurrection: The Power of God for Jews and Christians*, with Jon D. Levenson (Yale, 2008), *The Passions of Christ in the High Middle Ages: An Essay on Christological Development* (Oxford, 2007), *Ordained Women in Early Christianity: A Documentary History*, with Carolyn Osiek (Johns Hopkins, 2005), and *Olivi and the Interpretation of Matthew in the High Middle Ages* (Notre Dame, 2003). Another book, *Medieval Christianity: A Modern History*, is forthcoming from Yale University Press in 2014.

ANSELM K. MIN is Maguire Distinguished Professor of Religion at Claremont Graduate University, where he has been teaching in the area of philosophy of religion and theology since 1992. He is the author of, among other works, *Paths to the Triune God: An Encounter between Aquinas and Recent Theologies* (Notre Dame, 2005), *The Solidarity of Others in a Divided World: A Postmodern Theology after Postmodernism* (T & T Clark International, 2004), and *Dialectic of Salvation: Issues in Theology of Liberation* (SUNY, 1989). He is coeditor, with Christoph Schwoebel, of *Word and Spirit: Renewing Christology and Pneumatology in a Globalizing World* (Walter de Gruyter, 2014). Min has written numerous articles on Hegel, Aquinas, Christology, Trinitarian theology, liberation theology, interreligious dialogue, pluralism, globalization, and postmodern and Asian theologies. He is currently working on a systematic theology of globalization.

BARBARA NEWMAN is Professor of English, Religious Studies, and Classics and John Evans Professor of Latin Language and Literature at Northwestern University, where she has taught since 1981. Known for her work on medieval religious culture, allegorical poetry, and women's spirituality, she has written *Medieval Crossover: Reading the Secular against the Sacred* (Notre Dame, 2013), *Frauenlob's Song of Songs: A Medieval German Poet and His Masterpiece* (Penn State, 2006), *God and the Goddesses: Vision, Poetry, and Belief in the Middle Ages* (Pennsylvania, 2003), *From Virile Woman to WomanChrist: Studies in Medieval Religion and Literature* (Pennsylvania, 1995), and *Sister of Wisdom: St. Hildegard's Theology of the Feminine* (California, [1987] 1997), in addition to editing and translating works by Thomas of Cantimpré and Hildegard of Bingen. Among her current projects is a book titled *The Permeable Self: Medieval Meditations on the Personal.* She serves on the editorial board of the journal *Spiritus.*

PIM (WILHELMUS) VALKENBERG is Ordinary Professor of Religion and Culture in the School of Theology and Religious Studies at the Catholic University of America, where he has taught since 2011. He has also taught at the Radboud Universiteit Nijmegen, the Catholic University of Leuven, St. Augustine's College in Johannesburg, the University of Notre Dame, and, most recently, Loyola University Maryland. His special interests are Christology and Christian-Muslim relations. In addition to numerous articles and edited volumes on Islam and interreligious dialogue, he is the author of *Words of the Living God: Place and Function of Holy Scripture in the Theology of Thomas Aquinas* (Peeters, 2000), *Sharing Lights on the Way to God: Muslim-Christian Dialogue and Theology in the Context of Abrahamic Partnership* (Rodopi, 2006), and *World Religions in Dialogue: A Comparative Theological Approach* (Anselm Academic, 2013).

INDEX